# The
# FOUNDATION PILLARS
## for
# CHANGE

# THE
# FOUNDATION PILLARS
## FOR
# CHANGE

Our Nation, Our Democracy & Our Future

# K. V. PATEL

PARTRIDGE
A Penguin Random House Company

**To order additional copies of this book, contact**
Partridge India
000 800 10062 62
www.partridgepublishing.com/india
orders.india@partridgepublishing.com

# CONTENTS

This book is dedicated to my parents

Shri. Vaghabhai Makanji Patel (dec.)

&

Smt. Laxmibhen Vaghabhai Patel (dec.);

Without their shared values, behaviours and ways of living,

I would not be the person I am.

There are five factors to Wisdom:

Learning from your successes and failures;

Learning from your strengths and weaknesses;

Learning from what is happening around you;

Learning from what other people are telling you; and

Learning in an environment of honesty and truth.

*"We are responsible for what we are,*

*and whatever we wish ourselves to be,*

*we have the power to make ourselves.*

*If what we are now has been the result of our own past actions,*

*it certainly follows that whatever we wish to be in future*

*can be produced by our present actions;*

*so we have to know how to act."*


**Swami Vivekananda**

# PREFACE

*"Strive for perfection in everything we do. Take the best that exists and make it better. When it does not exist, design it. Accept nothing nearly right or good enough."*

**Henry Royce**

This book aims to share a set of view and opinions. It is based on my personal experiences; from individuals who have shared their thoughts with me; what I have seen, read, researched, and overheard is my many years of travel and work across the world and in India.

This book presents the components of change that leaders and citizens could execute in each of the six *'Foundation Pillars'*. These form the basis of what is necessary to ensure sustainable economic, social and personal development for citizens. These lead to a collection of suggestion and recommendation of activities and policies, once agreed, like *'Ashoka's edicts'*,[1] India could implement these to ensure change for the benefit for all its citizens and the nation. These six *'Foundation Pillars'* are not independent of one another, but are dependent and interconnected to each other. We cannot aim to successfully achieve any one, without succeeding in the others too.

As I researched material for this book, I realised that in this era of economic constraints and increasing citizen disenchantment, the more developed economies are beginning to question their priorities, and are now aiming to revert focus on to the basics, either on one, few, or all of the *'Foundation Pillars'*. My proposed priorities are not purely an Indian solution, as they are also applicable for any nation or group of citizens who wish to improve their quality of life and environment. This became more evident when looking at the more rapidly developing East Asian nations and those that are now considered *'Beyond BRIC's'*[2], which include amongst others Indonesia, Mexico, Argentina, Vietnam,

*"A man is but the product of his thoughts, what he thinks he becomes."*
Mohandas Karamchand Gandhi

13

South Africa etc., all these economies are aiming to align and bring improvements to their social and economic performance. This also provides direction to why some nations with considerable natural wealth of minerals, commodities and peoples are still significantly under-developed after many years of self-rule; the leadership is weak or corrupt, natural resources are siphoned off by powerful interest groups and small clusters of privileged families, supported by an internal security system with limited governance, and with the majority of citizens torn and kept occupied by internal strife and conflict, with poor education and healthcare, either engineered or as a result of differing cultures, tribes, religions or other factors. Our nation needs to take action to significantly improve on these six *'Foundation Pillars'*, and our citizens' needs to take action to ensure this happens in a more comprehensive and accelerated manner for all their benefits.

I am passionate about our nation, land of my birth, my domicile, and am enthusiastic about making positive change; change for improvement, whether it is behaviour change in our individual *'ways of working'* and *'ways of living'*, or change across an organisation or entity. The principles are the same. There are many examples from across the world, and within our own nation, where individuals have come together to form groups, communities and movements that have enabled a significant change for the betterment of the nation and its citizens.

My view is that our nation needs to make some fundamental changes, sooner, and in an accelerated fashion, in order to ensure a more secure future for all its citizens. This is a *'generational change'*. As a democracy, this cannot be delivered through revolution but through evolution of our existing systems, a more rapid evolution, than what we are currently experiencing. Changes and improvements will not be delivered by one, two or even three terms of a Government, or a cleverly crafted set of five-year plans. The six *'Foundation Pillars'* are the basis on which the new *'House of India'* can be build; we need these *'Foundation Pillars'* to be secured by ~2035 so that we have ~22 years to make the changes and improvements, and ~15 years to ensure sustainability. This requires a consistent and

*"The difference between what we do and what we are capable of doing would suffice to solve most of the world's problem."*
Mohandas Karamchand Gandhi

unwavering approach to the critical elements that provide for the foundations to a successful nation and a happy and content citizenry. It requires changes to some values, ethics, behaviours, 'ways of working' and 'ways of living'. We would also need a change in the governance of our nation: in its leadership, management, administration and the mechanisms for implementation of policy. Above all, it requires execution, the ability to make change happen and to deliver on it, in a timely manner.

My six priorities, the **'Foundation Pillars'**, may seem simple, and if they were easy, many nations would already have been successfull at them all. No nation is. Some nations are better at one than the other, while others have revisited each at intervals to ensure continued progress after relapses, and where policies in one have caused detriment to one or more of the remaining five. Using the analogy of a house, for the purposes of this book, a house we name India, these priorities form the six **'Foundation Pillars'** on which our new 'House of India' can be built, they are the necessary components before any nation can build the new super-structure 'House' above ground. The weaker these **'Foundation Pillars'**, the greater the chance of unevenness and movement, and consequently, the building blocks above ground will crack, damage and eventually either need rebuilding or redesigning. The Indian approach in many aspects follows the behaviour of 'build-neglect-rebuild', where leaders and citizens build something, not necessarily to last, but sufficient for a period, neglect it, and then have to rebuild it, as by that time it is beyond repair. This is where India is at this moment.

India has a younger population not only in comparison to advanced economies but also relative to large developing countries. As a result, the Indian labour force is expected to increase by 32% over the next 20 years, while it will decline by 4% in industrialised countries and by nearly 5% in China. This 'demographic dividend' can add to the growth potential, provided two conditions are fulfilled. First, achieving higher levels of education, health and skill development, and secondly, creating an environment in which the economy not only grows rapidly, but also provides the opportunities to meets the employment,

"Iron rusts from disuse; water loses its purity from stagnation . . . even so does inaction sap the vigor of the mind."

Leonardo da Vinci

15

quality of life and aspirational expectations of this younger population.

The simple tasks and services are usually the most difficult to do, especially when needed to be delivered consistently across the nation, and for the benefit of all citizens. The simple tasks, however, are easier to measure, monitor and report on, to gauge the levels of success in the implementation and benefits for all the citizens of the nation.

Many citizens have said that we cannot make positive political and *'anti-corruption'* type change in India through just changing one part of the political tree; you have to start from the top and work through to the deepest roots. Some say it will never be done, some that it cannot be done, and others that the whole tree needs removing and replacing. We need to apply both a *'Top Down'* and a *'Bottom-Up'* change to succeed.

We need a *'top-down'* change. We need a new breed of Leadership and Statesmanship, both as a President and as a Prime Minister; individuals who are natural leaders who command true respect across the nation; they need to be role models and have the characteristics, charm, charisma and intelligence: coupled with values, behaviours, ethics, *'ways of working'* and *'ways of living'* that our citizens would wish to emulate and replicate; and without this, we will continue along a path of mediocrity to decay and destruction. This leadership needs to appoint a credible Executive who are able to make difficult decisions for the benefit of the nation, with a Legislature that is a better representative of the nation and its citizens; its values, moral code, ethics and behaviours, which is then supported by a professional Judiciary and Law Enforcement: first and foremost, all servants of the nation and its citizens who they represent.

In parallel, we need *'bottom-up'* change. The true assets of our nation are its citizens, and civil society needs to participate more in making this positive change happen. We need newer, fresher and more able individuals, with energy, commitment, passion and enthusiasm to begin to support each of the six **'Foundation Pillars'** to make this change happen. We need new membership in the Legislature, a larger and more active Judiciary, enthusiastic and passionate Teachers and Medical professionals. We need honest and professional law enforcement and internal security forces, which are seen across the world as a beacon for how society is kept safe and secure and how the rule of law is enforced in the soon to be largest population on Earth. Our Armed Forces need to be further supported to ensure that they are equipped and capable of ensuring national security, protecting our environment and sphere of influence across the globe. We then need to provide our citizens with the mechanisms for them to securely live, work, trade and enjoy life in a clean and safe environment.

There are currently two India's. The increasingly wider gap between the improvement, growth and continuing acceleration of the *first India*, and the stagnant, deteriorating and constrained *second India* is a cause for concern. The Indian Government having focused on further developing *first India*, is now focusing on the greater challenge in helping the *second* to join the *first*; and this cannot be tackled and delivered by Government alone. This needs the support of the *first India*.

The statement, *"Power will go to the hands of rascals, rogues, freebooters; all Indian leaders will be of low calibre and men of straw. They will have sweet tongues and silly hearts. They will fight amongst themselves for power and India will be lost in political squabbles. A day would come when even air & water would be taxed in India"*, is very often ascribed to Winston S. Churchill, and is so prophetic to our current situation; however, it has never been attributed by the Churchill Archives or any historian, in anything he wrote or said in his letters, private papers, speeches, articles or books.[3] That does not mean he did not have those sentiments, because in the early years of his career he was genuinely doubtful about Indian independence and the Congress, which he considered elitist. Churchill had known Mohandas K. Gandhi from their time in South Africa and both had considerable mutual respect for one another, with G. D. Birla having been a communication intermediary for some of their letters.[4] Churchill recognised the distinction between independence and freedom, and was afraid that democracy would be compromised; so it was more *'imposed'* rather than *'introduced'* in India.[3]

*"A nation's culture resides in the hearts and in the soul of its people."*
Mohandas Karamchand Gandhi

In 1931 Churchill had said, *"India is an abstraction . . . India is no more a political personality than Europe. India is a geographical term. It is no more a united nation than the Equator".*[5] In 1946, India was described by Jawaharlal Nehru as *". . . four hundred million separate individual men and women, each differing from the other, each living in a private universe of thought and feeling . . . Yet something has bound them together and binds them still. India is a geographical and economic entity, a cultural entity, a cultural unity amidst diversity, a bundle of contradictions held together by strong but invisible threads".*[6] India needs to build on its progress to ensure that these common threads are recognised and understood, are stronger and bind together all its citizens, for their common good.

During the First and Second World Wars, Indians should recognise and appreciate that ~3.9 million Indian citizens and armed forces members volunteered to serve, and ~160,000 made the greatest sacrifice to ensure that democracy was upheld.[7] India rallied to support the Allies, and those with influence, including the Indian National Congress, believed that the Indian independence movement would best be served by helping Britain in whatever capacity possible. Should the Entente/Allied powers have lost these wars, then India may not have had either Independence, freedom or the foundation of democracy it has today, nor the principles of military subservience to the civilian government; an achievement some of India's neighbours have failed to succeed in upholding or maintaining.

Sixty-five years of Independence is a drop in the ocean of Indian history; however, all nations are at a time of human learning, technological development and global change, where the last 130 years has bought greater and more accelerated change than the world had seen in the recorded past of over 5,000 years. Some may view the ideas and solutions presented in this book as unacceptable, unpalatable and not digestible, naïve or impractical, even utopian; some may challenge the approach, the researchers, and the published data or anything else; however, the key issues are firstly the principle of the *'need for change'*, and then secondly *'improving the delivery'* of the changes; actually making the

*"I cannot conceive of a greater loss than the loss of one's self-respect."*
Mahatma Gandhi,

18

changes happens, so the citizens and nation see improvements. Inaction through *'the arguementative Indian'* type discussion, debate, arguments, pontificating, fine tuning and adjusting are merely delay tactics and behavioural manifestations of the inevitable continuing deterioration of Indian democracy and the nation, to the detriment of all citizens. The intent is always there; however, action and will seems to be lacking.

To quote Shashi Tharoor: *"India is not, as people keep calling it, an underdeveloped country, but rather, in the context of its history and cultural heritage, a highly developed one in an advanced state of decay".*[8] I am of the firm opinion that change is now due in our nation, or the decay will continue and accelerate. Without a positive change, our national condition and situation in 2050 will be significantly weaker from where it should and could have been. We have moved forward since Independence, but seem to have lost both the essence of true and honest public service, and the passion for supporting individual, community and national development. We see a more greedy, selfish, corrupt and myopic approach where it is more *'I'* and *'me'* rather than a *'we'* and *'us'*.

Our Indian history can be characterized as a work-in-progress, with a continuous process of reinvention; this is the essence of our character and strength of our culture and people. Regionalisation and caste-based social, economic and political behaviours are on the increase with ascendency, which is a potentially dangerous path towards an India that was once a region of princely State and warlord held lands prior to the arrival of the Greeks, Turks, Persians and Europeans. I would wish the citizens of India to question more, and demand more, for the nation as a whole, for our own joint benefit, and for those not yet fortunate to voice their opinions and be able to make their own demands.

At least four of the great *'faiths'* (Hinduism, Sikhism, Buddhism, Jainism) practiced across the world have emanated from the Indian sub-continent; be they called *'faiths', 'ways of life', 'ways of living'* or *'religions'*, their followers possibly account for over 1.5 billion humans across the world, nearly 1 in 4 of humanity.[9] There are many common themes across these;

*"You must do the thing you think you cannot do."*
Eleanor Roosevelt

as there are between these and Christianity, Islam, Judaism, Zoroastrianism and the Bahá'í faiths, and many others that have not originated within the sub-continent but are practiced by citizens across our nation and form a major part of our daily lives and communities, and have significantly contributed to our national culture. We are a secular nation, and this is strength not to be underestimated or undervalued.

Cohesion as a nation had been supported by the common attitude towards peace, tolerance and personal development that all its faiths support. Indian democracy was established on the values of secularism, equality for all regardless of race, gender or faith. Unlike many other nations, we have the luxury of having a deep, rich and wide heritage of accomplished individuals throughout our history; and a new wave of younger citizens should be able to glean at least a few lessons from these to apply to their leadership, governance, management and administration of our nation.

Individuals, families, communities, regions, companies, multi-national corporations and nation states that learn from their experiences, their successes and shortcoming, and apply and adapt that change and learning, for their future, generally have a better chance of success. The opposite is also true. It is the evolution India needs to begin to deliver, now.

This book is not an analysis of Indian history or an anthropological or sociological exercise, nor is this a piece of academic work or a theoretical exercise. This book deliberately does not compare India with others (only providing some statistics), neither the pro's and con's, nor dwells on examples from across the globe of other national citizens' experiences and outcomes from their actions on desired changes. Each of the six **'Foundation Pillars'** are an encyclopaedic volume in its own right; salient points have been selected, as many discussions, debates and information sources duplicate, overlap and merge. Observations and information are supported by data and information sources, and are then consolidated into the suggested *'edicts'* at the end of each of the six **'Foundation Pillars'** for change.

Citizens of any nation must seek out their own priorities and solutions and execute these at the pace they wish to, and need to. Everything is possible; it requires the support, commitment and participation from the majority of citizens who want to make the change happen; and ownership and clear objectives from a leadership, management and administration, and a governance and implementation model to ensure success. This is not an *expert* opinion, but that of a concerned citizen of India.

As a people and a nation we are able and capable of doing this; I will do whatever I can to help make this happen.

*"All compromise is based on give and take, but there can be no give and take on fundamentals. Any compromise on mere fundamentals is surrender. For, it is all give and no take."*

**Mohandas Karamchand Gandhi**

# INTRODUCTION

*"Men make history and not the other way round. In periods when there is no leadership, society stands still. Progress occurs when courageous, skilful leaders seize the opportunity to change things for the better."*

**Harry S. Truman**

Will the 21$^{st}$ Century be India's Century? If we were to see ourselves in ~35 years time, in a generation, say in 2050, would we be looking back and saying that the first half of the 21$^{st}$ Century gave us the *foundations and successes to achieve and maintain India as one of the most progressive industrial and agricultural economies, with an enlightened social and political system and with the most content (well-being/happy) citizens'*, where peoples from around the world would want to visit, stay and live; or one where we had the opportunity but something *"happened which was beyond our control"*, or we blame the *"corrupt politicians and administrators"*, or we take the fatalistic approach of *"what will be will be . . ."*, *"it was our destiny . . ."*, *"it was written . . ."*, the popular characteristic of inevitability.

Between 2008 and 2011 the local news was about the Indian economic boom, returning NRIs and expatriates; however, findings by a 2012 Gallup Study[10] show that the USA is the most desired destination for emigrants worldwide with 22 million Chinese and 10 million Indians wanting to move permanently to the USA. Regardless of the nationalistic and external outer voices, given the opportunity, we have many professionals and others whose inner voices would rather drive a taxi in a more industrialised nation than have a professional career in India. They prefer these better living and working environments, and for their children to grow and be educated, for their children's future security, opportunities and wellbeing. Can we really afford to lose these citizens, and their families? The brain drain has not

*"You must be the change you wish to see in the world."*
**Mohandas Karamchand Gandhi**

stopped nor significantly slowed down. We need measures to stop the outflow of capability, talent and competence.

As India entered the 21st Century a wider section of our population began to reap the rewards of both its liberalisation policies and increased globalisation. Our population demographic has changed over the last few decades, from a rapid growth with potential youth dependency to one where we have a higher share of workers as compared to dependents. If working-age people can be productively employed, India's economic growth can accelerate. Failure to take advantage of the opportunities inherent in our current demographic profile will lead to economic stagnation. Demographic profiles are no guarantee to economic and social well-being; growth in the number of working-age citizens will not directly lead to an increase and acceleration of economic growth. Our policy decisions, choices and ability to efficiently execute these will determine the realisation of the economic benefits due to demographics. Without such policies, we may find ourselves with large numbers of under-skilled, underemployed or unemployed working-age citizens. This scenario would be a demographic disaster, instead of a demographic dividend, and in some circumstances lead to a weaker more fragile nation, unable to successfully manage adverse political, social, economic and ecological changes.India's demographic cycle now lags ~25 years behind that of many East Asian nations. A purely demographic perspective suggests that the next three decades will be a period of catching up for India with respect to per capita income in East Asia. Education, health and security are essential to happier, more content and productive citizens.

We need to sustainably continue to create jobs at a scale to actively employ our increasing youth and those under ~40 years of age. As our current employment market is biased towards higher-skilled labour, the creation of more semi-skilled and lower-skilled labour will be our continuing challenge.

We are the 7th largest nation by geographical area with the 9th -10th largest by Gross Domestic Product and Gross National Product by value, which is a considerable achievement and a

*"Evil unchecked grows, evil tolerated poisons the whole system."*
**Jawaharlal Nehru**

major improvement in recent years, and our progress continues. However, on a Gross National Income per Capita basis, at approx. US$3,550 we rank at 111 out of 165, in the bottom third as we have a large population. We are better able to afford more food, goods and services as a proportion of our income, as costs are low, so on purchasing power parity we rank 3rd -4th in the world.[11] The key is in increasing per capita income and ensuring that the gap between rich and poor is as narrow as possible.

In 2012 we had the 2nd most populous nation with over 1.2 billion citizens (~17%, over 1 in 6 of all humans on the planet), and by far the largest democracy on Earth with ~714 million voting citizens,[12] so each are given the opportunity to contribute to their own and thus the nation's further development. By 2030, we are expected to have 1.5 billion citizens and the largest population on Earth, which is expected to continue to grow (1.8-2.1 billion by 2100),[13] further challenging our nation and citizens, as our high population growth may only result in increasingly impoverished and sub-standard conditions for growing segments of our population. Unless young people are provided good quality education, vocational skills and new jobs are created, population growth by itself will not result in prosperity. If we fail to generate meaningful employment our demographic dividend will become a demographic liability. This will also make significant demands on our already insufficient and ineffective infrastructure, as there will be an increase in the sizes and populations of the primary, secondary and tertiary cities across our nation. With a larger population living in dense conditions, water, sanitation and healthcare will become even more important, as will security and law enforcement.

The post-independence period saw us progress much slower than many other global economies, a 'Hindu' rate of growth of 1.4% GNP growth between 1960-1979 (which then increased to 4.1% between 1978-1988 and 7.6% between 1988-1991).[14] Socialist-inspired economic policies supported centralisation, extensive regulation, protectionism, licensing and public ownership; policies vulnerable to pervasive corruption and slow growth; coupled with the need for control, power, geopolitical

*"The inherent vice of Capitalism is the unequal sharing of blessings. The inherent virtue of Socialism is the equal sharing of miseries."*
Winston S. Churchill

and many other local internal and external international factors contributed to our leadership sustaining this policy for many decades. An era commonly referred to as the *'licence-permit raj'* and *'inspector raj'* period, which is often seen as the core source of corruption, as free market mechanisms were blocked and hindered, and corruption flourished through allocation of scarce and valuable natural and other resources amongst a group of entities in close collaboration with weak governments and regulatory regimes.

India's political leadership had regularly undertaken periods of *'liberalisation'*; 1945-47, 1965-66, 1980-82 and 1985-6. These were isolated episodes with no long-term benefits or implications. Each generated a burst of euphoria followed by retraction of policies for political reasons, or the perception of change did not last long enough for sustainable change and benefits.

The first period of liberalisation related to food controls, the second to agricultural failure and external shocks, which prompted an INR devaluation and trade liberalisation. The two in the 1980s due to the oil price, balance of payments trouble and an eventual IMF medium-term loan, and the fifth in 1991 was in response to the balance of payments and fiscal crisis. Overall the aim was to increase the efficiency and international competitiveness of Indian manufacturing industries by opening up Indian markets to global products, services and finance. Rapid growth and development in the South East Asian economies such as Malaysia, Singapore, Thailand and Indonesia etc., had also prompted the Indian government to make changes.

Given the Indian national financial position in the first half of 2012, India now needs either another dose of liberalisation, or more robust investments with focus on efficiency and effectiveness, in which citizen investors can deploy capital to generate goods and services for internal consumption, and ideally for export. Local businesses had begun to take advantage of the supply of lower cost educated labour, in manufacturing, technology and service industries, to the extent where Indian is now a major supplier in automotive components, knowledge, pharmaceuticals and information technology, to name a few.

*"Ask not what your country can do for you; ask what you can do for your country."*
John F. Kennedy

The continued successful development of India and the sustained advancement of our citizens is not a foregone conclusion. We are far from it. There are many internal and external factors that prevent and hinder our continued progress. To highlight a few, internally these would include corruption, criminalisation of politics, bureaucracy and security; and externally these include geo-political interests, global finance, investment and terrorism. We do not have the luxury to decide on the location for the *'House of India'*; we live in a relatively dangerous and unstable neighbourhood, and we have to ensure that we both develop and protect our property, as a priority, whilst beginning to support our neighbours in improving our neighbourhood. This is an endeavour we must succeed in.

There is an increasing and accelerating gap between rich and poor across our nation. There is always a gap in expectations between the *'haves'* and the *'have-nots'* within all countries and cultures; however, the wider the gap the greater the dissatisfaction and disenchantment. This can lead to a domino and cascading effect on the social and economic stability of the country. India is experiencing some of the first signs of this instability. As a culture, generally, we are not accustomed to revolution and revolts; however, economic strikes, protests and armed resistance are increasingly regularly events across our nation and evident regularly in the Indian press and television media.

Whether the definition of being *'poor'* and the *'poverty line'* is taken INR 28.65 per day, INR 22.42 per day or INR 32 per day;[15] at these levels India is doing a disservice to the vast majority of its citizens. As of 2010, more than ~37% (~450 million) Indian citizens lived below the poverty line, representing ~83 million families. More than 22% of the entire rural population and 15% of the urban population exists in difficult physical and financial predicament.[16] Studies, records and personal experiences from individuals who have attempted living at these rates clearly illustrated that this confines and de-humanises the existence of the weakest members of our society. We are confining 1 in 3 of our citizens and possibly more realistically, over 2 in 3 of our

*"Poverty is the worst form of violence."*
**Mohandas Karamchand Gandhi**

27

citizens, to a poverty trap which can be a vicious circle that it is difficult for many individuals to get out of, without increased non-welfare support from the wider society and the nation. Creating a welfare-state is not the answer to alleviating poverty in our nation. Wealthy nations have followed this path and many have created at least two generations of individuals who are unable to, and incapable of maintaining full-time employment. Their citizens do not have the education or motivation for personal self-development. No developing nation should begin to go down this slippery slope. Free hand-outs should only be provided for the most deserving; instead we need to provide citizens with the tools and capabilities to help themselves and their families. This starts with education, healthcare and security. Governments need to help their citizens help themselves. Happiness, contentment and well-being of citizens are directly correlated to life-style, health, education, crime and their opportunity for economic security

Almost 60% of the poor (by the above definitions) reside in the states of Bihar, Jharkhand, Orissa, Madhya Pradesh, Chattisgarh, Uttar Pradesh and Uttarakhand. Significantly, 85% of India's tribes'people and Dalits live in these states.[17] India has reduced poverty; however, it is not happening fast enough. Overall growth is essential to alleviating poverty; however, growth in itself is insufficient for poverty reduction on a sustainable basis.

Our nation's ills are a result of bad governance, misplaced priorities, unchecked corruption and a huge failure in increasing literacy and improving health. Weak, dysfunctional institutions provide an incentive for some citizens to loot national wealth, creating a parasitic or potentially a symbiotic relationship with those in leadership and power, which has been the dominant pattern in our post-independence history.

The last 60 years have been a challenge and we have had many name tags to classify our national status, be it 'non-aligned', 'third-world', 'developing', 'less developed' etc., for the majority of this period. We had been relatively insular, protective, conservative, blinkered and myopic in our approach to national

*"There is no limit to what can be accomplished if it doesn't matter who gets the credit."*
Ralph Waldo Emerson

and personal advancement. This is no criticism of the past, as we learned to lead, manage and govern a new nation, with one of the worlds' largest populations, in a democratic fashion. It is an achievement to have maintained cohesion in a post-World-War II environment where geo-political interests from far-away nations played for influence and interests in our backyard and neighbourhood. We have neither suffered the traumas that many other nations (including the majority of those in our neighbourhood) and their citizens have experienced, nor have we accelerated our changes and improvements that have benefits many other nations and their citizens.

Since the 1980s, we have begun to implement some changes. We recognised that in order to maintain a positive position in a global, interconnected and dependent economy and community, we needed to grow and develop our economy and people faster. We began a process of liberalisation and opening-up of our markets and economy to competition and up-skilling our citizens. We began to invest in our advancement as a nation and improvements for our citizens.

This has had some successes and been positive for India; however, India need to move faster and have a deeper change in order to ensure, at national and individual level, that this is both sustainable and these benefits will reach the vast majority, if not the whole population. In 2001 India was classified as one of the four 'BRIC' countries (acronym for Brazil, Russia, India and China), which were deemed to be in a stage of newly advanced economic development, and speculated that by 2050 these four economies would be wealthier than most of the then major economic powers. In 2010 these four have since added South Africa to form a 5-way BRICS emerging economies forum.[18] Some have speculated that the 'I' for India in BRIC could and should be replaced by Indonesia in BRIC.[19]

Will the first half of the 21st Century be a period when we can say India has achieved what its citizens have wanted and wished for? What sort of nation do we wish to be in 2050? In what type of environment would we wish our children and our

*"Life is like a game of cards. The hand that is dealt you represents determinism; the way you play it is free will."*
**Jawaharlal Nehru**

29

*"A small body of determined spirits fired by an unquenchable faith in their mission can alter the course of history."*
Mohandas Karamchand Gandhi

grandchildren to live? What do we need to do differently and better to achieve this

In a more interconnected world of rapid communications, media, travel, commerce and economics: Do we wish to be citizens of a nation where we are a major influencer and a positive contributor? Or one where we continue to disconnect from the facts, maintain our self-delusion of our own capabilities, look after number one, *'ourselves and our family'*, and believe that we will come out of this without any major changes on our own part?

According to the Indian government, most development spending fails to reach its intended recipients. It is either diverted or misused by a sizeable and complacent bureaucracy. Even if the national wish is for universal healthcare, water and education, there are only five other countries which have a lower portion of health spending in the public sector.[20] In his famous *'tryst with destiny'* speech on 14 August 1947, Jawaharlal Nehru articulated this challenge as *'the ending of poverty and ignorance and disease and inequality of opportunities'.* Sixty-five years later, the nation and its citizens are still waiting.

The world is looking at India's economic performance and growth with both respect and envy, and considers India and the BRICS as the current new wave of ideal economic growth models. This and other financial and economic performance has given Indian leadership, commercial houses and executives a level of *'can-do'* attitude and approach. This is positive and good; however, there is also a level of over confidence combined with arrogance, which could be dangerous. The Indian government have had sound reasons to initially focus on deploying resources to meet the demands of the growing middle class and business houses; however, India now need to take a deeper look into alleviating the causes of poverty, inequality and suffering, and for that India requires universal education, health and security; without the latter, the former will not be sustainable. We may lose the 'I' (in BRICs) to Indonesia, another regional neighbour whose governance, economic and social performance is likely to outshine India, and some economists stated in early 2012 that India now has only a 50% chance of ensuring continued development.

According to the World Economic Forum on Global Competitiveness we are still in the first of three stages of development: a 'Factor-Driven' economy where we still need to implement robust Institutions, Infrastructure, Macro-Economic Environment and Health & Primary Education. India is failing in the execution of policies and implementation of complete delivery of initiatives and programmes for improvement. India lacks a professional and honest approach across the vast majority of its public sector projects, and many private sector projects.

Could a vision be for an India where the vast majority of its citizens enjoy a living standard significantly better than at the start of the 21st century, an India being seen as benchmark for literacy, life expectance, security and the rule of law, a nation where all people feel safe, secure and content within our borders? A nation that looks after all its citizens, listens to their views and opinions. A nation where peoples from around the world would wish to visit, see, do business, trade, learn and aim to emulate our culture, heritage, behaviours, values, ethics, 'ways of living' and 'ways of working'. A nation and citizenry which do what they say, and say what they mean.

We need a leadership, legislature (management) and bureaucracy (administration) that are servants of the people, reporting to, and accountable to the people; that serve the needs of citizens and the nation as a whole, and are not using the democratic process to either provide themselves, their families or their associates with a platform for further personal gain, nor a vehicle for the elite to maintain power and status quo over the under-privileged and unfortunate. Many await a new breed of leaders, legislators, and administrators that can arise from the ~1.2 billion citizenry to accept positions of public responsibility without personal gain.

Our current legislature has an average age of ~63 years as of February 2013 (for 239 of 244 members of the Rajya Sabha).[21] This is not a reflection of our demographic, or of a nation of progressive forward thinking leaders, who are in-tune with their generation or the wider world. Few stand out as true statesmen and leaders; disappointingly, some of our younger political

*"Our chief defect is that we are more given to talking about things than to doing them."*
**Jawaharlal Nehru**

31

leadership are purely a younger version of their parents. Analysis for *'India: A Portrait'* by Patrick French in 2011, found that there is a direct linear relationship between age and hereditary MPs: a greater proportion of younger MPs have a family political background, in comparison to others. So, if a young citizen currently wishes to participate in national politics, one of the only available routes seemed to be through family connections:

- All MPs less than 30 years of age are hereditary
- More than two-thirds of MPs aged under 40 are hereditary
- 27 MPs are *'hyper-hereditary'* (where several family members who have made a career out of politics)
- 19 of them are in the Congress party

This is very unhealthy and potentially catastrophic for our nation. We need fresh ideas, fresh faces and individuals that are not constrained by corruption, insular, regional, caste or family perspectives. We need individuals that are Indian first, everything else second.

Indian citizens in the past have shown that we are totally able and capable of making this change happen. We can change ourselves and our nation, for the benefit of us all, and our future generations. Together we can do it.

*"One of the penalties of refusing to participate in politics is that you end up being governed by your inferiors."*
**Plato**

# 1

# GOVERNANCE

*"Just because you do not take an interest in politics doesn't mean politics won't take an interest in you."*

**Pericles**

As a nation of ~1.2 billion citizens we have generally maintained and upheld our Democratic freedoms. We have relatively free and fair elections. We have a relatively independent judiciary and a set of laws. We have an independent and relatively politically free media; and have supported the freedom of speech, expression and association. Our bureaucracy is mature, established and respected. Our policies have been aimed at developing our nation and some initiatives are focused particularly on the neediest. Our armed services have always reported to the civilian government, have amicable relations and been subservient to the elected officials. The Central government edicts and policies continue to be generally respected and followed by our States. However, each of these has being slowly and corrosively eroded.

Governance can be defined as the mechanism by which a government and its representatives are elected, monitored and replaced; how a government effectively develops, formalises and executes appropriate policies for the benefits of its citizens; and how a government maintains the necessary institutions that manage economic and social services among its citizens. An efficient, effective and democratic government is the best guarantor of social justice as well as an orderly society. India is far from it.

Corruption is the most important and most culturally difficult challenge our democracy faces. Criminalisation of the political process, the links between politicians, civil servants,

*"A change is brought about because ordinary people do extraordinary things."*
**Barack Obama**

33

and some commercial enterprises are having a destructive effect on policy formulation and governance. Our politicians are losing respect. There is a trust deficit. Our democracy is therefore, more impressive in form than substance.

Our electoral system and administration has widespread nepotism, cronyism, patronage, sycophantic behaviours and hereditary preferences. In the 2012 Lok Sabha, of our 543 elected MPs, we have approximately 162 MP's having criminal records and 14 MPs having at least one serious (murder, rape or similar) charge against them. National Election Watch analysed affidavits of 227 of the 238 MPs in the Rajya Sabha. Of these 227 MPs, 41 (18%) MPs have declared pending criminal cases against them, of these 13 MPs serious criminal cases. In the 2012 Presidential election, of 4,835 MPs and MLAs eligible to vote, 1,448 (31%) declared criminal cases against them in a self-sworn affidavit filed with the Election Commission. Of these, 641 have declared serious criminal cases such as rape, murder, attempt to murder, kidnapping, robbery, extortion, etc. The affidavits were analysed by Association for Democratic Reforms.[22] So, one in three of our MPs and MLAs could not claim to pass a 'moral code of conduct' test, or should legally hold a post of public service. This figure is probably on the low side, as bribery and intimidation coupled with the poor and lengthy legal system ensure some cases never see the light of day. This is a deep criminalisation of the political leadership and it makes a mockery of our Parliament, electoral processes and rule of law.

## ARE WE BECOMING A KLEPTOCRACY?

The sports field is the best arbiter for competence and capability. Be it in individual or team sports, across the world, children of leading sportsmen rarely succeed in competing and performing to the level of their parents. Sportsmen and women succeed through a combination of passion, natural skill, training, ambition, commitment, genetics, environment; and to an extent luck and timing. Nations aim to get their best available citizens to compete

*"The price good men pay for indifference to public affairs is to be ruled by evil men."*
Plato

34

for the nation, and citizens would want the best to be chosen to compete, in order to win. We try to select from the ~1.2 billion citizens available to compete in cricket, hockey, chess, tennis, badminton or shooting etc. This should be no different in any other profession, be it politics, administration, military, business, entertainment, law, medicine or science. Recent elections show that not all the offspring of existing or retired legislators are truly the new wave leaders our nation requires; they are either replicating their parents or merely using it as an easy option career move, basking in their parent's glory, or being used as an extension of politics being a *'corrupt family business'* where wives, sons, daughters, daughter-in-laws, son-in-laws, cousins and nephews can all become politicians. Some politicians have never been under any illusions that their continued power is maintained and extended through family and close associates.

Is this the law making body of an ambitious nation aspiring to a permanent seat in the Security Council? Is parliament a representative of Indian society and its citizens? Is this what the electorate of India wish for, and deserve?

Our elections are characterised by short-term policies (because a Government is often voted out of office by the following election), political violence and conflicts between various caste and sectarian groups (sometimes artificially created). Legislators seem to be more accountable to their political parties rather than the citizens. This is further exacerbated by many occasions where officials move from one political party to another, some in unison, and others flip-flopping between parties.

When in office, our mechanisms for feedback and monitoring of elected officials between elections are poor at best, and there are little avenues for citizens to provide feedback on performance and requests. Elected officials are regularly accused of political interference in the institutions and processes of governance in the pursuit of personal and partisan interests. This is a deep erosion of the rule of law and is a pervasive feature of most administrations.

The high levels of poverty and illiteracy that characterise much of the voting population do not assist the governance processes, as political funding and campaign strategies can focus

*"For a successful revolution it is not enough that there is discontent. What is required is a profound and thorough conviction of the justice, necessity and importance of political and social rights."*

**Dr. B. R. Ambedkar**

on *'vote bank'* politics; financial and other short-term incentives are used to ensure support during election periods, which in some regions and communities ensures maintaining the status quo against progressing or improving the standards of living among the majority of the electorate.

The proliferation of regional and caste-based political parties can be positive as it engages citizens to vote; however, we seem to also be moving towards community based parties, and this can be unhealthy for both these communities and the nation. Recently we have seen an increase in State and Central coalitions; coalition politics has further hampered governments as they are unable to make and take either long-term or tough decisions in the State or national interest, and when these changes are proposed, the leadership is often too weak to execute these; and the proposed reforms and changes are regularly retracted or reversed. Absence of bold reformist legislators, who act in the long-term interest of all their citizens, leads to a Parliament that is reluctant to make decisions which might affect their short-term benefit. Political pluralism is certainly present in India and a good thing; but we need to move away from agreeing and passing sub-optimal, short-term solutions and policies.

We need a *'top-down'* change where the President provides a credible long-term vision and works with the Prime Minister to agree the priorities for delivering that vision for the benefit of our nation; the Prime Minister would work with his chosen cabinet of Ministers to convert those priorities into strategies and action plans. Each Minister works with his Civil Servants to produce strategies, initiatives and delivery plans, including timings and measures, and these are jointly agreed across all Ministers with the Prime Minister being the final decision maker and arbitrator. Senior Civil Servants would be individually accountable for the delivery of each initiative and work plan. Ministers and Civil Servants would work with their counterparts in State Governments and their representatives to agree and re-cast these plans and deliver these for the benefits of the citizens in each State. The State and National Ministers and Civil Servants would present their final plans and progress to the Prime Minister and

*"It is not enough to be electors only. It is necessary to be law-makers; otherwise those who can be law-makers will be the masters of those who can only be electors."*
**Dr. B. R. Ambedkar**

Select Committees at regular intervals to evaluate progress and make course corrections if necessary, and reprioritise if required. The Prime Minister being the final decision maker; he or she would then update the President on progress towards the national Vision during his regular briefings. This should not be very different to what should actually happen already; however, in reality, there are many hurdles for this not to be happening as effectively as it should.

The *Panchayats*, State Governments and other stakeholders should be able to provide their *'bottom-up'* inputs into the Ministers and Special Committees to ensure the needs and expectations of the local citizens are considered and delivered.

# PRESIDENCY

Jawaharlal Nehru had stated, *"We have not given our President any real power but we have made his position one of great authority and dignity."* Dr. Ambedkar had declared, *"the President is merely a nominal figure head . . . he has no discrimination and no powers of administration at all.* At the time of writing the Constitution, the role of the President of India occupied the same position as the then King of England. He or she was the Head of State but not the Executive. He or she represented the nation but did not rule the nation. Like the British Sovereign, the role of the President was *"to advise, encourage and warn ministers in respect of the recommendations which they make."* [23]

Is a tried and tested British model still appropriate for an Indian Executive branch, with the challenges it faces? Is the way of governing an island of ~48 million people in 1948 (of generally one common language and culture), the most appropriate to govern a State of ~1.2 billion citizens (with many languages and cultures) in the 21st century? Do we need an amendment to further bring the Executive closer to the citizens and the electorate? How can we get the *'voice of the electorate'* and *'voice of the citizens'* fed directly and independently to the legislators?

*"When the effective leader is finished with his work, the people say it happened naturally".*
Lao Tzu (Laozi)

37

The President is a symbol of the nation, and has a constructive and meaningful role to play in the affairs of our nation, exercising a persuasive influence on the ministers and helping them through advice and experience, mediating between the Centre and States etc. The President's role as a figure-head is reflected in their indirect election by both Houses of Parliament; however as currently seen, this is an internal process as the election involves lobbying and trading by political parties for their respective candidates, and in order to get a majority vote, potentially a compromise candidate, or one that poses least cross-party resistance, or one which provides a minority coalition concession, could be nominated and elected for this very important and critical post.

We do not need a major re-write of the Constitution; however the role of the President could be better executed, enhanced and further developed. We need a Head of State to be a *'statesman'*, a *'visionary'*, the President should be an individual who:

- Exemplifies a role-model Indian, representing a set of values, behaviour, ethics, *'ways of working'* and *'ways of living'* that is both an inspiration and an aspiration for the young and old alike.
- Is a non-political self-made individual, who has succeeded in his or her own professional or field of expertise.
- Together with the Prime Minister, can create and articulate a long-term *'Vision for India'*.
- Works with the Prime Minister and ministers to ensure policies are developed to achieve the Vision, and appropriate measures and metrics are in place to assess progress and regularly report on these back to the nation.
- Works with the Prime Minister and ministers to ensure that the Civil Service Administration effectively and efficiently delivers these policies.
- Is able to challenge the Legislators when activities or laws are deemed not to be in the interest of our nation or its citizens.

*"A nation of sheep will beget a government of wolves."*
Edward R. Murrow

- Is able to communicate his or her *'Vision for India'* to our citizens and the progress towards this.
- Has weekly or bi-weekly physical communication meetings across the nation to listen to the *'voice of the citizens'* and provide feedback to the Prime Minister and Legislators at regular intervals.
- Is comfortable in, and able to, represent India on the world stage. Supporting the Prime Minister and other legislators in protecting and promoting Indian interests abroad.
- Is able to stand shoulder-to-shoulder with our friends and toe-to-toe with those who wish to harm us.

## STATE GOVERNANCE

India is a Federal Constitutional Republic governed under a parliamentary system currently consisting of 28 States and 7 union territories. Over the past few decades we have seen the more rapid progress of citizens in some states, and the continuing deterioration of the development of citizens in other states. We have the basis for sound institutions; however, the structures of governance seem to be ineffective in meeting and delivering the basic needs of our citizens. The states with Chief Ministers who are better administrators have stronger governance, less corruption and aim to represent all their citizens through delivering measurable, visible and tangible programmes for economic and social development, have been re-elected; the opposite is also true. We see the benefit of change in those States that have realised that the above practices works, and have begun to emulate them. Chief Ministers with a clear majority and bi-partisan consensus across political party lines have stable governments that are always better positioned to execute the vision and initiatives than those with fragile coalitions which make sub-optimal compromises on almost on a daily basis.[24]

Amendments to our Constitution have considerably increased the powers of local governments, including increased financial

*"Patriotism is supporting your country all the time, and your government when it deserves it."*
Mark Twain

and administrative autonomy. Key success factors have been shown to be a strong leadership with a vision coupled with and efficient and effective execution of policies by an administrative and support structure. Where initiatives have been implemented in a timely fashion, the introduction of information and systems technology has played a major role, while also providing a marked increase in the service to citizens.[25]

State Governments best serve their citizens when they self-govern and continue to take accountability to deliver services to their citizens, this trend of independence needs to continue; however, this needs to be balanced by a much stronger Centre that enforces nationwide policies and consistency in execution across all States and Territories. This also requires individual states to take accountability in increasing the learning and application of best-practices from one another.

There are planned initiatives towards further ground roots democracy and activities, by decentralising welfare and development schemes from the States to locally elected Panchayats for their districts or urban areas. We have ~3.3 million elected Panchayat representatives, of which ~1 million are women.[26] This is an excellent initiative to bring the strength of democracy through direct participation of individuals and communities. Albeit it supports delivery of policy and policy feedback at grassroots level; it will face both corruption and competence challenges. Governance and legal accountability during implementation has to minimise these.

Panchayats could be one of the mechanisms to deliver the 'bottom-up' change across our nation. These should ideally, but not exclusively, be led by younger informed individuals that are:

- Local to the region.
- Passionate about positive change for the citizens in their communities and across our nation.
- Incorruptible and with probity.
- Secular and independent in their views.
- Wanting to contribute back to society, and be part a of a democratic movement to provide consistent change across our nation.

*"People say, 'Why do you have this problem? Is it lack of good governance? Is it corruption? Is it attitudes, cultures, customs, mores?' The answer is it's all of those."*
Tom Miller

- Wanting to see the tangible and measurable short and long-term benefits of individual, social and economic change to their communities.
- Educated to a college or university level, ideally outside their region.
- Experienced in a working environment and successful a field of their choice, where they have made significant contributions.

We need to move away from Panchayats that are not reflective of the age, social demographics and the aspirational objectives of the communities they serve.

# CIVIL SERVICE ADMINISTRATION

The Indian Civil Service is the backbone of the government. Civil servants are an essential part of the policy making process; from policy formulation through to decision making and finally implementation of the component initiatives. They provide an important mechanism for implementing national and state policies of welfare and planned economic development.

The Indian Civil Service has had a reputation of being one of the best employers, providing the opportunity for variety, promotion and most importantly, interesting and challenging assignments with members holding strategic positions across the country. It provides some of the best quality training for personal and professional development.

Our Central and State government employs ~6.4 million civil servants. It is one of the world's largest employers. Of these, we only have ~4,500 of the elite IAS (Indian Administrative Services) staff, ~19,000 in the top Services and ~80,000 'Category One/A' staff, the decision makers.[27] These are some of the most important citizens that are necessary to deliver the changes required. We need more of the IAS and 'Category One/A' and less low level administrators, and many of these posts remain unfilled even after examination for a variety of reasons.[28]

"A few heart-whole, sincere, and energetic men and women can do more in a year than a mob in a century."
Swami Vivekananda

41

*"A great man is different from an eminent one in that he is ready to be the servant of the society."*
**Dr. B. M. Ambedkar**

Sardar Vallabhbhai Patel is remembered as the *'Patron Saint'* of the Indian Civil Service; he saw the importance of having a uniform administrative structure centrally organised, providing consistent services across the nation with *'complete loyalty and unremitting zeal'.*[29] Sadly, this mantra has also been eroded over time. Although a highly respected institution, a sense of *'Babu Raj'* has begun to pervade the population, as citizens experience an ever increasing, inefficient and ineffective bureaucracy.[30]

We have taken possibly an already complex British bureaucracy for managing their Empire, and enveloped this with Indian complexities for control, secrecy and security. This has created a paper trail monster that makes it difficult for a citizen to navigate the complexities and procedures for timely and quality delivery of services. A 2009 survey by the Political & Economic Risk Consultancy,[31] of the leading economies of Asia, revealed Indian bureaucracy to be not just the least efficient out of Singapore, Hong Kong, Thailand, South Korea, Japan, Malaysia, Taiwan, Vietnam, China, Philippines and Indonesia; it was also found that working with the India's civil servants was a *'slow and painful'* process. This ranking, done by 1,274 expatriates working in 12 North and South Asian nations, ranked Asian bureaucracies in the following order: Singapore, Hong Kong, Thailand, South Korea, Japan, Malaysia, Taiwan, Vietnam, China, Philippines, Indonesia and India.

Some ministers and politicians have misused their position and power, and have tried to influence civil servants to follow their bidding; non-compliant civil servants have been harassed, put under pressure, transferred (to perceived low priority, remote or insurgency-affected regions etc.), and their families have also been threatened. In extreme cases where civil servants have tried to defend the law, the individual has been even murdered.[32] The government has begun to put plans into place to eliminate the abuse by both Central and regional politicians on the civil service, especially the IAS and senior ranks. However, this is also a two-way street, where ambitious civil servants also use the support and influence of politicians to realise their personal objectives. The probity and independence of civil servants needs to be re-established. Civil servants and IAS members etc., should be in their allocated post for at least 2-3 years as a minimum to ensure they are able to implement and execute their initiatives and improvements; and these posts should be assigned independently, on merit, capability, competence and personal development needs, at the Centre without any state or federal political influence.

Civil Service recruitment needs to continue to be based on merit, although reservations are made for scheduled castes and tribes; the process of promotions and incentives have to be based on performance reviews against pre-determined expectations and 360° peer review, leading to a true meritocracy for development and continuation within the service. Civil Service positions cannot continue to have the guarantee of life-time job security; poor performers should be given the opportunity to improve and unprofessional behaviours should be grounds of temporary suspension for a minimum time period followed by rapid termination, and criminal convictions on confirmation of guilt. We need to establish personal accountability for performance and delivery for the majority of Civil Servants, and especially all the top tier staff. This has to be supported by mechanisms of oversight for all key initiatives by independent committees. This could begin help mitigate some of the current challenges, including incentivisation, frequent transfer of key civil servants, lack of accountability, political interference, consistent project management, skills exchange, use of tools and techniques, personal development etc. The Civil Service should use the same basis of employment as in the private sector. This may require changes in remuneration and incentives; however, the total wage bill should reduce. It is better to have fewer higher paid professional who deliver, rather than many poor paid, who do not deliver. In the short-term, this may be difficult and time consuming; however in the long-term we will have an effective and efficient Civil Service that provides significantly improved services and delivers value for money initiatives.

Civil Servant teams need to be established and implemented on a national basis, across states, and centrally controlled,

*"Justice will not be served until those who are unaffected are as outraged as those who are."*
**Benjamin Franklin**

to ensure successful execution of initiatives from conception through to final complete delivery and smooth operation post-implementation, to resolve any minor problems during and after implementation. Individuals would be assigned to these initiatives and personal performance would be directly linked to meeting their delivery metrics. This is not dissimilar to how large commercial management projects are delivered; usually on-time and on-budget whilst meeting the agreed objectives. If we can do it with the Delhi Metro System, sadly one of the few large public project success stories, we should use this as a template for others to replicate.

The institutions of Audits, Vigilance Commission and Ombudsman need to be significantly strengthened and given the executive powers and influence to investigate and take action in cases of corruption, interference and professional incompetence, independently and in a timely fashion.

In recent years, several States have harnessed information systems and technology to make it easier for citizens to interact with the authorities, and also increase the effectiveness and efficiency of service delivery. Value-for-money and effective service delivery can only be achieved through streamlining and use of technology. As a nation we are now the global leader in 'Business Process Outsourcing', where our home grown businesses have learned from companies across the world on how best to streamline processes and procedures, whilst maintaining compliance, security, governance and improving customer services. Our State and Central governments have begun to do this, but we need to leverage and apply this further. The use of information and technology systems is not the panacea to effective service delivery; we need to apply appropriate measures and reward mechanisms to ensure long-term institutionalisation of these processes and procedures to ensure ownership and sustainability. Most information and technology systems implementation across the world are over budget and delayed; however, experienced incentivised implementers can be commissioned to ensure timely delivery.

*"It often requires more courage to dare to do right than to fear to do wrong."*
Abraham Lincoln

# SUMMARY

Change in Governance and improvements for our citizens will not come from non-participation and walk-outs in our Parliament; this only delays necessary legislation and makes Parliament even less productive and effective, and is further seen as an immature and childish way to run the largest democracy in the world. Fasting protestors only benefit in their short-term health, and damage their long-term health. Strikes can result in lost wages, impacting the well-being and financial security of the protestors and their dependents, and protests that damage public and private property are least effective as they harm both our living environment and damage assets which eventually have to be replaced through the public purse. Venting anger and frustration can be done on a sports field or gym. Our history has taught us that peaceful protests and dialogue are effective and proven to deliver change.

Any real positive change would require the establishment of a much more authoritarian democratic regime that are servants of the citizens, focused on delivery of services for the benefit of the nation and its citizens, who are able to positively prioritise and take significant and difficult decisions at critical times, across the powerful interests groups, lobbies and dominant individuals.

Governance in India is evolving, its priorities and features will need to change, as we adapt to a growing population and economy, mistakes will be made; however, at each point of learning, we must further enhance and improve.

*"In politics we presume that everyone who knows how to get votes knows how to administer a city or a state. When we are ill . . . we do not ask for the handsomest physician, or the most eloquent one."*

**Plato**

**The *'Foundation Pillar for Governance'* could read that we will have:**

1. No individual with either a criminal record or outstanding legal cases in which, he or she are associated, to be able to apply for, or hold any public office.

2. A stronger more visible Presidency that provides for direct access to the *'voice of the citizens'*.

3. A stronger and more visible Prime Minister who takes accountability for developing and delivering the agreed services and improvements to its citizens.

4. A more transparent Executive and Cabinet that takes individual accountability to implement the initiatives necessary to deliver the agreed services and improvements, and to regularly communicate the progress of these to the citizens.

5. A more transparent and challenging Legislature which proactively proposes legislation to ensure consistent, faster and deeper improvements in services across the nation.

6. A more transparent and approachable Legislature which, listens to the *'voice of the electorate'* to ensure policy making is closer to the needs of the citizens.

7. A more transparent and humanitarian Legislature which is accountable for representing the needs of minorities, women and other neediest sections of society.

8. Civil Services and Governmental institutions that are accountable for planning and delivering effective and efficient initiatives and services.

9. Civil Service and Governmental institutions that are accountable for the significantly improvement in effectiveness and efficiency of their services.

10. All civil servants assigned to be in posts for a minimum 2-3 year term; individuals will be assigned by their central agency based on merit, capability, competence and personal development needs. There will be no state or central political interference in this process.

*"In a democracy you get the government you deserve and you deserve the government you get."*
Unknown

11. A mechanism for government employees to be recruited, promoted, rewarded and released based on regular and comprehensive performance appraisals.

12. Panchayats that are truly representative of their communities; led by incorruptible individuals who aim to serve the nation and citizens first.

13. Panchayats that are ideally led by young, informed and passionate local individuals who have had the benefit of work experience and education outside their region.

14. Local states that are reform-oriented, with an active, critical, vocal and highly politicised public.

15. Local states that propose and lead in the delivery of improvement initiatives in a consistent manner.

16. Local state with regional independent citizen watchdog organisations.

17. Oversight committees that robustly monitor all major initiatives to ensure value-for-money and effective service delivery.

18. Freedom of press and media to communicate the performance of governmental progress and citizen issues and concerns.

19. A significant expansion in the use of information technology and systems to improve the efficiency and effectiveness of the services to all citizens.

20. An independent legally authorised and accountable Audit, Vigilance Commission and Ombudsman to review and prosecute cases of corruption.

21. .........................................................................

22. .........................................................................

23. .........................................................................

24. .........................................................................

25. .........................................................................

Etc .......................................................................

*"It is any day better to stand erect with a broken and bandaged head than to crawl on one's belly, in order to be able to save one's head."*
**Mohandas Karamchand Gandhi**

# 2

# EDUCATION

*"I said to my children, I'm going to work and do everything that I can do to see that you get a good education. I don't ever want you to forget that there are millions of God's children who will not and cannot get a good education, and I don't want you feeling that you are better than they are. For you will never be what you ought to be until they are what they ought to be".*

**Dr. Martin Luther King, Jr.**

Data recently published in the 2011 Government Census[33] states that we have managed to achieve an effective 74% literacy rate for citizens over the age of 7; an increase of over 9% (from 64.8%) since 2001. Doubly beneficial was finding a significant rise in the literacy of females. This is excellent news; however, there was a debate on their definition of literacy.

We have made significant progress in many areas including raising school attendance, and there are several reasons for more optimism about progress of school education in the future. However, a very large amount of work still needs to be done. We have only scratched the surface. The number of independent private schools has significantly increased, and high visibility promoters and senior staff from commercial organisations have begun to take a greater interest in supporting this sector, as they recognise the importance of availability of quality education as a key factor to the long-term development of the nation.[34]

Education faces many challenges in parallel, and all need to be actioned in parallel, and each has a different need and a solution. We have illiteracy, poverty and low-attendance at one end and need for higher quality top-end research based universities at the other end of the spectrum, and everything in between.

Of our ~1.2 billion population at least 432 million could actually be classified as illiterate (36%, over 1 in 3); and we still have ~8.15 million (~57%) out-of-school children.[35] While the base of our education pyramid, primary education, may be weak; we have emerged as an important player in the worldwide information technology revolution on the back of substantial, absolute numbers, of well-educated computing and other graduates. We should be able to further leverage this as a learning tool for the rest of our citizens, and in particular rural India.[36]

Research information and analysis provides evidence to suggest that an individual's productivity and earnings depend not only on the number of years of education gained, but also on what is actually learnt at school. This evidence underlines the importance of ensuring that what schools do, leads to learning achievement. The key is not only the *'what they learn'* but the *'how they learn it'*. There are opinions and experiences stating that our system of *'teaching'* is more a one-way process from teacher to pupil, learning by being told, taking instruction, and not a *'two-way communication'*, where the students are challenged to think, apply and adapt, learning by doing. There are major differences in the outcomes of varying methods and cultures of teaching.[37] We need to make learning fun and enjoyable, and better than the other alternatives the children would have in spending their day-time. Being at school needs to be safer and securer than their alternatives; this includes the provision of meals, clean water and clean sanitation facilities. Behaviour, values and expectations start at a young age. Schools do not have sufficient basic facilities (water and sanitation): 265 of 304 (87%) schools tested, even in Delhi, by the Central Board of Secondary Education, have sub-standard facilities, at 33% below normal expected standards.[38] This forces students to urinate and defecate outside the designated areas; over time, circumstances drive practices, which lead to behaviours which over time become habits. Half of the ailments school children suffer are related to unsanitary conditions and lack of personal hygiene. This further reinforces the fact that we still need to get the basics right even in our nation's capital.

*"Education is the most powerful weapon which you can use to change the world."*
**Nelson Mandela**

With such large numbers of schools in poor condition, poor sanitation and school facilities, a simple idea could be to provide pre-fabricated schools, designed for different sizes of enrolment. The technology of pre-fabrication across the world has significantly increased and this provides all-weather protection and a consistency of quality of build, and therefore repair and maintenance. School construction and *'cost-of-operation'* could be significantly reduced; whilst most importantly, providing teachers and pupils with an environment more conducive to enjoyably teaching and learning.

# PRIMARY EDUCATION

We have made significant improvement in primary and secondary education, we perform better than countries in our region; however, we fall well short of the performance of other BRIC countries, especially in secondary school participation and youth literacy rates. Currently, we aim to raise college enrolment rates from 13% to 21% in five years, and to 30% by 2020,[39] and to do that we would need another 800-1000 universities and over 40,000 additional colleges. In contrast, the enrolment rate is currently 23% in China and 34% in Brazil, and is improving.[40]

1 on 5 of our primary schools are single-teacher schools. This is similar to many sub-Sahara African countries, and therefore a high pupil-to-teacher ratio of 45, which is higher than most South East Asian countries. Primary education is the base of the education pyramid, where the foundations for learning are laid, and this is also where the greatest challenges lie. Only 1 in 10 of those who enter the school system at primary level qualifies to college level. This is unacceptable. We will never further develop as a nation unless this is significantly increased.

In a 2011 survey by ASER Centre, one third of the teachers in government primary schools were absent on a given day, more disturbingly, even among the teachers who were present, only a small proportion were able to complete basic questions designed for the students, and to follow and use simple teaching techniques. In another survey, half of the schools had no teaching activity during the visit of the researchers. Inactive teachers were engaged in a variety of *'time-pass'* activities; drinking tea, reading comics, eating or just sitting idle. It concluded that some teachers placed a minimum of both time and effort in the task of teaching, and that this pattern was not confined to a minority of irresponsible teachers, but it had become a way of life, endemic in the profession. We need to re-establish teaching to its former, respected and rewarding profession. We need to significantly improve the recruitment and evaluation criteria and ensure teacher training courses are improved and nationally consistent, and teachers are regularly tested, accredited and licensed to teach. We need to supply teachers who have passion, enthusiasm and commitment with the equipment and resources to do their jobs, and pupils with the materials to do theirs. We need to ensure our university graduates, who are willing and able to contribute back to society and to support our nation's further development, are provided a fast-track means of getting the teacher training and experience necessary to be the *'guru's'* and role models of our next generation

The weak base of learning at the primary level makes it increasingly and unnecessarily more difficult for teachers, institutional managers and administrators as these children pass further up the educational system.

Experience across the world has shown that the key responsibility and accountability for primary education lies with the parents. It is essential to communicate, inform and convince parents for the need, and the benefits of sending their children to school; to ensure that they do go to school, and once there, parents need to take an active interest and participation in their child's performance and progress. Parents need to demand and ask teachers questions, for the benefit of their children. This is a big change that we must support. Many parents, especially illiterate day workers leave home prior to children getting to school and arrive after children leave school, and we need mechanisms for communities to work together in taking collective responsibility and accountability for the education and development of their children.

Tests and league tables are controversial and in many instances can help inform parents and communities and improve learning

*"No man should bring children into the world who is unwilling to persevere to the end in their nature and education."*

**Plato**

performance. While each State Examination board sets its own curriculum and examinations, there is no standardised national level common achievement test in India. We should introduce an age 7 and 11 set of tests to begin to establish teaching and learning standards across our nation. Each local community and school can benefit to see how they perform in a pan-India context.

## SECONDARY & HIGHER EDUCATION

Research and international comparisons have recorded the achievement levels of Indian students at secondary level to be well below international averages, albeit, the average value does include more industrialised nations.

With a significant proportion of our government's education resources focused on increasing rural literacy, through boosting primary education, the private sector has begun to fill a gap within secondary and higher education. However, many of these institutions, both private and public, are short of suitably qualified and motivated teachers, have poor equipment, facilities and libraries, and are working with outdated and inappropriate curricula and infrastructure.

There has been an exponential growth in the number of private schools, especially in cities, where aspiration, affluence and the benefits of good quality teaching and learning is better understood and appreciated. This further exacerbates the increasing inequality in educational provision and opportunity. Research and analysis also suggests that private schools are more effective in imparting knowledge and increased learning, whilst delivering this at a lower cost per student than government schools; their cost advantage seems to be primarily in being able to pay 'market wages'; it seems government school teachers have significant high minimum wages and total employment costs. The level of quality, productivity and effectiveness of government secondary schools and teachers has also been questioned. A similar set of solutions as with primary education in regards to teacher training, accreditation and student national tests at age 15 and 17 and league tables, could be beneficial.

*"It is the teacher—what the teacher knows and can do—that is the most significant factor in student achievement."*
Harry K. Wong

The government is currently working on at least 9 higher education bills to improve this sector, including allowing international universities to establish campuses and joint-ventures. These are demanding public education initiatives which suggest that we have begun to give greater priority to improving school education. However, as with most things in our nation, success will depend on execution of service delivery, against pre-determined criteria in a time bound fashion.

More than 5 million citizens will enter the 15-24 age groups every year, adding to the demand for more training, work experience, colleges and universities, and then employment. India will be the largest contributor to the global work-force; potentially increasing from 749 million in 2010 to 962 million in 2030. These are the individuals we need to immediately and urgently focus on. They will enter the work market as labourers, trainees, vocationally skilled, semi-skilled citizens, graduates and post-graduates. These are the citizens who should expect to benefit from our demographic dividend, which if successful will provide the sort of surge that sustained many of the Asian *'tiger'* economies. If by 2030 the current trends of education, labour participation and unemployment continue, 423 million citizens will be unemployed or unable to participate in the job market.[41] Our potential demographic disaster.

These citizens, once on the carousel of employment and success, will be better placed to focus their children and the next wave of citizens into the virtuous cycle of development and improvement.

We need to help these young citizens acquire both vocational skills training and to leverage the use and application of technology, towards excellence in all spheres of individual and collective activity so that the nation constantly rises to higher levels of endeavour and achievement. We have begun to develop in Information Technology and Systems, Biotechnology, Pharmaceuticals etc.; however, we need to maintain these and expand in many other industry sectors where we need to increase our global presence and be both leading edge and self-sufficient developers; these could include Automotive, Military, Aerospace, Environmental and Maritime technology to name a few. We need to better understand and have participation from Industry

*"Our progress as a nation can be not swifter than our progress in education."*
John F. Kennedy

53

to assess their real skill needs, and then align that with the expectations of the trainees, so they can be better motivated when they can see the potential job, employment prospects, career progression and personal development path.

We also need to improve the top apex of the education pyramid. We need to have a broader and deeper front-line in leading-edge research with more post graduates and doctorates; this is key for our next phase of industrialisation and advancement to high-value added products and services. It is essential for our universities to take on and succeed in leading-edge developments in the primary sciences, to further our knowledge and experiences, but also making it more applicable to day-to-day applications and support our critical national security type industries become self-sufficient. There is a direct correlation between nations that have universities and institutions which undertake leading edge research and the nation's technical and economic development. Many of the best brains employed in research institutions and universities in the USA and Europe, and many research papers and breakthrough ideas involve participation from Indian origin scientists. We should set ourselves a goal of increasing the numbers of approved patents, numbers of post graduate Doctors of Philosophy (PhDs), publication of research articles and also in the transfer of these ideas to practical applications. This will require a major change in the way these institutions are managed and run.

Our university system is in a deep crisis; if we do not create higher-quality colleges and universities for our young citizens, we risk reaping the results of a demographic disaster. In February 2012, activists in 6 states launched a campaign calling for a greater government role in monitoring higher education.[42] We await their progress.

# ASPIRATION GAP

Generally, self-respect is achieved when individual citizens are provided the opportunity to contribute and have sufficient earnings to feed, house and clothe their family: *'roti, kapda aur makan'*, the

*"Children must be taught how to think, not what to think."*
Margaret Mead

basic necessities of life. Increasingly, education is replacing muscle as the key component of personal development that is required to achieve this. Increasing aspirations has begun to create an *'aspiration gap'*, the gap between what citizens expect and what citizens are offered, if left unsatisfied, will result in social instability.[43]

The increasing shortage of high and semi-skilled labour will constrain productivity and economic growth. This shortage will further raise inequality. If we look at this from an economic perspective, to continue to provide the level of growth our nation needs, we must increase both the number of hours worked and the productivity (efficiency and effectiveness) of those hours; and this determines the output (amount per hour) of goods and services we are able to provide ourselves and the world. The more we are able to provide in a given work hour, the better for both the individual and the nation, be that in agricultural productivity, teaching, administration, science, transport, medicine, production line or a call centre; in any occupation or profession.

Higher value-added products and services, requiring inputs from more skilled citizens and more complex machinery and technology, will be the first to feel the pressure of the labour productivity gap and lower growth, even if we invested in technology, as this requires qualified citizens to operate, manage, maintain and repair. As the demand for skilled citizens increases, and if relatively lower skilled citizens are added to the workforce, they would reduce the overall workforce quality and impact productivity and growth. After a certain point, it does not help to increase the numbers of hours worked without increasing the workforce, as this negatively affect their productivity and can cause longer term motivation and self-respect issues etc. Should the business or organisation decide not to invest in technology as skilled staff is not available, then it will produce less value-added products and services, of lower value and quality, and we again loose out in the longer-term. This is why we are seeing ever increasing wage inflation, which in certain cases is reaching Western European and North American levels. This is not good, as it makes us as a nation, less competitive in the global market for both goods and services. We are becoming uncompetitive, as costs are rising, with poor infrastructure and other political and

*"A good head and good heart are always a formidable combination. But when you add to that a literate tongue or pen, then you have something very special."*

Nelson Mandela

socio-economic issues; these are driving international businesses towards our South Eastern neighbours.

Appropriate information technology and systems should be used, consistently, across our nation that meets the needs of each age group of students and their teachers. Use of computer based learning and teaching can make learning fun, support teaching, provide 24x7 accesses to better and standardised teaching and learning aids; benefits could include increased attendance, improved results and reduced long-term costs of education per student. We have begun to take the lead across the world in on-line tuition, with students from across North America and parts of Europe participating on-line with Indian tutors.[44] If we can do this for other nations, we should assess how best to apply this across our nation and in particular rural areas and primary school education.

If we are to sustain and increase our current economic, social and personal development, we need to increase the number of qualified citizens available to the nation.

## REGULATION & CERTIFICATION

Poorly regulated, unaccredited and often entirely fake colleges have sprung up across our nation as the growing number of young citizens demand higher education.

In 2012 the higher-education commission released a list of 21 *fake universities*', many of them with no more than a mailing address or signboard hanging over a shop or building. Another national survey of 20 States found 51% (1 in 2) of all private rural primary schools were unrecognised. A government regulator that focuses on technical schools named 340 private institutions that run courses without its accreditation, and of more than 31,000 higher-education institutions, only 4,532 (~15% = 1 in 7) universities and colleges are accredited.

There are accusations that a university in Southern India had awarded 2,660 doctorate degrees in just two years for subjects not taught there.

*"It is the supreme art of the teacher to awaken joy in creative expression and knowledge."*
Albert Einstein

There are claims by researchers that attendance in public primary and secondary schools is lower than recorded data as government supported school teachers have incentives to over-report their enrolments, when there is low demand for their services (since a school with smaller enrolment would lose teachers), and this in turn also reduces the apparent enrolment share of private schools; secondly, all official school censuses are undertaken only in the government recognised and accredited schools, and in most states, there is no requirement on private primary schools to be even registered, let alone be government recognised and accredited.

There are many bureaucratic and regulatory hurdles in establishing a college or university; it could deter honest individuals and groups, but encourage those who are willing to pay bribes and cut corners. We need clearer, practical, realistic and more rapid accreditation and recognition, clearer processes for approval, and more importantly the mechanisms and authority to ensure institutions cannot be established or operate courses prior to approval of accreditation.

The emergence of large numbers of unaccredited schools, colleges and universities suggests that schools, students and parents do not take government accreditation as a stamp of quality, compliance or authority.

# SUMMARY

We have made significant progress over the last 20 years; albeit, we started from a very low level. Much remains to be done, and there are considerable challenges amongst them.

The future of our nation will be decided in the classrooms. The better we construct the base of the *'Education Pyramid'*, the Primary education, the easier we will be able to deliver and enhance secondary and higher education.

We need to see more citizens move from primary, though to secondary and then on to further education. We can support this by application and use of technology, improving teacher training and providing a more standard set of teaching aids, equipment and curricula.

*"The foundation of every state is the education of its youth."*
**Diogenes of Sinope**

**The 'Foundation Pillar for Education' could read that we will establish:**

1. Schools with building, infrastructure and facilities that work, are always maintained, and designed to create an environment for learning and teaching.
2. Teaching styles and approaches that makes learning fun and creative for children.
3. Mechanisms for further parent participation in their children's school performance, especially in rural areas and in primary schools.
4. Compulsory school based education and attendance for all children between the ages of 5 and 15.
5. Simple, standardised, nationwide attainment and learning tests for ages 7, 11, 15 and 17.
6. Published league tables for attainment at learning tests for ages 7, 11, 15 and 17; at an individual, school, region, state and national level.
7. Provisions for learning multiple languages and sports at primary and secondary schools.
8. A consistent but flexible curriculum for all student age groups that supports learning and skills development.
9. A curriculum which includes healthcare, hygiene, social wellbeing, behaviours, values, ethics, 'ways of working' and 'ways of living'.
10. A vocational curriculum for secondary schools, in conjunction with Industry, that supports students to be inquisitive, creative and develop application based skills.
11. Improved teacher training colleges with appropriate leading edge teaching techniques and technologies.
12. Accreditation and refreshment courses for teachers to ensure teaching professionals are updated with teaching tools and techniques.

*"Teachers are the one and only people who save nations."*
**Kemal Atatürk**

13. Avenues for newly qualified graduates to get teacher training and work experience to begin to help craft the curricula and delivery of education in rural India.

14. Educational institutional leadership, management and teaching to be based on ability and competence rather than years of experience and qualification.

15. Educational institutions to have independent external governance through active participation from local businesses, stakeholders and parents.

16. Provisions for appropriate teaching aids and tools for teachers in each school to focus on learning.

17. Use of information technology and systems to support learning and teaching.

18. Use of information technology to support performance management and data capture.

19. More effective and efficient processes for accreditation of all government and private schools, colleges and universities.

20. More effective and efficient processes for accreditation of all courses at government and private schools, colleges and universities.

21. Provisions for adult education through evening school or on-line education, for any citizen over 18 who wishes to improve personal development.

22. Partnerships with commercial organisations to provide for vocational training, courses and direct work experience for citizens.

23. Partnerships with local commercial organisations to have employees support schools through experience share and career events etc.

24. More universities and research institutions which focus on primary sciences, research and development on leading edge technologies and sciences.

*"Too often we give children answers to remember rather than problems to solve."*
*Roger Lewin*

25. Partnerships between Universities, Research Institutions and commercial enterprises to develop practical applications for discoveries.

26. .................................................................................

27. .................................................................................

28. .................................................................................

29. .................................................................................

30. .................................................................................

Etc. ................................................................................

*"I cannot teach anybody anything; I can only make them think."*
**Socrates**

# 3

# HEALTHCARE

*"Growth in national income by itself is not enough, if the benefits do not manifest themselves in the form of more food, better access to health and education"*

**Amartya K. Sen**

Our healthcare system has gradually improved in the last few decades; however it is still in poor health. This could be attributed to the low level of government funding on initiatives; our absolute monetary level spending is low compared to all developing nations, and therefore our healthcare spending per capita is staggering low, estimated at US$33 per annum, far below international recommendations, and amongst the lowest in the world. Infant and Maternal mortality rates are still very high, and although life expectancy has increased to ~65 years, this is much lower than other developing nations.[45] Again, we started from a low base, and have a long way to go, and it is going to get more difficult.

As with Education, there are two India's. A small but growing number that can now afford healthcare and insurances, and the remaining majority who are serviced by Government funded healthcare. As in Education, the absence of quality and availability of Government healthcare has resulted in private enterprises filling the services, quality and availability gap.

We ranked 134 out of 187 nations in the 2011 Human Development Index (HDI) global ranking undertaken by the United Nations Development Programme (UNDP), this is a decline on the 128 ranking in 2009.[46] HDI is a composite index measuring average achievement in three basic dimensions of human development; life expectancy, education and standard of

*"Healthy citizens are the greatest asset any country can have."*
Winston S. Churchill

61

living. Despite all we have done, this is not good enough, as the rest of the world is moving faster forward, and we are falling further behind. This again reinforces the fact that we need to do more and need to do it better and faster.

As an industry sector, healthcare is one of largest, in terms of revenue and employment, and is still rapidly expanding with planned growth up to ~21% per annum.[47] With such spending trends, the healthcare system and infrastructure could eventually overcome the nation's health challenges. But when; and at what human and social cost? Are we willing to accept this? Data over time indicates this growth has been larger and faster than industry estimates over the last 10 years. Some of the major factors driving the growth include our increasing population, growing lifestyle related health issues, generic drugs manufacturing, medical tourism, disposable income, successful government initiatives and Public Private Partnership (PPP) models. We need to focus on the factors for improving healthcare for the majority of citizens who have no access to, or cannot afford healthcare; in rural and urban India.

We have much to be proud of in healthcare; we produce 80% of global generic drugs, we have taken leaps in biotechnology, we have begun to deliver high-quality low-cost healthcare, we have world leading medical professionals and institutions that have succeeded in attracting medical tourism from around the world, we have talented individuals now working on health care convergence, to create India centric solutions combining medical technology, information, medical diagnostic skills and telecommunications to provide healthcare solutions for our citizens. As we leapt from a low density land-line telephone nation to a higher density mobile telephone nation, without going through the *'one land-line'* per household model of other more developed nations, so we can also create new innovative models in healthcare provision for all our citizens across the whole nation.

*"Facts are many, but the truth is one."*
**Rabindranath Tagore**

# INFRASTRUCTURE

Our healthcare infrastructure has also seen steady improvement, but much remains to be accomplished. It has not kept pace with the growth in the economy or population. Lack of adequate healthcare is reflected in the low density of healthcare personnel. Although we educate ~32,000 professional physicians and ~10,000 professional nurses per annum, we need more. We have on average 0.7 doctors to 1,000 citizens, where a world average is ~1.5 and there are ~1.8 doctors to 1,000 citizens in more industrialised nations. We fall further behind in nursing, with 1.3 nurses per 1,000 citizens, to a world average of ~3.3 and more industrialised nation averages of ~1.8.[48] We expect to see a shortfall in physician of 700,000 by 2025; however, more acute will be the shortfall for nurses, laboratory technicians, radiographers and other specialists for providing primary and secondary, estimated by 2015 to be ~350,000.[49] The majority of doctors and nurses we produce however wish to practice in the urban cities (or go abroad, with many even working in rural areas of more industrialised nations), and this further skews the number of professionals available to service our rural areas. ~66% of medical professionals practice in urban areas and ~88% of towns have healthcare facilities as against 24% of villages, which is where we have ~70% of the patients.[50] We can do little to increase medical professional numbers besides having increased education and aspirations, as reducing standards of entry and qualification will prove catastrophic.

Despite a steady increase in the number of medical establishments, there still remains a severe shortage of primary health and community health centres. The infrastructure of these government health centres is well below medical building regulations with dilapidated buildings and rooms, lack of electricity and access, insufficient drugs and essential supplies and equipment that is not operational. To reach the current levels of density (4.3 per 1000 population) in hospital beds as our South East Asian neighbours, we would need an additional ~3 million beds, and ~2 million beds to meet WHO average levels.[51]

*"People are like dirt. They can either nourish you and help you grow as a person or they can stunt your growth and make you wilt and die."*

Plato

Although the principal responsibility for public health funding lies with the State governments, with the Central government contributing mainly through national Health programmes, the Centre not only significantly increases its contribution, but also ensures more control through governance and delivery, to realise a consistent quality and service for all our citizens across the country.

# ACCESSIBILITY GAP

Poor access to availability of government healthcare leads citizens to reach out to private healthcare suppliers out of necessity and desperation. Studies and surveys recorded that ~40% of those hospitalised have borrowed money or sold assets to pay for their services, and ~24% of those were below the poverty line due to hospitalisation. About 65% of citizens that incur expenditures on major health problems become indebted for life.[52] Our healthcare system is predominately financed *'out-of-pocket'* and for most people, that is a significant barrier. Private healthcare accounts for over 80% of total healthcare spending. This is an extremely high proportion even by international standards. There are observations that the insurance system has extensive problems; with claims often being challenged, significant delays in payment or even claims being unpaid (it is unclear whether this is due to fraudulent claims), which exacerbates the problem as citizens have to pay the charges before claiming from the Insurance companies. Current projections indicate that private health insurance sector will continue to expand.

While the rural poor are underserved, they are beginning to be able to access the limited number of government supported medical facilities; however, the urban poor could fare much worse, as government healthcare can be less accessible and because they are also unable to pay for the private facilities in the cities.

The Government launched the National Rural Health Mission 2005-2012 in April 2005, to provide effective healthcare to the rural population, focusing on 18 States with low public health indicators and inadequate infrastructure. They aimed to increase the capabilities of primary medical facilities in rural areas, and ease the burden on the tertiary care centres in the cities, by providing equipment and training to primary care physicians in performing basic surgeries. This has been relatively successful.

Launched in 2007, the *Rashtriya Swasthya Bima Yojana* (National Health Insurance Programme) is an innovative government sponsored PPP to provide health insurance to our poorer citizens. Families receive US$700 in medical care for a nominal premium, and as they use the services, the costs are deducted from their account using '*smart card*' cashless processes. The government pays the premiums directly to participating insurance companies, and has allocated ~US$1 billion over five years. At the time of this writing, it had enrolled over 15million families and 4,384 hospitals across 26 States. This programme should grow to cover more of our population; this can also help collate data and information on health issues and incidents, which will help better provide for planning and delivery of services.

The government have also launched many other creative initiatives and programmes over the last few years, such as Village Health Guides etc.; however, corruption and poor execution are cited as the main reasons for failure of some of these initiatives. There are several healthcare centres of excellence across the nation; however, these centres are limited in their ability to improve healthcare standards due to the poor infrastructure across most of our nation.

There are large professional private hospital chains that can support the expansion of the government programmes; however, the concern is on the levels of quality and services that will be provided by the newer healthcare providers that aim to build and operate the smaller hospitals in rural areas. Will they operate on and provide consistent professional standards?

*"I do not believe in a fate that falls on men however they act; but I do believe in a fate that falls on them unless they act."*
Siddhārtha Gautama Buddha

# QUALITY AND COMPLIANCE

India is internationally recognised as a producer of high-quality physicians and healthcare professionals, with Indian doctors and nurses practicing in nearly all countries across the world. As with many nations, but particularly more so in India, the position and title of *'Doctor'* is highly regarded for both social and economic reasons. This is a double edged sword. There has been an increasing deterioration in the provision of health services across our nation which needs to be urgently improved. There is also a growing concern over the training for medical professionals and the quality and competence of the *'Doctors'* that graduate from private universities. Over many years, these private institutions have been accused of taking bribes (or 'donations') to admit less qualified students, and providing them with substandard education. As with the growth of private schools, colleges and universities, we also see a growth in these types of *'Medical Schools'*. In Maharashtra, a recent inspection report indicated that 9 of 17 of its private medical colleges were severely understaffed and lacked essential infrastructure, including teaching beds and clinical materials.[53]

Professionals who work in Public Healthcare have been known to *'moonlight'*, simultaneously offering their services on a private basis to supplement their income; this leads to the continuing deterioration for the Public Service, and the misapplication of its scant resources. This also means the public sector ends up subsidising unofficial private practices.

There is also a thriving *'black market'* in healthcare which is causing long-term demographic and social challenges; these include organ trading, transplants and abortions based on sex determination (whole villages and communities in some parts of our nation face a future without daughters, and at some point, their sons may need wives). The effects of parental decisions and medical malpractice of female foeticide, resulting in more males than females, is only now being felt, and it is expected to get worse; human trafficking, rape, violence, crime, abuse etc. Widespread corruption, bribery and other illegal practices are themselves caused by an ineffectiveand broken health system, with low income of health workers, further undermining these systems.

It is estimated that nearly 70% of all hospitals and 40% of hospital beds in the country are in the private sector. Governance and Compliance of all private and public institutions and healthcare providers need to be strengthened, with increased supervision to meet established quality, teaching, ethical and service standards.

# PREVENTION

Whilst we have not won the battle against reducing maternal and infant deaths, eradication of polio and malaria etc., we still need further improvements in education on hygiene, health, nutrition, gender and social inequality. We will continue to face diseases and illnesses that can more easily be reduced and eliminated through improvements in environmental sanitation, safe drinking water, balanced nutrition, living conditions, and access to preventive and curative health services. All this will significantly help improve the health of our citizens.

Vaccination coverage across our nation continues to be low, and falls short of the target; there needs to be an increase in the range of vaccines provides, and a concerted effort, as with Small Pox, to provide our citizens with these preventable diseases vaccines, such as DPT (for diphtheria, pertussis (whooping cough), and tetanus), Polio, BCG (for TB), Measles, Hepatitis B and H influenzae type b (Hib for under 5 infants).[54]

The next wave of new and growing medical conditions in our country also needs to be planned and prepared for, the so called 'life-style diseases'. The World Health Organisation (WHO) estimates between 2-3.1 million people are living with HIV; 1 in 5 of all diabetic in the world is an Indian. Our nation is called the 'diabetes capital of the world', and we have ~41 million sufferers forecasted to rise to ~70 million by 2025.[55] An increase in disposable capital, coupled with poor lifestyle also results in at

*"Any man may easily do harm, but not every man can do good to another."*

Plato

least 30 million obese and 70 million overweight citizens (in 2012, in urban areas almost 1 in 5 men and over 1 in 6 women were overweight, in some areas as high as 40%; and 24% of children surveyed between ages 14-19 in Delhi);[56] prosperity and obesity are bedfellows in our nation, and a dramatic increase in heart related illnesses, accounting for nearly 25% of all deaths of citizens aged 25-69 years. 20,000 citizens die annually through a disease caused by sandflies, called Leishmaniasis (*kala-azar*), one of the world's deadliest parasitic diseases. Nearly 2.2 million people develop tuberculosis each year, a quarter of all global incidents, and of those, ~73,000 develop an infectious form of the disease and ~432,000 die annually.[57] Overreliance on antibiotics, and prescribing high doses, leads to a vicious circle of resistance by the bacteria and the human body, which some leading medical forecasters are suggesting will lead to strains of bacteria that cannot be managed by our existing and planned range of antibiotis.

We have to manage these issues, so they do not become larger problems than they currently are. A 2010 Lancet study predicted that by 2030, nearly 70% of all global deaths will be from non-communicable diseases like cancer, diabetes, respiratory and heart disease. Of these 70% of deaths, 80% will be in the less industrialised nations like ours.[58]

The increase in the numbers of people smoking, drinking and taking drugs also contributes to a higher level of health issues; in the majority of cases this is confined to those who can afford their healthcare; a possible result of increased affluence and life style preferences and changes. The challenge is to reduce this amongst those that cannot afford their healthcare, to stop further damage to their health. Education is the only long-term solution to reducing and minimising the effects of these; prevention is neither possible nor proposed, education to use in moderation may be practical and realistic.

Generally, our poor sanitation and personal hygiene behaviours, coupled with the high density in urban areas also makes us prone to other serious contagions such as SARS, N5H1, bird flu and other drug resistant and mutated pathogens, whilst

*"The highest patriotism is not a blind acceptance of official policy, but a love of one's country deep enough to call her to a higher plain."*
George McGovern

dengue fever, hepatitis, tuberculosis, malaria and pneumonia are still present and potentially increasing.

Our own behaviours and *ways of living* contribute significantly to our health and that of others. As a nation we do things in public that we would never do in our own home. Generally, around the world it is the other way around. We seem to be the only nation with excess throat and nose mucus. Are we that genetically different to other human beings? Citizens regularly clear the contents of their throats and nose in public places, pavements, roads and inside buildings, regardless of consideration for others. We should have learned with TB over our many years of suffering from it, and from the newer television media broadcasting that SARS, N5H1, Bird Flu and other such diseases are spread not only though touch, but, are airborne through coughing, sneezing and spitting. Basic hygiene behaviours such as using a handkerchief, cloth, ideally a tissue or at last resort, hands are better than not using anything at all to stop our coughing, sneezing and spitting to be shared with others.

We are a nation and culture that have pride in their presence and appearance. We look after ourselves, but not the environment around us, we somehow believe that we are not responsible for it; it is someone else's problem. Be it the industrialists or high-powered corporate citizen walking their dogs in a city, and do not dispose of their pet's defecation, or the citizens in our cities, towns, and villages that urinate and defecate in public and in secluded areas. The end result is the same; an environment that is unhealthy leads to illness and diseases. It is the same with litter. We need a change in our behaviours, values and *ways of living*.

Sanitation and clean drinking water should be a priority, and the provision of more lavatories and clean water in urban and rural areas should be given a priority. This will be discussed late in Infrastructure.

*"Ultimately a genuine leader is not a searcher for consensus, but a moulder of consensus."*
**Dr. Martin Luther King, Jr.**

# PRIVATISATION & PUBLIC-PRIVATE PARTNERSHIP

Despite the size and reach of the public healthcare system, we score poorly on many health indicators. PPPs have been tested as an option of meeting the citizen's healthcare needs whilst maintaining public service objectives. The main objectives of PPPs are to improve quality, accessibility, availability, acceptability, effectiveness and efficiency of healthcare services. There have been some marked successes with these initiatives and it is expected that the private sector will continue to play an increasing role in our healthcare system.[59]

There are many benefits that private healthcare and PPP have bought to the nation; supporting government health programmes through services to the poor, establishment and expansion of world-class centres of excellence, speciality hospitals, and the provision of medical tourism are all excellent achievements for our nation.[60] They should continue to provide these services to those growing numbers of citizens who can afford private services and also those who are insured and covered by their employers. However, on a national basis, this does not really help the citizens without means, so the private and PPP models will have to continue to contribute particularly in providing services to the needy whilst government services are improved.

Some private hospitals have used technology and talent to reduce administrative costs and surgical operating costs to a level that is significantly lower than other counterparts in North America and Europe. This is excellent news. Efficient and effective services and processes created in the private sector should be applied to the public sector.

# TELE-MEDICINE

Driven by need, our nation is inventing new ways to use information and medical technology to improve health care. The combination of medical technology, information, medical

*"Minds are like parachutes—they only function when open."*
Thomas R. Dewar

professionals and telecommunications can provide a range of innovative solutions and applications in healthcare. We have the potential to develop innovations that can be adopted in other parts of the world, including the more industrialised nations in North America and Europe where cost and access are becoming increasingly important issues. Telemedicine provides remote diagnosis, monitoring and treatment of patients via videoconferencing or the Internet. High patient volumes can be serviced with telemedicine, remote diagnosis, monitoring and treatment via video-conferencing, internet or mobile telephones and through use of low-power hand-held medical monitoring devices. This provides a possible solution to improve the services to the 70% of citizens who cannot access quality healthcare and diagnostics etc. We have over 900 million mobile telephone users and over 120 million internet users;[61] telephone signal coverage and handset density in rural India is increasing rapidly, and with almost 80% of adult citizens with a mobile telephone, we can significantly increase health awareness and prevention, and provide appropriate access to the right healthcare.

The government has made a major commitment to the growth of telemedicine. Starting in 2001 with pilot projects to prove the technology and systems, the Indian Space Research Organization (ISRO) has supported private hospitals to connect via satellite across the country, and has already connected major hospitals to district hospitals.

There are many PPP initiatives in this area and early successes have provided confidence, resulting in the many telemedicine centres across the country today. It is estimated that ~800,000 tele-consultations have been undertaken as of April 2011 from the existing 650 telemedicine centres and 30-35 mobile vehicle telemedicine units. A leading private healthcare provider has planned to open 1,000 telemedicine centres by 2015.[62]

Other new models are also emerging: membership-based telephone medical advice services that offer family plans for 3-6 months, during which period, members are entitled to unlimited phone consultations and discounts at select diagnostic centres. Subscription based telephone medical

*"You can't cross the sea merely by standing and staring at the water."*
Rabindranath Tagore

advice services that offer access to basic medical guidance on non-emergency health problems for INR50 (US$1) for each consultation. Other where subscribers who call to seek health advice are visited by paramedics who come with a laptop and medical diagnostic equipment and conduct consultations via video conferencing. Some call centres are taking more than 50,000 calls a day, manned by registered nurses working under physician approved protocols and guidelines; they also provide triage, medical information and counselling services.

There are also new products that have been developed, driven by the need to provide low-cost 'Indianisation', 'frugal innovation' and 'jugaard' type solutions. An innovative low-cost ECG machine was developed that takes digital images which are emailed to cardiologists. A mass pre-screening portable, non-invasive device that helps in early detection of eye diseases like cataract, diabetic retina, glaucoma and cornea related issues, available at one-sixth the cost of present diagnostic devices. It can be operated by a minimally trained technician, where the digital information is transmitted electronically, using only 10 watts of power and can run for 4 hours on a single charge, making it ideal for rural areas.[63] Such creative initiatives, if successful, need to be expanded and rolled out across our nation.

There are clear benefits in using internet technology and health information across the nation, and to connect all medical establishments to a Health Grid. We would be able to exchange information, share experiences and cases, get access to the best available advice, better respond to pattern of increased instances and causes etc. This would also support maintaining standards and improving services and control of this nationally critical sector.

## MEDICAL TOURISM

Medical tourism is one of the major success stories of Indian Healthcare. It has successfully leveraged our nation's well trained English speaking professional medical staff, with state-of-the art medical equipment, technologies and diagnostics, within a world-class infrastructure, all at a relatively low cost. Best-in-class services are provided at ~35-50% of the costs incurred in North America or Europe.[64]

It is estimated that by the year 2015, we will treat in excess of 600,000 medical tourists annually, generating over US$3 billion by 2015 and US$12.5 billion by 2020; a growth rate over 30% per annum.[65] This is a major source of external income and revenue. This should further assist the nation as the leading private hospital chains continue to give back to the nation and citizens through their provision of high-quality low-cost healthcare for the rural and poor, and through PPP initiative.

In addition to the surgery based medical treatments provided, we have also successfully expanded services in wellness tourism, meditation, alternative and ayurvedic medicine; all part of a holistic healthcare provision and approach.

# EMERGENCY MEDICAL SERVICES

Emergency Medical Services (EMS) are essential for a robust and efficient medical care system. EMS are still in their infancy across our nation, and the current infrastructure is ineffective and inefficient due to the lack of critical components such as a centralised administrative body, trained emergency medical personnel, a centralised emergency phone number (similar to 999, 911 or 121), infrastructure and quality ambulance services. There are, however, signs of change in EMS due to an increase in the number of government initiatives.

An ambitious telemedicine and emergency-response initiative, run by an IT company, succeeded in saving many lives in Andhra Pradesh. This medical service answered up to 35,000 calls a day, providing medical advice over the telephone on how to manage common health conditions and recognise symptoms.[66] It is claimed that EMS respondents were physically at the scene of an accident within 15 minutes of receiving the telephone call. As with a call centre type of operation,

*"It is health that is real wealth and not pieces of gold and silver."*
**Mohandas Karamchand Gandhi**

performance was tracked, measured and improved on a daily basis.

# RURAL HEALTHCARE

The provision of medical services to rural India must be simple and effective. As with the Panchayats, we need a *'bottom-up'* participation and delivery of change and services. We need to ensure our medical university graduates, both doctors and nurses, which are willing and able to contribute back to society and to support our nation's further development, are provided a fast-track means of getting the training and experience necessary to provide multi-level medical care in rural regions.

Healthcare is currently delivered on 3 levels: primary, secondary and tertiary, but underlying those are village-based health sub-centres, which the WHO describes as *'the most peripheral health institutional facility'.*[67] We need to accelerate improvements and make medical services available to a higher proportion of the population by taking the primary and secondary services even closer to the patient, building on previous research:

Nurses and paramedics could take the lead and accountability for providing Clinics/Health Centres in small rural regions (for ~7,000 citizens vs. current 3,000-5,000);; they would provide preventative support through education, information, hygiene, diagnostics, vaccinations (as discussed the need for DPT [for diphtheria, pertussis {whooping cough}, and tetanus], Polio, BCG [for Tuberculosis/TB], Measles, Hepatitis B and H influenzae type b [Hib for under 5 infants]), basic medication, wounds, injuries and other medical support including pregnancy and delivery.

The role and activities of paramedics and nurses in more industrialised nations is being re-evaluated, due to advances in medicines, information technology and medical equipment; they now provide wider primary care services, and are the first person a patient would see, with doctors then being the second or even third person, should the paramedic or nurse not be able to diagnose and treat the patient.

These Clinics could then report into a regional small secondary hospital, (for ~30,000 citizens) staffed by doctors and other medical professionals who would be the next level of care that the Clinics could not support. These hospitals would provide beds and cater for minor operating facilities, including an Accident & Emergency (A&E) type service. A rota of specialist medical staff would be required to provide support to these small hospitals on a regular basis to treat patients that require specialist treatment and complex surgical operations.

For extreme and speciality cases, the specialist would refer the patient to a major urban hospital that provides tertiary services and specialist medical staff and support for the medical condition.

In remote Indian villages, people sometimes have to travel or walk for many miles to visit a qualified doctor. This solution or option potentially provides better medical services closer to the patient. This solution could see significant improvements in our health care system. This requires an increase in the numbers of larger and better equipped clinics/health centres and primary hospitals; however, the ratio of paramedics and qualified nurses to doctors would he higher; which in the short-term is challenging, but potentially better for the nation in the medium and longer term.

As with schools, the government could provide pre-fabricated Clinics and Small Hospitals. This has all the benefits of appropriateness, functionality, scale, cost, quality, consistency, repair and maintenance etc., with medical staff provided a market rate salary, with appropriate incentivisation.

The use of simple but high technology diagnostic, therapeutic and preventive interventions in the field of medicine and surgery could be undertaken at these Clinics and Health Centres. Telemedicine technology can be utilised to support treatment and reduce costs of delivery and significantly improve quality and efficiency of services.

*"Many ideas grow better when transplanted into another mind than in the one where they sprang up."*
Oliver Wendell Holmes, Sr.

# CONCLUSION

If a vision of *'Health for All'* is to be achieved, we will have to significantly increase spending in the healthcare sector as a percentage of GDP. Our Government possibly views healthcare as a cost, when we should be viewing it as an investment. Government fiscal constraints may be driving the growth of PPPs to help meet our growing demand for healthcare infrastructure; however, it is only one of many strategies, and in the long-term, we need to continue to provide the option of free or low-cost healthcare for all our citizens. In parallel, technology-enabled health care networks can play a significant role by bridging the distance between doctors and patients through Internet and other telecommunication technologies. We can better leverage the existing human resources available in health care. Scale, however, can only be achieved through effective government intervention.

There are significant unmet healthcare needs, especially in rural India and amongst the increasing urban poor. The challenge is to provide affordable health care for the masses whilst at the same time making the service attractive to the providers. We have succeeded in leveraging the private sector through PPPs; however, there is fine balance that has to be reached and maintained in operating PPPs and their growing role in healthcare. We cannot become like the USA and other nations where private healthcare and Insurance are the major routes to access healthcare for our citizens. That model and system does not support the under privileged, unfortunate or poor. It creates a schism in society.

Health drives the nation's economic and social growth through four avenues:
- A healthier workforce is more productive.
- Healthier children have less childhood illnesses, physical and mental disabilities and so have better cognitive functions, supporting increased school attendance and duration, which ultimately results in a more educated population.

*"Each indecision brings its own delays. What you cannot do or think you can do, do. For boldness has Magic, Power, and Genius in it."*
Johanne Wolfgang von Goeth

76

- Healthy and more educated populations have more stable and deeper social connections and activities outside of the work environment; positively contributing to a more secure society.
- Healthy and educated populations attract global investment and confidence.

The statement, *'healthier means wealthier'*, has being proved correct in that health is a strong driver of economic and social growth. We will have to address our healthcare access challenges if economic growth is to be sustained, and social order maintained.

We are also poised to become a major exporter of pharmaceuticals, and drug intermediates, particularly generic and over-the-counter drugs. Indian manufacturers maintain efficient process development and modern manufacturing equipment; we have labour, equipment and capital cost advantages; we have a highly skilled labour force, with excellent chemical synthesis capabilities. Together with the growth in Biotechnology, we should be better positioned to provide lower-cost drugs and treatments to our citizens.

We have the technology and talent; we need to apply it better. We have islands of excellence in our own ocean of humanity. We need to focus on scaling what we do to service ~1.2 billion people, with a sustainable model that covers our whole nation.

*"Man's mind stretched to a new idea never goes back to its original dimensions."*
Oliver Wendell Holmes, Sr.

**The 'Foundation Pillar for Healthcare' could read that we will establish:**

1. Access to healthcare for all citizens.
2. A national healthcare system that provides consistent services for all citizens.
3. National professional service standards and enforced regulations.
4. Modularised health centres and hospitals to ensure hygiene, physical infrastructure and services standards for our citizens.
5. Market rate salaries and incentivisation for all healthcare workers.
6. Sufficient educational establishments to produce the highest quality and wide range of medical professionals our nation needs.
7. Appropriate medical curriculum and education to service the needs of our citizens and nation.
8. More robust registration and regular evaluation procedures for all medical professional to ensure citizens are provided professional services.
9. Retraining and regular additional training of professional medical staff to ensure they have, and can apply the necessary skills, tools and technologies.
10. Mechanisms to promote creative and innovative solutions to deliver healthcare services.
11. The nation as a world leader in lower-cost high-service healthcare.
12. Public Private Partnerships that maintain a commercial, efficient and effective focus on government healthcare services and initiatives.
13. New and creative medical equipment, information and telecommunication technologies to become a world leader in medical services.
14. An integration approach to healthcare and town planning to support Emergency Medical Services.

*"Change doesn't take time, it takes commitment."*
Thomas F. Crum

15. Leading edge research organisations to advance pharmaceutical, biotechnology and medical applications.
16. Information and educational programmes to improve personal hygiene.
17. Information and educational programmes to improve personal health and life style.
18. A centralised healthcare database and medical records system that supports diagnosis, conditions, trends and planning.
19. .....................................................................................
20. .....................................................................................
21. .....................................................................................
22. .....................................................................................
23. .....................................................................................
Etc.................................................................................

*"Success in life comes not from holding a good hand, but in playing a poor hand well."*
Denis Waitley

# 4.1

# LAW & ORDER— THE JUDICIARY

**The roots of Crime & Violence are:**
—**Wealth without Work,**
—**Pleasure without Conscience,**
—**Knowledge without Character,**
—**Commerce without Morality,**
—**Science without Humanity,**
—**Worship without Sacrifice,**
—**Politics without Principles.**

**Mohandas Karamchand Gandhi**

Three common themes emerge in conversations on the Indian legal system: *'Money buys justice'*, the rich, powerful and influential have easier access to justice, due to the legitimate costs involved as well as the ablility to afford the bribes and corrupt payments necessary to make cases *'go-away'* or be delayed in the *'system'*; *'justice delayed is justice denied'*, referring to the slow, antiquated, elaborate, complex, corrupt and long-winded processing of cases; and *'laws are not fully enforced or enforceable'*, in many cases our laws are seen as mere guidelines rather than legally enforceable laws, and in many cases our law enforcement is not as robust as our laws require.

Our nation's judicial system is comprised of a number of layers. We currently have a Supreme Court at the national level and 21 High Courts at the state and territory level. Below the High Courts we have a hierarchy of subordinate courts including Civil, Family, Criminal and various other District Courts. The High Courts are the principal courts of jurisdiction in a State along with District Courts, which handle all matters including those designated specifically as State or territory law.

Prior to the arrival of the British in India, India was governed by a set of laws at two levels; The Executive, Legislature and Judiciary were the same person, the King, Warlord or Ruler of the Land, and villages were governed by Panchayats, independently resolving disputes among its members. Larger issues were managed through multi-village Panchayats. There were also two codes of laws, one for Hindus and the other for Muslims; the central philosophy was based on tolerance and pluralism. Both were replaced by 'Common Law' when India became part of the British Empire. Since Independence, over the last 65 years we have seen an increasing complexity in our legal system, a vicious cycle of administration; self-generating inefficient processes and requirements to meet an increasing set of ineffective rules and regulations. No judgement is made here on the pro's and con's of either system.

The Judiciary in India represents one of the three central planks of democracy in our Republic, together with the Executive and Legislature. Historically, the Judiciary was seen as the most respected of the three, but its image has undergone steady and significant erosion. Given the overt and covert criminal constituency of our current Legislature, this leaves little for the victims to hold on to, for confidence and faith in the current legal system.

The lack of fair and timely justice, corruption, excessive costs, unresolved disputes, poor judgements and high visibility failure of the legal system to convict, have all contributed to the erosion of confidence, within our nation and abroad. The judiciary is seen to have lost sight of the social and economic consequences of its actions, or the lack of them. This is now leading to a grave threat to constitutional and democratic governance of the country. Justice often remains a mirage.

*"A state is better governed which has few laws, and those laws strictly observed."*
**Rene Descartes**

# PENDING CASES (BACKLOG AND DELAY)

It is estimated through official government figures that more than 30 million legal cases are still pending, with some claimed to be dating back many decades. Of these, ~25million are at the lower district and sub-ordinate courts, and of these, over 18million are criminal cases, whilst only ~750,000 civil cases.[68] These cases should not be viewed as major or minor, each is a case, and each citizen, under our law, deserves the same right to justice and to be heard and judged by his or her peers in a court of law.

An unfortunate side-effect of this is also the long lead time lag, between the crime and the conviction, in many cases it can be over a decade. A major consequence of this unacceptable situation is that millions of citizens are still awaiting justice.

It seems that both the government and the senior judiciary come out with intentions, statements, promises and platitudes but no concrete steps to resolve these problems, again, the absence of implementation and delivery.

A major factor in the slow speed and extent of improvement is in the poor execution of the recommendations of multiple studies and reports by the Judiciary themselves.

Some reasons and solutions cited for the pending cases are:[69]

1. **Large number of vacancies in trial courts:**
   - There are up to ~40% unfulfilled vacancies in judicial staff.
   - Unsurprisingly, according to the 120th Law Commission Report, our population-to-judge ratio is one of the lowest in the world. While the United States and Britain have about 150 judges for every million of its population, we have only 10.5 judges per million. Only Guatemala, Nicaragua and Kenya have a lower ratio than India.

2. **Salary Differential:**
   - There is a significant salary differential, with advocates in the Supreme and High courts earning a daily fee

equivalent (over INR1 lakh) to over a month's salary for the majority of judges.

- Salary for judges in the lower courts is lower than the higher courts and subsequently, this makes it even more unattractive to advocates.

- Poor pay scales have triggered corruption, widespread bribery and political interference which deny millions their right to a fair trial.

- Quality of justice is as, if not more important, than the speed of justice. Judges need to be paid a salary commensurate with their value and contribution to law and order in Indian society.

## 3. Unwillingness of lawyers and advocates to become judges:

- Our archaic process of promoting judges on the basis of seniority, which is effectively time in post, is ridiculous for any profession (like waiting for a dead man's shoes), where competence and capability should be amongst the key criteria.

- Promotion should ideally be from the lower courts to the higher courts as judges' gain and bring their experiences to bear on conclusions and decisions; however, the scope for promotion is claimed to be very limited to negligible.

- Department of Justice data indicated that 66% (2 out of 3), a significant proportion, of higher court judges seem to have gained direct entry to the Bench directly from the Bar.[70]

- The Supreme Court also decided in a judgement that all promotions to the Supreme Court would be based on the number of years of service as a judge in the High Court, therefore the years of service and experience in the lower judiciary is removed from the acceptability criteria for promotion. Therefore, lower court judges would find it extremely difficult to advance through promotion to the highest levels of their own profession.

*"Justice delayed is justice denied."*
William E. Gladstone

- An analysis from the 2009 *'Handbook on Judges of the Supreme Court of India'* further reinforced this opinion as data validates the number of judges in the High and Supreme courts originated from the Bar rather than through promotion from within the court system.

4. **Failure of the Judiciary in filling vacant High Court judges posts:**
   - There are ~300 posts for judges that remain unfulfilled. This is an issue for both the government and the judiciary. They share equal responsibility and accountability. It is unacceptable over the past few years that 50% of posts for judges in the country's largest High Court, in Allahabad, are vacant. Unsurprisingly, 25% of all pending High Court cases are also in Allahabad.
   - We currently have ~10.5 judges per million population; in 2002 the Supreme Court had suggested 50 judges per million population. If we were to project our population to 2030, we would need 125,000 Judges dealing with 300 million cases.
   - The shortage of judges could result in the overall calibre of judges being compromised as we seek to fulfil posts.

5. **The dragging of feet by the Central government and States in keeping their promises:**
   - At one point, 5,000 judges were to be inaugurated to eliminate the pending cases (backlog); another idea was to encouraging plea bargaining and finding ways to prevent stalling techniques; *Alternative Dispute Resolutions* (ADR) and *'fast-track'* courts are also seen as options. Several other ideas have been proposed, but the majority have not been implemented, or if implemented, are incomplete in their delivery; whilst the cases continue to accumulate.
   - State Legislators have also been delinquent in taking action and they should be the first public officers to make change happen for the better for their electorate.

*"Better to fight for something than live for nothing."*
George S. Patton, Jnr.

## 6. Complex and Inefficient Court proceeding:

- Strict formalities slow down every step of our legal processes and are common across our vast bureaucracy. Processes have been established over time, whether though *'custom and practice'* or by design, where even the task of simply registering a case takes considerable effort and energy, wastes time and denies the ordinary citizens access to the court.

- Many kinds of objections are raised, as the bureaucracy justifies its own non-value added existence; the copies are dim, the margins are not wide enough, it's single-spaced instead of being double-spaced etc., for the average citizen, this is impossible and frustrating to understand.

- Long verbose commentaries and summaries by both lawyers and advocates, to explain their cases and circumstances, elongates the duration of the cases and time in court.

What should be most concerning and worrying most to our citizens and civil society should be the recent *'Rights of Information Act'* released data highlighting the additional consequence of this. Un-sentenced prisoners account up to 70.1% (~232,400-250,000) of the prison population, the highest in the recorded world, of which ~2,069 have been incarcerated for more than 5 years, neither as guilty nor innocent. A sound assumption would be that these were the poor rather than the privileged. This can breed resentment and further criminalisation of innocent victims as so many prisoners are held un-sentenced. Nigeria comes second with 64%, followed by Turkey, Kenya and Mexico, with the USA at 21% and Brazil at 33%.[71] Given the issues discussed earlier with *'pending cases'* and judicial and law enforcement corruption this should be a priority; with the aim of releasing the innocent and replacing them with the guilty

According to the *'Global Corruption Report 2007: Corruption in Judicial Systems'* an estimated $600 billion was paid as bribes to our judiciary; this was higher than the bribes paid out in any other sector in the country. All the above factors prompt people

*"Law and order are the medicine of the body politic and when the body politic gets sick, medicine must be administered."*
**Dr. B. M. Ambedkar**

to pay bribes, citizens pay middlemen, clerks and administrators, and there are also many lawyers who are bribing judges; it is a lucrative business for all parties; to either speed-up or slow-down the judicial processes and get favours, or they resort to short-cuts through unconstitutional and other illegal behaviours to get justice; this leads to further unlawful behaviour. This exacerbates the overall situation as citizens' resort to extra-judicial methods to sort out their disputes. It is a vicious cycle. It can make an honest man turn to crime.

# DEVELOPMENT & EXPECTATIONS

Recent research and analysis of civil litigation rates,[72] dating back to 1977, in all States across our nation has shown two very interesting trends:

Citizens in our more developed and wealthier States are more often likely to file civil cases, in both lower and high courts; wealthier States had a higher number of civil cases filed per 1,000 people, and the data also showed that as the States grew more prosperous, their civil litigation rates rose. Two hypothesis were put forward; that the more active economic States would have more interactions and transactions, which could lead to an increase in the numbers of disputes; and wealthier and literate citizens were more empowered and would have the means to go to Court, and the judiciary and Courts may also be more trusted by people in more developed States.

The litigation rates seems to have levelled off, even in States with GDP growth; this is likely to be caused by the numbers of pending cases and the consequent delays, beginning to have a dampening effect on citizens going to court. States with the largest numbers of pending cases have extremely low filing rates over the last five years, while States with the lowest backlog have the highest civil filing rates.

Our civil litigation rates (filed cases per population) are far lower than those of more industrialised nations, and the number of pending cases is having a dampening effect on new filings, and our citizens, and this in turn, will affect our nations long term growth and prosperity. Increasing backlogs are correlated with decreasing filings. The number of new cases has a direct relationship with increasing literacy rate and awareness, a link back to the Education *'Foundation Pillar'*.

# CORRUPTION IN THE JUDICIARY

Corruption is unchecked in the vast majority of our courts. Most distressing is the reality that corruption has reached the Supreme Court, our highest judicial body, and it has been claimed that 50% (1 in 2) of our nation's most recent senior judicial individuals, Chief Justices themselves, did not possess the values, behaviours and probity required for someone in that position. Some have even had impeachment motions bought against them, but these were never brought before the Parliament; ironically, one of these Chief Justices had retired from the Judiciary and taken up a position in the Legislature as Member of Parliament. It is only in late 2009, that the judiciary reluctantly agreed to declare their financial assets; and in our nation, this should include all close family, for all individuals who hold a Public Service post. In our nation, our judges are protected by the *'contempt of court'* act, which prohibits raising any questions about judges or their actions; this is dampening some of the debate around judicial corruption; however, the judiciary cannot and will not be cleansed unless these matters are brought into the public domain and action taken in a democratic fashion. Judges have been fierce in using the independence of judiciary as a sword to take action in *'contempt of court'* cases against their critics, whilst they also using the same law as a shield to cover a multitude of their sins, some abhorrent.

In November 2011, a former Supreme Court Justice provided an insight into the higher judiciary, and highlighted many of the inadequacies in some of our most senior judges, in what she termed *'the seven sins'.*[73]

*"Once a government is committed to the principle of silencing the voice of opposition, it has only one way to go, and that is down the path of increasingly repressive measures, until it becomes a source of terror to all its citizens and creates a country where everyone lives in fear."* —Harry S. Truman

1: **Turning a blind eye**—To the injudicious conduct of colleagues and brushing things under the carpet. They have either ignored the unacceptable conduct or refused to confront the judge in question, and have suppressed any public discussion on the issue often through use of the *'Law of Contempt'*, in the wish to silence the issue.

2: **Hypocrisy**—The complete distortion of the norm of judicial independence. Judges claim that the law is above all, *'howsoever high, the law is above you'*; however, in reality judges who enforce the law for others often break that law with impunity. This could include traffic regulations and any other regulation to which the *'ordinary'* citizens are subject to, including, issuing a rule of contempt against the unfortunate police constables who may have been diligently following their duties.

3: **Secrecy**—When enquiries are made into judicial work or conduct, judges would aim to either delay or prevent further questioning or investigation, this includes the *'best kept secret in the country':* the process of appointment of judges to the High and Supreme Courts.

4: **Plagiarism and prolixity**—There is very little original thinking or reasoning to support the concluding judgements; very often and unnecessarily, Supreme Court judges lift whole passages from textbooks and earlier decisions by their predecessors; this results in long worded compendia of decisions on decisions. They do this without acknowledgments to the original sources of the materials.

5: **Personal arrogance**—While the Supreme Court had laid down standards of judicial behaviour so that members of the subordinate judiciary are conscientious, studious, thorough, courteous, patient, punctual, just, impartial, fearless of public clamour, regardless of public praise; some members of the higher judiciary exempt themselves from complying with these standards. This, it was stated, stemmed from judicial arrogance as to their intellectual ability and status, in office and chair; therefore, the higher judiciary has claimed superiority and independence to mask their own indiscipline and transgression of norms and procedures.

6: **Professional arrogance**—A degree of intellectual dishonesty, whereby judges do not do their homework and arrive at decisions of grave importance ignoring precedent or judicial principle.

7: **Injudicious Conduct and Nepotism**—Wherein favours are sought and dispensed by some judges for gratification of varying manner. These includes known examples of judges using guest houses of private companies or a public sector entity, for a vacation, or accepting benefits like the allocation of land from the discretionary quota of a Chief Minister, or land allocation at preferential rates for close relatives from a private company.

Where the judiciary have taken a logical and rational stand on an issue, or a case, and in the public interest, in some instances, the Legislature and/or the Executive have either connived or blocked the conclusion; where the judiciary have taken a stand that has not been logical and rational, nor in the public interest, or has reached an irrational judgement, the Legislature and/or the Executive have not taken action against the tainted judiciary and they have not been penalised. All three of our democratic planks could be seen as tainted with corruption and potentially incompetent.

In any nation, a judiciary's independence depends on the judge's integrity, and judicial independence cannot exist without accountability. They need to be beyond reproach. What is required of a judge is independence, a degree of detachment, not only with the litigants but also in relation to the lawyers. Litigants also include the Executive and Legislature. There is a need for an effective mechanism for enforcing judicial accountability and independence.

Citizens who are part of the court system are part of our society where corruption is currently now common. The magnitude of corruption however in the higher judiciary has a very destructive effect on the entire fabric of our society, and

*"No civilized society can thrive upon victims, whose humanity has been permanently mutilated."*
**Rabindranath Tagore**

*"A 'No' uttered from the deepest conviction is better than a 'Yes' merely uttered to please, or worse, to avoid trouble."*
Mohandas Karamchand Gandhi

makes a mockery of our democracy and the sanctity of our Constitution. The judiciary has received serious criticisms from both the current and former Presidents of India, Smt. Pratibha Patil and Shri. Abdul Kalam, for failing in its independent duties; and the current Prime Minister, Dr. Manmohan Singh, had also stated that corruption was one of the major challenges facing the judiciary, and suggesting urgent action to eradicate this.

The National Judicial Council, chaired by the Chief Justice of India, was to probe allegations of corruption and misconduct by either current or retired High and Supreme Court judges. However, this seems to enable judges themselves judging the judges. Across the world, self-regulation has been proven not to work. It seems that this is an exercise in dampening the citizens' concerns.

The Supreme Court is taking notice and beginning to change itself and the nation. The majority of its rulings over the last two years have dealt with corruption related issues. It has begun to push for clarification and repatriation of *'black money'* overseas, the 2G scandal, the 2010 Delhi Commonwealth Games etc., and it has progressed with the arrest of a horse dealer who it is claimed has US$8 billion in Swiss bank accounts, amongst others. It is also pushing for the reduction in *'pending'* cases and the recruitment of lower and higher court judges etc., all of these issues require follow-through to conviction, sentencing and to see these sentences are fully served. Only then should we be truly able to say we live in a democratic nation that observes the rule of law.

# CORRUPTION IN LEGISLATURE

The more dangerous threat to India's democratic governance is from the significant number of citizens with criminal backgrounds and criminal associates, convictions and pending cases, who are entering into both the State Legislative Assemblies and national Parliament. The major cause of concern is that corruption is weakening the political body and damaging the supreme importance of the law governing our nation and society.

Corruption within our legislature, the pinnacle of our democracy is a result of corruption being endemic within our society. It is continuing the spread of the disease the blights our nation and our future development. Our citizens encounter it from the time they are born through to the day they die. It pervades our society, be it our protector in *Khakhi*, the policeman, wanting a *chai*, or *'baksheesh'* for a traffic violation, or the administrative official wanting a *'commission'* to obtain a business license, or legislators wanting *'facilitation'* fees for a business transaction. It is a system we ourselves perpetuated through its acceptance and participation. Change comes when we all say *'No'*, *'No'* to accepting it and *'No'* to offering it.

A political culture seems to be taking form in which membership of State legislature and national Parliament is viewed as offices for seeking personal and private gain and financial benefit. In an era of coalition politics, these individuals have become members of the Council of Ministers and a weak Prime Minister or a weak Chief Minister is unable to take decisive and necessary action in the belief that it may lead to the downfall of his or her government.

Our nation, the largest democracy in the world, with the second largest population has a recent history of corrupt behaviour with a former Prime Minister convicted for bribing fellow MPs, a former Chief Minister (CM) convicted of corruption in a land deal, and another CM with some of his ministers charged in a number of corruption cases and facing trial, and a third CM convicted on grass fraud.[74] This is only a small selection of successful examples. Many of the most recent are larger scandals involving Cabinet Ministers and Chief Ministers, such as the 2G spectrum auction issues, the 2010 Commonwealth Games issues, the Adarsh Housing Society issues, Mining and Cash-for-Votes issues. The Head of anti-corruption himself was to step down because of his corrupt actions.[75] We are close to becoming a Kleptocracy. This needs to stop. The Legislators are draining the national purse to fill their own.

By one estimate, two-fifths of a particular State's paraffin subsidies are stolen, earning a *'fuel mafia'* US$2 billion a year. In

*"Even a little untruth destroys a man, as a drop of poison destroys milk."*
**Mohandas Karamchand Gandhi**

another State it is reported that over US$40 billion of food and other subsidies have been misdirected over five years, which is US$8 billion per annum. [76] Where is all this money? In which bank account or deposit lockers? Or spent on which assets?

Whether since independence or just the Top 10 Scams in India, the numbers are probably close to nearly 100,000 Lakh Crore. There are also many land deals involving Central and State governments and even the military that would make this list longer; however, that is not the issue. The issue is what are we going to do to stop this? How are we going to stop this? Who is going to stop this?

The Indian illiterate voter is sometimes too easy a prey to dynastic and powerful local and national names leading to awe, reverence and 'vote bank' politics. Gifts of a free bottle of alcohol, food, cash, clothing, and electrical items including free television sets easily sway those that are not able to make informed decisions, sadly, even if they are literate. Should they be informed that these gifts only form a small amount of funds that could be used for the benefit of themselves and their families, they could vote in an informed manner. The total values of these 'scams' could have significantly improved the future prospects of many of our citizens and the nation as a whole.

It is mandatory for a candidate contesting an election for Parliament or State Assembly to declare whether he or she is accused for any offence punishable under law, within the last two years or more, for which charges have been issued. Candidates should also disclose whether they have been convicted for any offence in which a sentence of one year or more has already been given. These are initial steps taken to inform the voting citizen, with the aim of reducing the number of criminals in politics. This has not worked, nor is it appropriate. It is therefore, necessary to prevent citizens with criminal records and accused citizens from contesting elections or holding any public office. The law needs to change where no candidate who had had a criminal record, or any pending cases, should be allowed to contest or hold public office, including State assemblies and Parliament. The individual citizen who does not have a criminal record, but does have a pending case/s, can reapply as a candidate, once he or she has been proved innocent in their pending case. Should a candidate be in office, and a case is made against him or her then he or she would be provided the right to stay in office, until the end of their term, to clear their name. This change in law has to be controlled by the Centre and executed by the Supreme Court and supported by our law enforcement agencies.

Of our current 4,835 MPs and MLAs eligible to vote, 1,448 (31%) declared criminal cases against them in a self-sworn affidavit filed with the Election Commission. Of these, 641 have declared serious criminal cases such as rape, murder, attempt to murder, kidnapping, robbery, extortion, etc., these numbers could still in reality be an underestimation, given the time it takes for cases to get to court and the more realistic practices of *out of court* settlements, and other methods used to potentially get the claimant to drop the case even before it gets to be registered.

In both local and national elections, candidates and elected members have multiple, pending and actual criminal charges, with some with well over 10 criminal cases.[77] These are professional, practiced multiple offenders, not the result of political or unfortunate circumstances. Ironically, a number of these elected citizens have Law and Order and Prisons as their portfolio.

While none of them are yet to be convicted, they have doubtful credentials to hold public office positions and manage government administration. It has also been stated that many Law and Order ministers are also illiterate, posing additional challenges.[78] It is in the interest of these and corrupt politicians to delays improvements in the legal system, as a poor system maintains them and their colleagues in power for longer and they can further profit from it for longer.

How can we ask a professional Police Department and upstanding law enforcement officers to do their duty and implement the law when they are reporting to, and their career and livelihood depends on, repeat offenders yet to be convicted.

This is not a chicken-and-egg scenario. This is the responsibility of the Government and the Citizen; when the

*"First they ignore you, then they laugh at you, then they fight you, then you win."*
Mohandas Karamchand Gandhi

citizen is illiterate, government has to bear greater accountability and responsibility for the outcome. A mandatory clean record must be required for all public positions of office and responsibility. The Executive and the Judiciary are going to have to make some hard decisions and have these enforced.

# CORRUPTION IN SOCIETY

We have become a society where there is no shame in being convicted of a crime, where an individual has no fear in being called a criminal, committing a crime, or even going to jail. There is no real fear of being tried, prosecuted and sentenced. There is a blatant disregard for the law, as it, and its law enforcement officers are not viewed as credible amongst many individuals within our society. There is no deterrent. These individuals continue to break the law and this sends a negative message to others, so there is no deterrent for any *'new to crime'* citizens from breaking the law.

Corruption is present in all nations. However, as nations and individuals in a society have progressed, developed and evolved, corruption in which ever form, has moved from being overt to covert, with fewer and fewer individuals being corrupt; what you see is sporadic corruption rather than endemic or systemic corruption, which we see across our nation at the moment. Our values, behaviours, ethics, *'ways of living'* and *'ways of working'* need to change and mature to one where we are a society in harmony with ourselves, where all are safe and secure, knowing that the laws of the land are just and fair, and are being implemented diligently. Many other nations face similar issues to ourselves, some have been able to largely address the problem; however, it has taken multiple attempts with sustainable actions each time.

Bribes were originally paid for getting the wrong things approved, but now bribes seem to be paid for getting the right things done in time. Apparently, if a person wants a government job he or she has to pay many lakhs of rupees to the higher officials irrespective of satisfying all the eligibility criteria. Additional payments have to be made to officials for work that is carried out as part of their normal day-to-day activities; citizens are short changed from their food hand-outs, welfare payments, and some even cut corners in food and safety, to save money, whilst risking the lives of fellow citizens. The list is endless. Corruption has become respectable in our nation, because 'informed, educated and respectable people' are now involved in it, it is not just the criminals. Social corruption pervades all levels of our society, and our citizens seem to cower and be afraid to raise their voices against the politicians, criminals and the anti-social elements that form the controlling influence in much of their lives; only now are we seeing some traction against corruption; however, there are little signs of sustainability. Other nations that have had programmes to reduce corruption are geographically smaller and with fewer citizens, our solutions will have to be different and radical to make positive sustainable change.

Corruption by civil servants also breaks down the confidence of the citizens as the whole chain of command and control within our nation is corrupt. All the 'links' in the 'chain' of governance and administration of our nation are corrupted, making them rusted and weak, which in turn makes our nation, the 'Indian chain', weak and vulnerable. The Indian Revenue Service (IRS) officials top the Central Bureau of Investigation's (CBI) list of most corrupt bureaucrats.[79]

Unofficial estimates and comments suggest that Indians had over US$1,456 billion (INR72,80,000 crores) in illicit 'black money' stored in Swiss and other foreign banks.[80] There are many other similar estimates and comparisons. This could be money removed from the official economy, usually as a result of corruption, bribery, tax evasion etc. All this money may not have to be bought back; its sources must be broadly ascertained, and if legal, then taxation would be due, and if not, then an agreement needs to be reached with the Swiss and other authorities and the bank account holding individuals or entities to repatriate it, for some degree of amnesty. Positive and honest behaviours should be recognised and rewarded. This is not only a matter of bringing this money back to the nations purse, but then in effectively and

*"Good actions give strength to ourselves and inspire good actions in others."*

Plato

95

efficiently using it to pay for goods and services for the benefit of the nation and all its citizens, or for the *'owners'* of these funds to utilise these of their own accord, under supervision, to the benefit of the nation. They could build and fund hospitals, schools, power stations, wild life parks, irrigation canals etc. People generally will be willing to pay taxes for provision of efficient and effective services.

The *'auction'* of 2G mobile licenses has caused an estimated loss of INR1,76,000 crores, and two Supreme Court Justices requested the Central Bureau of Investigation (CBI) to ascertain who the beneficiaries and conspirators were and where the funds were being held. It transpired that some of these were in foreign bank accounts; however, it is claimed that the Government refused to disclose details of Indian citizens holding accounts with these banks.[81] This is a classic example where the Judiciary has to take the lead and be seen as the source or reason, sanity and vehicle for law enforcement and democracy in our nation.

The 2012 Transparency International's *Corruption Perceptions Index* (CPI) ranked India 94 out of 177 countries (deterioration from position 95 out of 183 countries in 2011, and 87 in 2010 and 71 in 2001). Transparency International claims as many as 77% of the Indian citizens believe the nation's judiciary is corrupt and 36% acknowledged paying bribes to the judiciary. The Index is closely monitored by investors, economists, and civil society campaigners and is based on expert assessments and data from 17 surveys and 13 independent institutions, covering issues such as access to information, bribery of public officials, kickbacks in public procurement, and the enforcement of anti-corruption laws.

Foreign businesses have been investing in India; however, over the last 2-3 years we see a trend towards India being short-listed but the major investments then being made in other countries. Our complex legal and administrative processes, corruption and poor infrastructure are often the reasons cited behind their decisions. It is also clearer to see which Indian State receive the largest investments from both our home grown enterprises and foreign investments, and they too cite the reasons for their investments; these being, simpler administrative processes, no or limited corruption and good infrastructure and workforce.

It is claimed that in many cases, citizens choose corrupt practices out of compulsion and not by choice. Some individuals state that their salaries are insufficient to meet the needs of themselves and their families, and if they were paid more, they would not be forced to accept bribes. This is a major stumbling block to the culture change required and necessary. Salaries should be at market rates and are a reflected by the supply and demand of capable resources and alternatives. Bonuses should also form part of this equation. Many salaries may need to increase; however, that purely stokes inflation and it does not help in the longer term. The key to increased salary should be performance and behaviour and that is bought about through improving their work processes to improve the services to the other citizens or customers, observing the rule of law, and doing the tasks and jobs assigned to the best of their abilities. The behaviours, values, ethics, 'ways of living' and 'ways of working' should be judged by their peers and superiors of being a standard that sets the example of performance benchmarked to other work colleagues. Reward and recognition mechanisms in government and other institutions should follow the better practices amongst our home grown and international commercial enterprises.

There seems to be an increasing and larger scale of corruption, probably because India is getting richer faster, and the faster the economy grows, the more opportunities present themselves for the corrupt minded citizens.

In their book 'Corruption in India: The DNA and RNA' economists Professor Bibek Debroy and Laveesh Bhandari claim that public officials in India may have siphoned ~INR92,122 crore (US$18.42 billion), or 1.26% of GDP, through corruption. They estimate that corruption has virtually enveloped India growing annually by over 100% per annum and most bribery is accrued from the transport industry, real estate and other public services. They estimate the total quantum of corruption money in 1990 stood at INR31,546 crore (US$6.3 billion), shooting up to

*"True patriotism hates injustice in its own land more than anywhere else".*
Clarence Darrow

INR1,00,095 crore (US$20.01 billion) in 2000 and to a much higher INR4,61,548 crore (US$92.3 billion) in 2010.

The government is planning to spend over US$1 Trillion on infrastructure (road and railway transport, sea and airports, rivers and dams, water and sanitation) and more on re-equipping the armed forces and on improving social welfare, over the next few years. A governance mechanism has to be created and executed to ensure these programme funds are efficiently utilised and effectively delivered.

# SENTENCING STANDARDS AND BENCHMARKS

Two senior lawyers were convicted in the Delhi High Court trying to influence a key witness to change his testimony in a high-profile case involving a hit-and-run that left six people dead. The lawyers were barred from appearing in Court for four months and fined 2,000 rupees (US$ 50), the case took nearly 10 years from action to conviction.[82] This is a light sentence by any measure, and purely an example of scale and timing.

There are many cases where when convicted, the sentence is not reflective of the crime. Be it murder, fraud, corruption, rape, incest, molestation, bullying, threatening or robbery.

We need to re-evaluate our sentencing parameters and guidelines. The law should be simple yet effective. Sentences should be preventative where the consequences of an action would result in a sentence and penalty that does not make the crime rewarding; it should make the crime insignificant relative to the sentence. Simple laws and severe sentencing need to be created and enforced which gives no room for the guilty to escape. We need to be tough on crime, and tough on the causes of crime.

Albeit India has laws of asset recovery, seldom have they been implemented to successfully repatriate and recover the significant funds stolen, lost or misdirected. Laws of Confiscation have been successfully introduced in some countries which allow the

*"Nothing is more destructive of respect for the government and the law of the land than passing laws which cannot be enforced."*
Albert Einstein

courts to confiscate all earnings from the convicted citizens and their businesses or associated interests, for a number of years prior to arrest, and all income over that period, regardless of source, which has to be proven and justified though original legal documentation and records. The onus of responsibility to provide proof of the sources of the funds and assets should be with the defendant and the accused, rather than the government. In India, the Law of Confiscation should also be extended to include direct family members and associates, so the trail of illegal activities and finances can be caught in a net of transactions and assets.

Our citizens should not live in fear to walk in their own streets, communities or villages in which they live, at any time of day, or in the places of work, study, leisure or recreation. Many parts of our nation are increasingly becoming unsafe for young children, girls and women, and even able bodied men. We cannot let our nation or citizens be held to ransom, abused, violated, be threatened or intimidated.

Judicial accountability has succeeded in sending a number of Legislators and Ministers to prison; however, new methods have also been created to circumvent the existing and new processes of law. Accused criminals facing prosecution get out on bail and even go free during the bail processes. During the trail or when on bail, their doctors are able to find a new serious ailment that enables the accused to escape the discomforts of prison by admitting themselves in the care of doctors at luxury hospital. We need to simplify the law and the legal processes to make them efficient and effective, and the consequences severe enough to discourage.

Our sentencing laws must be recast to remove these individuals from our communities until they have completed their full sentences, have reformed, and their illegal and unaccounted for assets confiscated. These assets could be managed by a new division in the Home Ministry which would provide funds to the Indian Treasury for investment in the nation for the benefit of its citizens.

We also have a large number of laws that are either impractical or not enforceable, with many dating back decades and to

*"A wrong decision isn't forever; it can be reversed. The losses from a delayed decision are forever; they can never be retrieved."*
J.K.Galbraith

independence. Some laws, including one where male traffic officers cannot arrest women drivers, even when they are under the influence of drink and are driving dangerously, are designed for an era which has long past.[83] These must all be removed and our legislature simplified, and made to reflect the behaviours, values, ethics, *'ways of living'* and *'ways of working'* we wish to have in the 21st century.

How can we expect to have a common belief, value and respect for the nation, when the Indian Flag Code prevented ordinary citizens from displaying the flag on homes and other buildings for over 50 years after Independence; with only government officials and government buildings being able to unfurl the flag. Thanks to Naveen Jindal, a leading businessman, who had to win a court case in 2001, for the Supreme Court of India to give Indians the right to unfurl the flag publicly. The flag code was updated in 2005; some new provisions still include that the flag cannot be worn under the waist or on undergarments. Our citizens should be allowed to feel proud of the flag and unfurl it where ever they wish. Many citizens sacrificed their lives so we could have a national flag, and not for it to be restricted in use. Desecration by burning by a citizen should be the only illegal act. The rest should be up to the citizen to respect the flag as he or she sees fit. In some countries schools raise the national flag every morning during assembly, this also happens in some offices and companies; it creates an environment and culture for respect for the nation, its citizens, sacrifice, respect and reaffirmation of the values, behaviours, ethics and ideals they strive for. It seems to form a much more cohesive community of citizens, bringing together and building on their similarities rather than their differences. We as a nation could do something similar. What benefits would we gain if all our schools, colleges, universities and some businesses across the nation raised the tiranga daily to the sound of *Vande Mataram* or *Jana Gana Mana*?

*"It will be necessary for us Indians—Hindus, Muslims, Christians, Jews, Parsis and all others to whom India is their home, to recognise a common flag to live and die for."*
**Mohandas Karamchand Gandhi**

*"There is no such word as 'can't'. The word is 'won't'."*
George Cooper

# MECHANISM FOR LEGAL & SOCIAL CHANGE

It is acknowledged that judges do impose their values, preferences, 'ways of working', 'ways of working', likes and dislikes on a society through their conclusions and decisions in particular cases. We need more Supreme Court and High Court judges who have made the lives of the Executive, Legislature, corrupted officials and citizens uncomfortable with sharp questions and even sharper judgments; for which fighting corruption, inequality and the rule of law is of primary importance. In our nation, it is currently the only front line defence for Democracy. Judicial activism is not new to India, and we need more of it.

Under the proposed 'National Mission for Justice Delivery and Legal Reforms', in the 5 years to 2016, the government is proposing that their new 'fast track courts' will reduce the period of 'pendency' (delay and backlog) of cases from the average current length of 15 years to 3 years. It wishes to have all cases to be decided within 3 years and within 3-6 months in the new 'Fast Track' courts. The government is also proposing to create 200 additional family courts to settle matrimonial disputes and child custody matters etc., in a timely manner, and to focus on those crimes related to women, children and disabled: all good intentions. The aim is to increase access to justice, reduce delays and increase accountability through structural changes and by setting performance standards. This would include making changes in policy and legislation, simplification of procedures to make them more effective and efficient, hiring of more judges and court staff, improving physical infrastructure of lower courts and promoting use of computers and other information technology in delivery of justice.

'Social audits' are a grievance-redressing mechanism that gives the poor an opportunity to seek justice. These audits were first made statutory in the 2005 Rural Employment Act. Since more than half of the Government's budget goes towards welfare schemes, it is important to understand how and when the monies are utilised and most importantly, that these are going to the

"There's only one real sin, and that is to persuade oneself that the second-best is anything but the second-best."

**Doris Lessing**

intended recipients; to that end, *'Social audits'* should be exercised for all major welfare schemes across the country. The process they use is to increase transparency and gain traction as individual citizens take interest in the proceedings listing civil works, and this encourages the beneficiary villagers to question transactions, which also breaks social barriers. The Government is supposed to takes action against those found guilty of misappropriation of funds. This unique effort at accountability begins to help ensure good governance. Most States have delayed conducting social audits, despite their availability since 2006.[84] They are held back by a lack of political will and entrenched vested interests. However, one State, has taken a lead and set up the *'Society for Social Audit, Accountability and Transparency'*, an autonomous body insulated from government interference, where over the years, contractors and middle men have been removed, with government dealing directly with the beneficiary citizens. It has undertaken over 3,200 social audits and more than 38,000 disciplinary cases have been brought against officials involved with the jobs scheme, many being suspended. In the past three years, the team has been able to recover almost a quarter of the US$24 million of the irregularities detected.[85] This is a small start.

Welfare cannot and should not be used as a mechanism to try to bridge the gap between rich and poor, privileged and underprivileged, have and the have-nots; as it cannot help bridge the gap between educated and uneducated, literate and illiterate, healthy and unhealthy, or even safe or unsafe. What the nation requires are mechanisms to help individual citizens help themselves. We cannot and must not have a welfare dependent nation with welfare dependent families, communities and societies. Citizens should be provided the education, healthcare and information to help them make the right decisions for themselves, and to help themselves get from where they currently are, to where they wish to get to, to meet and achieve their personal expectation. Citizens should be able to do this in a secure and safe environment where the rule of law is observed and implemented to help them realise their aspirations

For the long list of *pending cases*, a simple solution to begin supporting the reduction could be to extend the hours our courts work; the High Courts generally hear cases for just over 5 hours a day for ~213 work days per annum. The Judiciary and the court staff could suggest working longer hours to support the citizens and nation; they would be paid for their additional contributions. This could help kick-start an improvement in the ethos, work culture and introduce more efficient processes, to help significantly reduce the pending case load.

In 2010 the Supreme Court passed an interim order on a private boundary dispute that the parties should attempt to resolve this dispute through mediation. It was the first time a boundary dispute in the country had been referred for mediation, and this had therefore validated mediation as a form of grievance resolution. Since these mediation centres opened in Delhi in 2005 and Bengaluru in 2007, they have seen 60% of their ~31,000 mediation cases settled within two months. Mediation offers an alternative to a potential multi-year expensive court case; however, both parties need to be willing to accept a slightly sub-optimal solution. Mediation should also not see Justice being short-cut in the interest of time and costs.

Public Interest Litigation (PIL) has proved to be useful initiative, but it also has its limitations. It has been beneficial in bringing access to legal recourse for the citizen where a public interest is being contravened; however, experience has also shown that it is also used for frivolous suits and accusations by disenfranchised individual or political point scoring. PILs should be screened and scrutinised under a set of standards and benchmarks prior to going to Court, as they are beginning to further clog and delay an already over committed legal system.

Justice at the higher courts is both expensive, time consuming and the poor or needy have little to benefit from this; they have to depend on the lower courts and these in turn are where corruption and stalling by lawyers and middlemen is most prevalent. The government is setting up more *'Lok Adalats'* (People's Courts), with the aim of bringing justice to the doorsteps of all citizens; however, implementation of such

*"If money help a man to do good to others, it is of some value; but if not, it is simply a mass of evil, and the sooner it is got rid of, the better."*
Swami Vivekananda

initiatives can be both time consuming and costly. Citizens should also get consistency and quality in justice, which may not be possible when diluting the legal system, so this has to be managed to successful resolution during and post implementation.

The *Jan Lokpal* bill for 2012 would create an independent Ombudsman which would be empowered to register and investigate complaints of corruption against politicians, government and other public officials without prior government approval. However, these type of bills have been proposed and introduced several times since 1968 but have never been passed by Parliament.[86] After a series of fasts by veteran social activist Anna Hazare, coupled with widespread protests by citizens across the nation, the government constituted a 10-member Joint Committee of ministers and civil society activists to draft an effective Jan Lokpal Bill. Until this bill is passed as a Constitution Amendment Bill, the ombudsman will be a *'glass half full'* solution, a *'toothless tiger'*. Amendments generally result in dilution through compromises resulting in a Bill and Ombudsman without the necessary teeth and muscle this body requires to implement the necessary actions to improve governance across the nation. The Legislature supported by the Executive and Judiciary need to pass this law, with appropriate powers, to help begin to heal itself, the citizens and the nation they represent.

Information and technology systems can play a significant role in reducing corruption and improving the effectiveness and efficiency of the courts and government administrative processes. Some states use online auctions and reverse bidding for contracts, allowing anti-corruption bodies to monitor them. One state does this for all contracts over INR 5 lakhs (US$11,000).[87] It has also registered and input all land records and death certificates online; this reduces petty corruption at the ground level.

Rules and regulations are not, by and large, deterrents to corruption, but a source of it. Simpler, easier and more robust processes and procedures are possible while maintaining control and compliance. We need a concerted effort to simplify each

*"The only thing necessary for the triumph of evil is for good men to do nothing."*
Edmund Burke

major process and procedure to support the reduction of corruption and costs to the nation.

The *www.ipaidabribe.com* website is innovative in that citizens openly reveal the levels and nature of corruption they encounter. There are many other web based social forums and magazines that are seeking change in our nation; *www.tehelka.com, www.indiaagainstcorruption.org, www.canarytrap.in,* including *face-book* and *twitter* to name a few. Social media has proven to be a vehicle which can galvanise citizens to make change happen, as the North African and Middle East 'Arab Spring' changes have recently proven.

A single, standardised, Biometric Identification and Unique Identification Number (UID) through a computerised identity system would prove invaluable for multiple reasons and have significant benefits for citizens across all day-to-day activities, and for the administrative operations of government. This is a number that is linked to a citizen's fingerprints, iris scan and facial photograph. The primary motive is not national security, but social benefits, where the majority of government funds are invested. This would work in conjunction with each individual holding a bank account, so funds transfer from government can be traced to ensure the correct citizens receive the correct support they require and need. It is being introduced as a pilot now across some states.

The 'Right to Information Act' (RTI) is aimed to provide a citizen with all information he or she requires about the Government. Under this act, the citizen has the right to ask the Government to help on any problems or issues that are being encountered. A 'Public Information Officer' (PIO) has been appointed in all Government departments, who are responsible for providing this information for a nominal fee. Should the PIO refuses to accept the application or if the applicant does not receive the required information on time, then the applicant has the right to make a complaint to the information commission, which has the power to impose a penalty of up to INR25,000 on the errant PIO. Effective implementation

*"The man who believes he can do something is probably right; so is the man who believes he can't."*

Unknown

and delivery in operating this initiative is key to its success and credibility.

A 'Central Vigilance Commission' (CVC) has also been established by the Government to advise and guide Central Government agencies in reducing and eliminating corruption. The CVC has the accountability and responsibility to increase the awareness among the citizens of the consequences of giving and taking bribes and of corruption, and this body should take action against those when reported. Again, effective implementation and delivery in operating this initiative is key to its success and credibility.

## CONCLUDING COMMENTS

The Judiciary is the third branch of our government. Our citizen's faith in our judiciary is declining at an alarming rate, posing a grave threat to constitutional and democratic governance of our country. Each nation and community creates its own dispute or conflict resolution institutions; ours are the Courts that resolve both civil (between private parties) and public disputes. We have installed both legal and regulatory mechanisms; however these should reflect our economic environment, our civil society and the cultural values of the citizens. This is failing. It has not done as well as it could have. It has not moved with the citizens' progress, our expectations or our position relative to the world environment, and in parallel it is obstructed by our own Legislature and Executive, as well as its own judicial shortcomings. There is a need for a fundamental improvement to our Judiciary and its supporting mechanism for maintaining Law and Order through our Law Enforcement agencies.

We have a rusted judicial system that has long been plagued by corruption, inefficiency and lack of accountability, often making the rule of law unattainable for all but the wealthy and the well-connected. Some senior advocates and judges have stated that the system has *completely collapsed* and that the country *only lives under the illusion that there is a judicial system*.

Indian courts are inefficient. Our judiciary should be the guarantor of fairness and a defence against corruption, but our citizens' experiences have fallen far short of this ideal. Corruption in the judiciary goes beyond the bribing of judges. Court personnel are bribed to slow down or speed up a trial, or to make a complaint go away. Judges are also subject to pressure from above, with Legislators or the Executive using their power to influence the judiciary, starting with the skewed appointment processes.

In our constitutional system, every person is entitled to equality before law and equal protection under the law. No person can be deprived of his life or personal liberty except according to the procedures established by law. Thus, the State is legally bound to protect the life and liberty of every citizen and human being. This is all good in theory. In reality, access to timely justice is difficult for the majority of citizens. There are a high number of 'pending' cases and shortage of judges, resulting in delays, and opportunities for demanding unscheduled payments to fast-track a case; coupled with the complex legal processes and costs, and when this is further aggravated by corruption, the significant resources employed in seeking justice means that real justice is almost unavailable but for a limited few, and that at a considerable and excessive cost. In effect, only those who can afford to pay to speed up the process, and sometimes the outcomes they require, can get justice. There is also a significant increase in the use of non-judicial processes to resolve disputes, as legal transparency and accountability have deteriorated. It is also highly likely that as some citizens are often unaware of their rights, coupled with their many negative experiences of the legal system, they could be resigned to their fate before a corrupt court. Many an innocent citizen could have been convicted, and are awaiting trial in our prisons. This is a serious threat to our constitutional and democratic governance system, as discussed in the next chapter.

Citizens may be more inclined to break the law and have little respect for rules and laws, or find ways around them, if they believe that they are not being served or protected by the law,

*"The administration of justice is the firmest pillar of government."* George Washington

not listened to, or feel they are not part of the civil society. This happens when civil society, the citizen, and the State live separate lives; with the State and Central government continuing to set the policy agenda much on their own and the agenda does not meet the expectations of the citizen and civil society. This leads to disenfranchised citizens, insurgency and rebellion. We need to bring the citizens and civil society closer to the State and Central governments through the *'top-down'* and *'bottom-up'* processes I have identified, to help them become more active in deciding their own destiny through their shares values, behaviours, ethics, *'ways of living'* and *'ways of working'*.

The sources and reasons for corruption can be understood and its mechanism known. It is then possible to manage to reduce and eliminate most forms of corruption efficiently and effectively. However, we need a determined, focused, dogmatic and systematic approach, as a culturally emotional reaction and approach will most likely result in reducing some forms of corruption whilst pushing other corruption further *'underground'*, not really solving the problem, but delaying it by moving it, while making us feel better in the short-term.

In general, the vast majority of us Indians are not corrupt; when we go abroad for vacations, work or emigrating, we do not generally create, promote or participate in forms of corruption, illegal or unethical activities, as we reflect and observe the laws of the environment we live and operate in; when in India and working for a foreign organisation or a local ethical corporate, we also observe the law, as is our human nature. The vast majority of our citizens have bettered and developed themselves wherever we have settled. They have positively contributed to both the peoples and countries where they reside, and have risen to positions of leadership in these nations, their businesses and military, in medicine, mathematics, music, astronomy, architecture, social service, science, technology, engineering, education, art, literature and many others. Literally, in all fields necessary for personal and national development. It could therefore be hypothesised that poor governance; the complex and lengthy application of law, poor law enforcement, unethical social and weak economic policies could be some of the reasons behind our nation's current level of corruption and unethical practices.

Citizens need to be assured that the applied and implemented law is proper, fair, transparent, impartial, and unbiased, and we have access to a variety of anti-social regulations to take strong, deterrent and timely legal action against the offenders, irrespective of their political influences or financial power. Each citizen should be treated as an equal; none are more equal than others.

Wealth is no antidote to corruption: some relatively rich countries, including Russia, fall at the bottom of the global corruption league table, while some of the world's poorer States do comparatively well: Botswana, Bhutan and others appear among the 50 *cleanest* countries. This is again, therefore, a result of values, behaviours, ethics, *'ways of living'* and *'ways of working'* of their Executive, Legislature and Judiciary.

Some citizens may claim that corruption has not stopped our nation from growing; what they fail to recognise, or do not wish to recognise is how much better we could have done without it, and the longer-term impact it is having. Given the value of funds embezzled, say over the last 20 years alone, how much better would we have now been as a nation; our education, healthcare, security, infrastructure, roads, rail, water, sanitation, recreational areas, living conditions? The same question we have to ask ourselves when we think about us standing in the year 2050 and looking back.

We are taking action, but is it enough? Is it exhaustive and comprehensive to change and impact our nation? Or is it just another temporary feel good solution?

Systematic solutions are, therefore, needed for strengthening access to justice. At the same time ad hoc measures are required to provide immediate assistance to the needy citizens.

Corruption will be eliminated from our nation when the Executive, Judiciary and Legislature are all truly aligned and focused on resolving this issue, and citizens in each can look at themselves in their mirrors and claim to be representing the

*"The duty of youth is to challenge corruption."*
**Kurt Cobain**

nation as a servant in the service for the betterment of all our citizens and the nation. History has informed us that in all nations, individuals and movements arise that can make a difference. It starts with each individual, one by one, making a stand and doing and standing up for what is right.

*"No man is above the law and no man is below it; nor do we ask any man's permission when we ask him to obey it."*
Theodore Roosevelt

# 4.2

# LAW AND ORDER— LAW ENFORCEMENT & INTERNAL SECURITY

*"Every society gets the kind of criminal it deserves. What is equally true is that every community gets the kind of law enforcement it insists on."*

**Robert Kennedy**

Law enforcement can be defined as the maintenance of public order and the prevention and detection of crimes. In our nation, law enforcement and internal security is undertaken at both the Central and State levels. Our Constitution provides the states and territories with the responsibility and accountability for law enforcement within their boundaries, and the Centre provides overall co-ordination, security and central government law enforcement functions and facilities. There has been increasing friction between these two over the last few years culminating in the Centre having to negotiate with the States on new legislation and central control over the newer more recent challenges such as terrorism and Maoist insurgencies. The States believe that our federal system is being undermined by the Centre, whilst the Centre believes that further coordination and consolidation of some security is necessary to meet the newer cross-state, cross-border and other complex terrorism threats that exist.

Whilst both are correct, what is becoming much clearer are the significant differences in performance of each state and

*"We cannot expect people to have respect for law and order until we teach respect to those we have entrusted to enforce those laws."*

Hunter S. Thompson

111

territory in their capability, capacity and competence in providing security and law enforcement for the citizens (each has their own rules and regulations governing their law enforcement agencies). There is also an increasing and dangerous tendency and trend that the law enforcement and security apparatus of each state is now more under influence, direction and the control of local politicians rather than the leaders of the law enforcement and security services. Given the recent increases in corrupt, criminal and illiterate legislators in some States, coupled with the generally perceived corrupt nature of some members of the law enforcement agencies, this poses a grave challenge to agreement and implementation of the necessary improvements and changes, which in the meantime will continue to result in poor execution of law enforcement, internal and personal security.

Law enforcement and security for citizens is inadequate, ineffective and sometimes corrupt, and it also dependent on influences and pressures. At the Centre, the law enforcement and security agencies are part of the Ministry of Home Affairs, and these are to support the states and territories in their duties. States and territories also have their own state law enforcement and security agencies under the control of a State Minister.

High crime rates, violent gun related crimes, suicides by women, students and farmers, domestic violence and dowry deaths, child abuse, communal and sectarian violence are all symptomatic of India's failure to develop evenly in either social or economic terms. Terrorism, insurgency and secessionist movements are rooted in poverty, social inequality and ethnic tensions that are neither adequately recognised nor managed effectively. Terrorist, insurgent, secessionist and violent crime share similar underlying causes; it makes sense to tackle the problems together.[88]

Girls and women form nearly half of our population. They are generally the glue and thread that binds and brings our families and communities together. They represent an untapped skill and resource within our nation, and are an undervalued and underappreciated group within many parts of our nation.

*"Justice without force is powerless; force without justice is tyrannical."*
Blaise Pascal

This must change. We must provide all avenues for girls and women to leverage and build on their skills, interests and capabilities. In the short and medium term, in our nation, we still need to ensure that law and law enforcement are used to help make this happen.

A comprehensive and holistic approach to the problems needs to address not only the immediate dangers, but also the social, economic and infrastructure development needs. We need to provide basic education, healthcare and social services, whilst providing for more effective democratic representation and improved governance. These same solutions are necessary to address armed violence, insurgency, State based violence, gang and neighbourhood violence. There also seems to be a lack of official coordination to armed violence, between bureaucrats, Central and State governments, and limited collaboration between the law enforcement agencies, and between the government and non-government agencies.[89]

Although some issues presented in this book seem unique or exceptionally severe in our nation, they resemble problems faced by other nations; however, we seem not to have benefitted fully from experiences and lessons learned elsewhere across the world through international communication and dialogue. Not surprisingly, only two issues are India specific, caste violence and dowry crime. Both outlawed, and not resolved successfully.

The government appears willing to increase spending on reducing and eliminating armed violence, intimidation and security challenges; however, it needs to develop a coherent strategy to deal with these issues; addressing the full range of these issues and the root causes, and providing a comprehensive Centre, State and citizen based approach to the solution. This type of approach is being used in other countries successfully.[90]

All senior police officers in the Federal and State police law enforcement agencies are either members of the Indian Police Service (IPS) or the Indian Revenue Service (IRS). Both are civil service agencies. The IPS consists of 4730 staff reporting to the Ministry of Home Affairs, while the IRS consists of two divisions, each reporting to a separate controlling Central Board; the IRS

*"It doesn't matter if you are on the right track. You'll still get run over if you don't keep moving."*
**Will Rogers**

(Customs and Central Excise) reporting to the Central Board of Excise and Customs and IRS (Income Tax) reporting to the Central Board of Direct Taxes.[91] In many developed nations, these entities have been bought together under a single governance and leadership; as increasingly they face issues and overlaps that bring them more closely to one another.

We have multiple federal agencies, and each State has their own version of its law enforcement and security. In a nation such as ours, with the challenges it faces, and with the inherent issues of corruption, incompetence and a lack of willingness to make things happen in a timely fashion, any improvements will require a group of committed professionals to set the benchmark examples to provide a mechanism of support to others, for making improvements across our nation. We may need to simplify the numbers and remits of these agencies, as there does seem to be overlap amongst some, and in others there is conflict between State and Central agencies. This is not a recipe or foundation for success. Many of these law enforcement and security agencies are new, established in the last 30 years, and some within the last 5-10 years, and set-up as a result of our nation experiencing a particular catastrophic event, which is a national tendency to follow a soft reactionary approach rather the necessary harder pro-active approach which plans and prepares for eventualities before they happen. A more standardised approach is also required, across the states to provide for consistency in service, experience and implementation for the benefit of all citizens. As a nation we should move at a faster evolutionary speed, rather than revolution; the Centre should have more influence and accountability to ensure and enforce improvements across all States and territories. The Centre would need to have the competence, capability and credibility to do this in a timely fashion.

It is unacceptable that a small band of disenfranchised individuals have grown into terrorist, secessionist and insurgent type movements that covers nearly one third, 33% of our nation and 22 of our 28 states,[92] controlling areas of the nation where our own law enforcement and security forces either fear to tread or it is mortally unsafe for them to tread. This level of expansion does not happen by itself, it requires support and a level of disenfranchisement of the citizens. This is not a situation that should be found in a nation wishing to be a member of the UN Security Council, and with one of the largest standing volunteer armed forces in the world

This situation will only continue and maybe expand, unless dialogue with the disenfranchised individuals is started and firm action taken in parallel against anti-social and illegal activities and behaviours.

# FEDERAL LAW ENFORCEMENT— INTERNAL SECURITY

There are seven main law enforcement and internal security forces officially defined as 'Central Armed Police Forces' or paramilitary forces:

**1—Border Security Force (BSF):** Is responsible for guarding our land borders during peacetime and preventing cross-border illegal activities, predominantly along the Western border with Pakistan. More recently, the BSF has also the task of aiding the Indian Army in counter-insurgency and counter-terrorism operations.

**2—Central Industrial Security Force (CISF):** Is responsible for guarding industrial installations, seaports and airports owned by the Central government. Recently, the CISF has also started providing its professional services to non-government private organisations. This also includes the Railway Protection Force (RPF) which is responsible for law enforcement and security on Indian Railways; this includes security for stations, platforms, trains, railway lines, equipment people and goods transported.

There are concerns that this extended role moves it from a Public Service organisation to a semi-commercial organisation, as these central services should only be used for government

*"When you have police officers who abuse citizens, you erode public confidence in law enforcement. That makes the job of good police officers unsafe."*
Mary Frances Berry

and critical national security industrial installations, and not for private company use; private companies should commission their own private agencies. These security agreements have to be reviewed to ensure governance and probity are monitored and maintained. If it is revenue generating then premium commercial market rates should be charged and the CISF then operates as a commercial entity providing some Central Government installation protection.

**3—Central Reserve Police Force (CRPF):** Is responsible for assisting states and territories in maintaining law and order, law enforcement, insurgency containment and anti-terrorist activities. This also includes Rapid Action Force (RAF) and Commando Battalion for Resolute Action(CoBRA).

**4—Indo-Tibetan Border Police(ITBP):** Is responsible for securing the Indo-Tibetan land border.

**5—National Security Guards (NSG):** Is India's premier counter-terror unit created for counter-terrorism and hostage rescue missions, modelled on the SAS of the UK and GSG-9 of Germany. It is a task-oriented force that has two groups; the Special Action Group (SAG) comprising Army personnel and the Special Ranger Group (SRG) drawn from the central and state law enforcement and security forces.

The NSG, however, is now also increasingly tasked with the protection of members of the Legislature and other citizens deemed VIP or VVIPs (very or very very important persons). It is claimed that this role has been further expanded in recent years, as members of the Legislature have come to view NSG protection as a status symbol, and this has caused concern among senior NSG officers and Home Ministry officials.

The NSG, unlike its SAS and GSG-9 counterparts on which it is modelled, is therefore more likely to become a personal protection force for influential individuals rather than a counter-terrorism unit. As the premier counter-terrorism unit it should be used in the many counter-terrorism and

*"As important as the will to win, is the will to train to win."*
Knute Larsen Rockne

counter-insurgency activities within our borders, and in the remainder of its time, it should be practicing and improving its performance, skills, capabilities and competencies; rather than the protection of individuals, which is not either what the SAS or GSG-9 do on a regular basis.

**6—Sashastra Seema Bal (SSB):** Is responsible for security along the Indian land borders with Nepal and Bhutan.

**7—Central ParaMilitary Forces (CPMF):** Such as the Assam Rifles etc.

There is also the **Special Protection Group (SPG)**, which is responsible for protecting the government Executive, the Prime Minister and other top officials, and their immediate families.

Could there be scope in simplifying or better setting-up these entities, to improve the way they function and operate to ensure more effective outcomes?

# FEDERAL LAW ENFORCEMENT— CENTRAL AGENCIES

There are nine Central Law Enforcement agencies that provide services to the Central government.

**A—Central Bureau of Investigation (CBI):** Is India's premier investigative agency, responsible for a wide variety of criminal and national security matters, it handles intelligence matters, criminal investigations and is the national security agency for the nation. It is India's official Interpol unit, and draws its officers from the IPS and IRS across the country. The agency specialises in investigating crimes involving high ranking government officials and politicians, and is divided into three Divisions which are Anti-Corruption, Economic Crimes and Special Crimes.

Albeit lower than most industrialised nations, criminal violence caused more than 14 times as many violent deaths as

*"Poverty is the parent of revolution and crime."*
Aristotle

terrorist activity in 2009, the most recent year for which reliable data is available; there were 32,369 homicide victims and 2,231 deaths linked to terrorism and insurgency. Approximately, 33,000-38,000 citizens die violently each year, nearly 5% of all violent deaths worldwide. Some of the most extreme violence in our nation are concentrated in particular cities, including the national capital, New Delhi. According to the National Crime Records Bureau criminal gangs are heavily involved in the trade of illegal firearms, and most crimes are committed with these weapons. During a ten-year period police seized 4,500 Illegal firearms; in 2009, 371 murders involved licensed firearms, while 2,722 murders involved unlicensed firearms that were possibly made in Uttar Pradesh and Bihar. [93] Only a small proportion of illegal guns are manufactured abroad and smuggled into the country.

There are a potential group of citizens who are more vulnerable to becoming *new to crime* candidates. The majority are in the more prosperous states, between the 18-30 age groups, relatively wealthy, with some education; however, this is insufficient to get the high paid jobs they seek, or they are too qualified for the lower salaried work available, or they fall out of contention for jobs due to caste or background. Their parents could have farm land or other commercial businesses which these children are not interested in running. These individuals are most at risk to drugs and alcohol and the associated addiction and crime that this entails. An initiative is needed to ensure these individuals are gainfully employed or occupied in work and contributing more positively to the nation.

**B—Income Tax Department/Indian Revenue Service (IT/RS):** Is responsible for a wide variety of financial and fiscal matters and is our nation's premier financial agency. It is India's official Financial Action Task Force unit, an inter-governmental organisation set up by the G7 to combat money laundering and terrorism financing. Through the Central Board of Direct Taxes, it sets and implements taxation policies and parameters, and is responsible for the collection of direct taxes, and investigating

*"Look back over the past, with its changing empires that rose and fell, and you can foresee the future, too."*

Marcus Aurelius

economic crimes, tax evasion, terror financing, revenue sources and transactions that pose a threat to national security. It works with the Directorate of Criminal Investigation and Central Information Branch.

If a comprehensive set of Laws of Confiscation were introduced; all financial moveable and non-moveable assets, within the last 10 years from case being registered, should be confiscated from all convicted criminals, their associates and immediate family; these would only be returned after a pre-agreed time, say 6 months, in which period the individuals or their businesses would need to have provided sufficient written proof that these assets were not from illegal, corrupt or unaccounted sources. After precisely 6 months, all financial moveable and non-moveable assets would be confiscated. These would be managed by a new Asset Management Department, where these are either sold by open auction or managed, where the proceeds would be provided to the Treasury for the national purse.

The IT department would need to work with the forensic finance departments to identify assets and sources of funds of convicted criminals, their associated and immediate family.

**C—Directorate of Revenue Intelligence (DRI):** Is responsible for providing information for the co-ordination of India's anti-smuggling efforts. Officers in this organisation are drawn from Indian Revenue Service (IRS).

All nations gain the majority of their income through forms of taxation and income from government controlled assets and entities. The IT and DRI, under the Ministry of Finance should be one of the key vehicles to bring about the improvements and change necessary in our nation.

On the one hand we are constrained on how much we can *'spend'* on our nation's most important issues and have to prioritise and budget for these, and on the other hand, we have the *'income'* we can generate though taxation and national assets. Our annual national budget is always a challenge to *'balance our books'* whilst maintaining a healthy balance of payments,

*"Our duty is to encourage everyone in his struggle to live up to his own highest idea, and strive at the same time to make the ideal as near as possible to the Truth."*

Swami Vivekananda

borrowings, INR level, and ensuring sufficiently healthy foreign exchange reserves etc. We are not decoupled from the global economy, its trends and its impacts; albeit, we have been slightly insulated in the last 20 years as our growth and consumption to date has been predominantly internal. However, this is now rapidly changing and we have a significant trade balance deficit in our national accounts of ~INR1,086.12 billion in January 2013 alone, and this has been a long-term trend. The value of imports far exceeds our exports.[94] This is unsustainable and leads to a vicious cycle. We need to reduce this trade balance. Budgeting is a very complex undertaking, and our recent experiences and trends have shown a slowing down of our economy, tighter financials and insufficient income to meet our potential spending needs and expectations. We need to flourish as a nation and citizenry, now, at the time of our demographic dividend, without having to prioritise unnecessarily and put into place severe austerity plans, which many of the more industrialised countries are currently doing.

We can either maintain the current high level of the nations *'black economy'*, which does not pay taxation, is illegal, and not recorded; or move towards a more transparent system of providing openings to bring this *'black economy'* money into official circulation (and a large part of this is in physically printed paper notes, whilst others are in hard assets such as land, building and commodities such as gold and diamonds etc.); bringing more of these under the taxation net and generating income for the nation, which would in turn provide for benefits for all citizens. Neither over reaching welfare nor subsidies, whether for social stability or political vote bank policy, will support the growth of the nation and citizens in the longer-term. Improved industrial and agricultural productivity, effective and appropriate employment policies and higher value-added outputs are necessary. We operate in a global economy and need to be competitive globally across all economic sectors.

Significant investments, more so than those planned at the moment, will need to be made to successfully implement any of

LAW AND ORDER—LAW ENFORCEMENT & INTERNAL SECURITY

the changes in the six *'Foundation Pillars'*. Each *'Foundation Pillar'* will require investments, and these must be generated from industrial and agricultural growth in parallel with improved revenue and taxation recovery; and for these funds to be effectively and efficiently deployed, will require more robust mechanisms of governance and financial transaction records to ensure compliance. We will need an increase in investment into our nation, from both foreign and domestic sources, to create jobs and value; this must also help the Indian Rupee gain strength, as a weaker rupee will continue to result in higher inflation losing us some of the benefits of growth generated in last few years.

We need a more simplified, but focused approach to taxation through revenue and records, building on the General Anti-Avoidance Rules, and experiences from other nations.[95] Tax minimisation through legal means is a valid practice; however, tax avoidance should have its severe consequences and deemed illegal. The statement of *'India is a rich country of poor people'* can be construed in many ways, and we need to fairly and constructively reduce the gap between the *'haves'* and the *'have-nots'*.

The UID scheme in parallel with a number of our existing agencies working in unison, to an agreed strategy and plan of action, could ensure we become more honest and transparent in our financial and operational behaviours, values, ethics, *'ways of working'* and *'ways of living'*.

**D—National Investigation Agency (NIA):** Is responsible for combating terrorism in India. The agency is empowered to deal with terror, drug trafficking and currency counterfeiting related crimes across States without special permission from the States. The NIA was created in response to the 2008 Mumbai attacks as the need for a central agency to combat terrorism was essential and absent. Drawing its officers from the IRS and IPS, it is divided into three divisions; the Investigation, Policy Research and Coordination, and Administrative Divisions.

*'Terrorism'* typically refers to politically motivated secessionist violence, or to internationally sponsored political violence,

*"You can't succeed in beating the insurgents unless you can convince the people that they can be protected."*
Rand Beers

it usually does not include communal or sectarian violence, however, with religious extremism, this is now also categorised as terrorism. According to the 2011 USA Department of State assessment, India *'is one of the world's most terrorism-afflicted countries and one of the most persistently targeted countries by transnational terrorist groups'.*[96] Terrorism and insurgency undermine both security and economic development and not just the direct deaths and injuries caused. Surprisingly, and disappointingly no government agency is known to keep comprehensive records of casualties from terrorist violence in India.

There are literally hundreds of factions across our nation that support or have religious and political ideologies that are considered extreme, as they conduct or sponsor violent acts and because they seek to undermine the legitimacy of our nation's government while instilling fear in the hearts and minds of the citizens.

Through to November 2011, there were over 1,550 incidents involving Naxalites that resulted in over 500 deaths as compared to 2010, when 2,006 incidents involving Naxalites resulted in over 93 deaths.[97] Many of the masterminds and perpetrators are yet to be brought to justice.

The *'House of India'*, our nation, is directly and indirectly affected by problems spilling over from our *'neighbourhood'*. Many of our neighbours are either plagued with armed conflicts, terrorism, separatism or illicit arms trafficking, such as Afghanistan, Pakistan, Myanmar and Sri Lanka.

The Maoist/Left Wing Extremists (LWE) insurgency began as a peasant uprising in 1967 in the village of Naxalbari in West Bengal. Although it declined in intensity in the late 1970s, when most senior leaders had died or were imprisoned, the movement is expanding once more. The Maoist/LSE or Naxalite insurgency and violence has significantly increased in terms of both number and lethality of attacks in recent years. Terrorism is our most prominent armed-violence issue, but it is not the cause of most deaths. Insurgent and terrorist dangers across our nation are complex and multi-faceted; some are nationalist and independence based, and others are social and economic based. Important groups in the multi-ethnic and multi-cultural states like Assam, Arunachal Pradesh, Manipur, Meghalaya, Mizoram, Nagaland, Sikkim and Tripura have never fully accepted integration into our nation, and they remain politically sensitive and prone to revolt. Almost all these conflicts are decades old with strong local roots. The many forms of secessionist warfare and terrorist conflicts involve old-fashioned nationalist or ethno-nationalist movements, as in Kashmir and the North-Eastern States, as well as more present-day issues such as the lack of effective governance that are generating and accelerating the Maoist/LWE insurgency. We have also not actively helped and supported these citizens integrate into our nation, and there is much we could have done, and can now do, to ensure all our citizens feel part of one great nation.

Although the Maoist/LWE insurgency was concentrated and had previously been confined to tribal and rural areas in the large 'Red Belt', it has spread to 20 of our 28 States and roughly 200 of the 626 districts, most of them relatively remote and impoverished, it is now beginning to be felt in Indian cities.[98] In 2008, some 400-500 Maoists/LWE attacked police facilities in the towns of Nayagarh and Daspalla in Orissa, killing 14 citizens.[99] In dealing with these threats, our governments have used strategies of both negotiated settlement and military force, although the latter has been more prominent.

The results have been mixed: in places such as Punjab the government has almost entirely used military means to contain the militancy, while in Mizoram the insurgents were brought into the mainstream through their participation in the electoral process. The government has begun to address the Maoist/LWE insurgency by using a mixture of development incentives and military force, but it is unclear how long this will take, or how many lives will be lost before the threat is contained.

There are schools of thought that are linking some of these insurgencies to local politics and commercial organisations and interests; who as a troika are sustaining the economics of

*"In India we only read about death, sickness, terrorism, crime."*
Dr. Abdul Kalam

funding insurgencies through indirect payments, support and protection.

The Maoist/LWE movement feeds off the tribal areas, where illiteracy levels are high and where there is a lack of basic facilities (the six **'Foundation Pillars'**, governance, education, healthcare, law & order, infrastructure and security) and very poor or non-existent government or governance present. According to the Ministry of Home Affairs: "*Left Wing extremists operate in the vacuum created by functional inadequacies of field level governance structures, espouse local demands, and take advantage of prevalent dissatisfaction and feelings of perceived neglect and injustice among the under privileged and remote segments of population*".[100] Maoist/LWE insurgents have now begun to target development works in an effort to undermine the government's authority and perceived effectiveness, they are targeting school buildings, railways, roads, power and telecom infrastructure. The Maoist/LWE affected states contain 85% of the nation's coal resources, and since coal constitutes more than 70% of our current needs for electricity generation, the Maoist/LWE threat is therefore both a manifestation of the economic and social underdevelopment that has plagued rural India for decades and an obstacle to the future development of those same areas. It is an example of how '*a sense of injustice, related particularly to gross inequality, can be a good ground for rebellion, even bloody rebellion*'.[101] Improving the lives of the people in these rural areas requires concerted developmental efforts from the government, but these efforts are being, and will continue to be, compromised by the Maoist/LWE threat, until it is managed.

**E—Narcotics Control Bureau (NCB):** Is responsible for anti-narcotic, drug trafficking and abuse of illegal substance operations across the nation. The officers in this organisation are also drawn from both the IRS and the IPS.

Narcotics have already become a major issue in our large cities and these drugs are now pervading into our secondary and tertiary cities. Unlike other crimes, narcotics can induce addiction in a very short time period; and in severe cases, only a few uses

*"Drugs are a waste of time. They destroy your memory and your self-respect and everything that goes along with your self esteem."*
Kurt Cobain

of a drug can cause irreparable long-term damage through addiction. The prevention of use and abuse is therefore more a priority than managing the after affects; although this should not be understated.

We have one of the world's youngest populations, our demographic dividend, however, Punjab is already an example of a potential demographic time-bomb that awaits us, as an overwhelming majority of addicts are between the ages of 15-35, with many of them unemployed and frustrated by unmet expectations. According to the Punjab State government, figures submitted to the Punjab and Haryana High Court in 2009, suggested that 75% of its youth, 1 in 3 students, and 65% of all families had direct experience of addiction in some form, and 30% of its prison population of 18,000 have a drug related history or crime.[102]

Under a mix of complex social conditions, alcohol abuse can lead to drug abuse. Easier access alcohol and addiction to alcohol, leads these individuals to seek out more effective, quicker, pronounced and more sustained means of getting the effects they seek. There are approximately 8,000 government liquor stores operating in Punjab and according to India's comptroller, liquor consumption per person in Punjab rose 59% between 2005-2011. In one village, of the school's 656 students, ~70% have lost a parent to drugs, in another village there are 48 hard-core addicts in a village of 2,000 inhabitants. The use of intravenous drugs has also compounding health affects through the rise of AIDS, HIV, Tuberculosis, Hepatitis B and C and other transmitted diseases. This one proud state is liable to become a shell of its former self. Other states such as West Bengal, Andhra Pradesh, Uttar Pradesh, Bihar and Haryana are not too far behind.

We had nearly 70 million drug addicts across all socio-economic groups according to a 2006 estimate by the National Survey on Extent, Pattern and Trends of Drug abuse in India conducted by the Centre in collaboration with United Nations Office on Drugs and Crime. Our local produced pharmaceuticals (stolen from manufacturers or distributors, and

*"Terrorism is the tactic of demanding the impossible, and demanding it at gunpoint."*
Christopher Hitchens

sold via pharmacies), heroin, and alcohol are amongst the most abused drugs. However, drugs like Methamphetamine, Ecstasy, Cocaine and Crack are increasingly being used on a daily basis throughout our nation. This increase in use and addiction has also increased the need for dealers and distributors to traffic these drugs, and many citizens and criminals are seeing this as an opportunity to make fast and easy money. It has been claimed that by 9th grade, ~50% of Indian students across the country have tried at least one type of drug as per Alastair Mordey a reputed drug counsellor of The Cabin: Chiang Mai. These youth begin to damage their physical and psychological health and their intellectual growth, especially when their curiosity turns into abuse. These youth that continue to abuse drugs will normally begin to use harder drugs and develop addictions to them. Some of them may eventually join gangs or drug related organisations. Most of the youth that get caught up with drink and drugs normally do not continue education through college.

The border with our western and north eastern neighbour is porous to drugs (from Afghanistan and Myanmar amongst others) and other illegal substances and activities. These drugs and other products find their way throughout our nation's cities, towns and villages, and this is a problem that will only accelerate and accumulate as it impacts the daily lives of our citizens through commercial, criminal and social consequences. Approximately 60% of all illegal drugs confiscated in India were seized in Punjab. In the first three months of 2012, 127 kg of heroin were seized by the BSF, double the value of the seizure in the whole of 2011. We need to re-evaluate and improve our security along the land borders and coast to have a much tighter barrier to trafficking. It is claimed that part of the electric fence along Punjab's 553 kilometre border is only switched on after 6 pm in the summer and 4 pm in the winter, it also has gaps in ravines. This is unacceptable for a national border, especially to one of our most important neighbours. There is no explanation that can be acceptable. We also have home grown drugs and we need to have a more concerted effort in eliminating this through confiscation of all land and assets of the cultivators.

**F—Bureau of Police Research & Development (BPR&D):** Is responsible for the modernisation of the Central and State Police Forces. It is involved in research on the challenges confronting the Indian police, including training and introduction of new technology at both Federal and State levels.

To improve policing, we need to improve the basic working conditions and standards of our men in *khaki*. We need to ensure rotas and working hours are reduced, working conditions improved, and they are provided better crime fighting equipment. In between work, we need to ensure that the law enforcement and security agency staff have better housing, enough time to rest and recuperate, and periodic training to refresh and renew skills and competencies. We will need many more better organised and equipped training institutions across the nation.

The government is working on importing appropriate weapons and the introduction of 3D imagery and scanning technology to help all agencies; however, the quality and scope of the outcome will depend on the quality and timeliness of the implementation.

There are technologies available across the world that have a proven track record in law enforcement and security; however, the introduction of new equipment cannot be undertaken without the appropriate training and application of the outputs and outcomes from these tools and technologies. There is a vast range of equipment that is required, this included; range finders, better GPS devices, thermal imagers, night vision, surveillance and recording equipment, close combat and assault weapons, data processing machines for crime records; equipment for forensic science laboratories, finger print bureaus and technology, centres for examination and questioning, documents and scientific aids to investigation; wireless equipment for police; equipment for police training institutions; and vehicles for increased police mobility etc., the list is very long, and will have to be prioritised and time phased to ensure both value-for-money and application through practice and outcomes.

*"Out of every one hundred men, ten shouldn't even be there, eighty are just targets, nine are the real fighters, and we are lucky to have them, for they make the battle. Ah, but the one, one is a warrior, and he will bring the others back."*

**Heraclitus**

This agency needs to be more pro-active in supporting State and Centre agencies in mapping and implementing a plan to reach world-class law enforcement and security standards of service and performance for all citizens in a given time frame, say 15 years.

**G—National Crime Records Bureau (NCRB):** Is responsible for creating a central database for sharing, consolidating and maintaining crime and criminal records consistently from each individual police station across the nation. Theoretically, this should enable a common format to be used and shared at all levels of law enforcement and security, improving the effectiveness and efficiency of crime prevention and detection. This bureau would incorporate the IT systems, finger prints, DNA, photos, data and statistics.

This agency could be the central agency providing a consistent set of information and records to be available to all State and Central law enforcement agencies; it should also be the agency that provides real-time data and information via information and technology systems to all police stations across the country, to connect them to the records, surveillance information, photo, fingerprint, personal identity and DNA databases etc. The Home Ministry has recognised the importance of networking Information and Technology systems across the nation's law enforcement offices. They have created plans to use wired and wireless networking technologies to connect 15,015 stations and 7,000 offices nationwide.[103] This will be done as part of the Crime and Criminal Tracking Network System initiative aiming to provide seamless access to a repository of crimes and progress across the nation. The issue as always is complete, effective and timely implementation. Coupled with the proposed National Intelligence Grid, 11 law enforcement agencies should have real-time access to information and data from 21 sources to be more effective and efficient in the execution of their tasks, to reduce crime and acts of violence.

*"Ten soldiers wisely led will beat a hundred without a head."*
Euripides

According to the NCRB, the most frequent motives cited for murder and culpable homicide are financial gain, disputes over property, personal vendetta, sexual affairs and dowry. The victims tend to be young adult men, with 45% of murder victims aged between 18 and 30 years. Since young adult men are the most economically productive segment of the population, their deaths represent a significant loss of productive human capital for the country.

Dowry deaths are specific to our nation. Official statistics show that there were 1,438 deaths from dowry and caste deaths, in 2011.[104] Despite the stigma and a harsh punitive regime, dowry gifts remain a local custom. According to a study by the Institute of Development and Communication, *'With get-rich-quick becoming the new mantra, dowry became the perfect instrument for upward material mobility'* and consequently dowry harassment has become a part of family life, *'the quantum of dowry exchange may still be greater among the upper classes, but 80% of dowry deaths and 80% of dowry harassment occurs in the middle and lower strata'.*[105] This must be weeded of our 21st century society. We need a more active and vocal citizenry, especially in the rural areas.

**H—Central Forensic Science Laboratory (CFSL):** Is responsible for undertaking forensic work and holding the DNA repository. There are a number of these laboratories across the country. The laboratory in New Delhi is under the control of the CBI and investigates cases on its behalf, whilst the others report into the Directorate of Forensic Science in the Ministry of Home Affairs.

Medical, Chemical, Financial and Information forensics is the key to unravelling many criminals, terrorists, financial fraud and trafficking etc. India is a large nation and with our size of population, science and information technology capabilities, we should have a vision to be one of the world's leaders in Forensic Sciences. We need to significantly increase our personnel and equipment resources and expertise in this area; each major investigation and incident should have forensics expertise available on site from the start to support the investigators. A

*"War is what happens when language fails."*
Margaret Atwood

national DNA database for all citizens should be captured in parallel with the UID.

**I—National Institute of Criminology and Forensic Sciences (NICFSC):** Is responsible for the application of education, training and research in Criminology and Forensic Science to support the Criminal Justice System.

Could there be scope in simplifying or better setting-up these nine entities, to improve the way they function and operate to ensure more effective outcomes?

# STATE LAW ENFORCEMENT

Each state is accountable and responsible for administering the criminal justice system and deciding on the most appropriate level of policing. Currently, the Centre can only try to support, share best practices and provide checks and balances, by creating and monitoring state and central governance commissions and institutions; however, even though the Supreme Court has laid down a set of minimum measures for police reform, some states have not put these actions into place, are behind schedule, or have not implemented these as well as they should be. These include the mechanisms to decide on hiring, transfers and postings at State level, legislation, community policing and to how to deal with complaints against the police etc.

Each state and territory of India has a State Law Enforcement Police Force, responsible for maintaining law enforcement and security; headed by the State Commissioner of Police or Director General of Police. It is under the control of the Home Minister reporting to the state or territory Chief Minister.

There are considerable variations in the competency, capabilities and effectiveness of these law enforcement and security forces. Some are excellent and respected, whilst others not so. There have also been growing concerns between the states, the CBI and NIA on jurisdiction and who takes the lead and credit for some cases. These could be *growing pains* as these agencies learn to work with one another, and in some cases due to political interference at state level. Either way, all three have the same overall objective; to implement the rule of law and ensure conviction and incarceration of criminals and their associates.

The Centre, working with each State needs to agree a set of consistent tools, techniques, technologies and equipment that should be provided to, and used by, the law enforcement agencies to undertake their duties. We need a vision of Indian Law Enforcement where its agencies are seen as one of the most respected and recognised around the world; one where the criminals and their associates, home grown or visitors, will always be caught and sentenced in a timely fashion, where the crime will be recorded and documented for robustness and learning.

We should still have professional law enforcement officers with *lathis* patrolling our streets, day and night; however, we also need a professional force that is armed and equipped with the most appropriate defensive and offensive equipment. It is not acceptable that our largest cities do not have sufficient officers that are weapons trained, technology trained, nor have bullet proof vests and other equipment. We cannot accept that our law enforcement officers are going into duty, putting their lives at risk, and are being sent out without the appropriate equipment to get the job done, without potentially losing their lives or with risk of serious injury.

We should have a consistent set of approaches that provide our officers with safety and defensive equipment, armaments and weapons, telecommunications, surveillance and other necessary equipment. This will help significantly improve morale, performance and increase the calibre and numbers of new recruits to transform this service into one of the most professional in the world. This has to be coupled with a more appropriate salary, performance and service related public recognition. The infrastructure for police stations and housing for all law enforcement officers need to be significantly

*"Each man must for himself alone decide what is right and what is wrong, which course is patriotic and which isn't. You cannot shirk this and be a man. To decide against your conviction is to be an unqualified and excusable traitor, both to yourself and to your country, let men label you as they may."* —Mark Twain

improved; and as with education and healthcare, these could be provided through a modular approach to speed up the improvements.

# POLICE CORRUPTION

According to Transparency International January 2012 report, an anti-corruption advocacy group, the police are reported as the most-bribed public-sector individuals, perverting the course of justice.

The National Human Rights Commission reported in 2012 that over the past two decades, it has received more than 20,000 cases of citizens allegedly dying in judicial custody, and more than 4,000 complaints of citizens dying in police custody.

There are many cases of corruption within the police force and other law enforcement agencies. It is part of the endemic disease our nation faces as it now permeates all aspects of our society. The Judiciary supported by Law Enforcement agencies are our first line of defence and change. We can only reduce corruption within and across our society if we first truly outlaw it, and then have the police and law enforcement agencies equipped to apprehend and convict the criminals, and then sentence the criminals to take them out of our society until they have reformed.

Torture and custodial misconduct by the police has been widespread, resulting in many deaths whilst citizens have been in custody. It is claimed that the police often torture to get a confession. What is most disturbing is that some of these citizens could be innocent individuals victimised to save influential and wealthy offenders and criminals. Human Right activists and legal representatives are insufficient to deal with the current scale of the problem. The main issue seems to be that there is a lack of accountability in police violence.

There were almost four deaths in custody every day, recorded in the period 2001 to 2010. The National Crime report lists just under 62,000 complaints against the police in 2011 for activities such as interrogation, beatings, torture, rape in custody, illegal detentions and extrajudicial killings. This does not allow for the many incidents, which are not recorded or registered.[106]

This level is too high. This could be accounted for by many factors: law enforcement and security in these states are more accountable; it is easier to register cases against law enforcement and security officers; law enforcement and security are genuinely worse in some states than in others; or simply that these states collect their statistics better. The NHRC is right to be concerned as custodial rapes have almost disappeared from the crime reports. Just two rapes reported in the entire country in a whole year, and a third reported case was declared false due to a mistake of fact or law.[107]

Extra-judicial killings and *fake encounters* were supported by large parts of the informed and educated citizenry as they had first-hand experience of the judiciary, law enforcement and security systems not working, and were frustrated; they supported taking the shortcuts necessary to kill individuals suspected of criminal activities. The issues of *fake encounters* have made national headlines and caused controversies; however, these events and each individual case has to be examined on its own evidence and circumstances. Vigilante and extra-judicial justice must be never be condoned, and our law enforcement agencies must be given the equipment and support to do their job more effectively, efficiently and following the rule of law.

Over the years, numerous recommendations have been made to reform the police, law enforcement and security agencies. These include top law enforcement and security officials, consecutive police commissions, eminent jurist Soli Sorabjee and finally even by the Supreme Court in 2006. The Supreme Court ordered the Central and State governments with seven directives to begin the process of police reform. The main objectives of this set of directives were two-fold; streamlining the appointment and transfer processes of policemen, and increasing the accountability of the police through the introduction of civilian monitoring committees to

*"If we desire respect for the law, we must first make the law respectable."*
**Louis D. Brandeis**

*"You're not supposed to be so blind with patriotism that you can't face reality. Wrong is wrong, no matter who says it."*

Malcolm X

investigate complaints against the police. However, less than half of our 28 States have passed these reforms or any previous recommendations, and have historically been reluctant and unwilling to change and take steps to improve policing. Why would this be?

A sense of *'goonda raj'* now pervades some of the law enforcement and security agencies, especially the police force, where once a particular political party comes into power in a region or state, it replaces police officers posted by the previous government in various district, with its own subservient individuals. Endemic corruption has reportedly made the police more susceptible to the influence of criminals, unscrupulous politicians and local entrepreneurs. It has become common practice for politicians and bureaucrats to use the police and law enforcement agencies in their own power struggles thereby further undermining police independence and accountability, potentially leading to police and law enforcement agencies to under-report crime and potentially avoid thorough investigations. The link between political influence and commerce over the independent police and law enforcement agencies is then complete. The link between the potential criminals in politics, entrepreneurs or their representative and the police and law enforcement agencies is complete—democracy and the rule of law dies; and the innocent pay with their lives, livelihood, independence and security.

# PRISONS

In 2011, India had ~357,000 prisoners, the 5th largest prison population in the world (USA ~2.24 million, China 1.64 million, Russia 701,000 and Brazil 549,000); on a per capita basis, we are one of the lowest, ranked 152 out of 155 with only 30 prisoners per 100,000 citizens; USA still highest with 773 per 100,000, China at 118, Russia at 615, and Brazil at 193. We have the 3rd highest prison occupancy density at 139% of capacity, which is behind Kenya at 285%, Brazil 150% and just above South Africa at 138.6%.[108]

We will have to significantly increase our prison capacity to provide humane accommodation for our existing inmates and to accommodate the potential significant increase in inmates we will have to accommodate if our Judiciary and law enforcement agencies do what they are sanctioned to do and take the criminal elements off our streets, and out of our cities, town and villages.

We may need to build larger prisons, in locations that support rehabilitation and reduce re-offence. There has to be an increase in prison population in the short-term to begin the change that is necessary across our nation. We need to take the convicted, corrupt and criminal citizens out of our society for the remaining citizens to live in a relatively safe and secure environment. We need our Judiciary and law enforcement agencies to do their jobs to ensure that sentences and time in prison are not worth the corrupt and criminal behaviours

The prison system can be used to ensure these criminals are productive and benefiting the nation whilst incarcerated, and that all prisoners are treated as equals. Incarceration should be incarceration. Currently, we see a categorisation of prisoners where we have a *'VIP'* or *'VVIP'* type category where prison is treated like a *'home-from-home'*, hotel or country club for a short vacation, where prisoners are able to continue their business and political activities, hold personal meetings, conferences, at a time of their choosing, and are provided a separate menu driven kitchen, or their own food can be brought in. This does not send a message of deterrence or unacceptability. All prisoners must be treated as equal and made to live under the same conditions. This would begin a sense of deterrence as citizens need to be afraid and concerned of the consequences of being incarcerated. Incarceration in prison should be a preventative behaviour tool to begin the behaviour change across our nation. The consequences of entering prison, even for a short time should have a long lasting effect on the criminals to avoid re-visiting the prison. The *'Shuanggui'* type approach that China had used to some

*"As long as the world shall last there will be wrongs, and if no man objected and no man rebelled, those wrongs would last forever."*

Clarence Darrow

success,[109] may not be appropriate for India; however, we need a mechanism that is present in some countries where there is ground roots hatred towards corruption, especially official corruption, support for stronger legal and sentencing action, and little sympathy for convicted criminals.

We cannot and will not change our nation for the better unless we begin to reduce and remove the endemic corruption and criminality in our society.

## MECHANISMS FOR CHANGE IN LAW ENFORCEMENT AND SECURITY

Currently, we do not have the capacity, capabilities or competencies to execute the level of law enforcement and security needed across our nation. According to Human Rights Watch and the NCRB, as of 2011 we still had insufficient numbers of law enforcement officers; our police officers cover three times as many people as the global average (137 officers per 100,000 population against the global average of 350 officers), and just 52.4 police personnel for every 100 square kilometres of our nation.[110] Coupled with the ~380,000 vacancies in the police constabulary, which is also too large a number, a high workload, poor pay, poor living conditions, poor equipment etc., with little respect from citizens and bad press, this is currently not the most respected and sought after profession. The law enforcement agencies and some of its officers have not helped themselves either; corruption is seen as the most cancerous attribute of the men and women in *khakhi*.

We have to change this. We need to make changes that ensure we begin to recruit a higher calibre of individual and a new batch of officers to ensure that they are the first stages in the transformation of the law enforcement agencies and the police force.

We need to modernise, rejuvenate and reinvigorate our law enforcement and security agencies, and we can do this by *'reinventing'* them; this requires transforming them and building them into a more respected and credible service in the eyes of the citizens. This will take time. This change for improvement starts

*"When a person is humiliated, when his rights are being violated, and he does not have the proper education, naturally he gravitates toward terrorism."*
Shirin Ebadi

from recruitment, meeting the necessary standards to maintain existing roles, through to promotion. Mechanisms for recruitment have already been developed by the Centre to ensure minimum human interference and subjectivity in the process; these currently include minimum education and physical fitness standards; however, this needs to be enhanced with a personality profile to ensure that the individual *'has what it takes'* to wear the important *khaki* uniform and serve the citizens of India. It would be necessary to ensure all current law enforcement officers are retrained, revaluated and then if necessary reassigned, to ensure they meet a set of standards the nation would expect from a professional law enforcement agency. These should be physical, mental and developmental assessments to help our existing law enforcement officers contribute to society in the best way they can and wish. Promotion for law enforcement officers should be based on merit, feedback and performance. Recruitment, promotion, performance and discipline for non-conformance to the service standards have to be managed and implemented without local or central political influence or control. The police, law enforcement and security agencies have to be managed by themselves, with oversight from appropriate central and local citizen committees, not a political body or individual.

The State and Central Police Commissioners and heads of agencies should be the individuals personally held accountable for the improvements in the performance, management and control of their agencies and report directly to these independent committees, free of the political parties in power at any given point in time; however, the political parties in power can set expectations on police, law enforcement and security performance. These committees must be independent, citizen and professional led. The membership of these state committees would be agreed with both the State and Centre to ensure independence, governance and compliance to a set of standards of citizenship. This committee can then jointly report to the State CM and his ministers, and the central agencies. This would help the nation move towards adopting more pro-active community policing for effective and pro-public friendly initiatives and actions.

*"A good plan violently executed now is better than a perfect plan executed next week."*

**George S. Patton, Jnr.**

# CONCLUDING COMMENTS

The Home Ministry is taking concrete steps to upgrade India's law enforcement infrastructure. There remain very real problems with political, caste and religious violence, crimes against women, terrorism and insurgency. There are wide variations in the performance and ability of the individual states and territories to reduce violence, crime, terrorism and insurgencies. Armed violence is much more serious in the North, the North-East, and the Maoist/LWE-affected regions. We need to spend more on addressing armed violence, and the Central government must lead an integrated response, coordinating institutional cooperation amongst ministries, between the Centre and State, and between government and private organisations.

A culture change is required throughout the nation and national law enforcement agencies, especially the police forces. Recent and on-going events continue to highlight the difficulty of trying to *'clean-up'* the nation's notoriously corrupt crime-fighting forces.

The police system is still the first point of call for the citizen in an emergency; criminals are caught, crime is prevented and law and order is maintained in large parts of the nation. We are making progress. We have to build on this good work, and better support the hard working and honest individuals and aim to help them transform their service through their inputs and suggestions.

Our nation is seen as a *'soft'* nation, not a *'hard'* nation. It is viewed as one which negotiates with terrorists, and caves in to their demands and releases the terrorists and other criminals who our law enforcement officers have given their lives to capture. The Air India, Kandahar hijacking and Maoist/LWE kidnappings etc. are just two of many examples. We need firm and strong leadership, and to take steps to reduce the atmosphere of insecurity and vulnerability, and to create an atmosphere where positive, patriotic, intelligent individuals come forward to serve their nation with pride, virtue, and honesty for the welfare of the citizens of India.

*"Better no law than law not enforced."*
Danish Proverb

**The *'Foundation Pillar for Law & Order'* could read that:**

1.  The Law will be simplified to make it more practical, applicable and implementable for the needs of 21$^{st}$ century India.

2.  The judicial processes and procedures within courts and of cases will be simplified to make them more practical, efficient and effective for use in 21$^{st}$ century India.

3.  We will recruit and retain sufficient numbers of appropriately qualified and experienced judges and arbitrators to meet the needs of the citizens.

4.  A minimum time will be provided for all citizens for first hearings of new cases once the case has been registered and recorded.

5.  All citizens will have the equal right to timely justice and legal representation should they require.

6.  All citizens will be treated equally in the eyes of the judiciary, courts system, law enforcement and security agencies.

7.  All citizens will have the right to demand justice and have their voice heard in a court of law.

8.  Lok Adalats and the lower regional courts will be the first point of justice for all citizens.

9.  High Court and Supreme Court justices will be appointed on a performance and merit system, without tenure, length of service and political influence

10. All government judicial, court, law enforcement and security employees will be servants of the nation, and will be paid a market rate salary with benefits, in accordance with their performance and abilities.

11. All government judicial, court, law enforcement and security employees will be provided with the most appropriate world class tools, technologies and equipment in order to execute their roles and tasks.

*"Laws control the lesser man . . . Right conduct controls the greater one."*
Mark Twain

12. No government judicial, court, law enforcement, security employee will accept a bribe, payment, inducement or favour or any additional benefit above and beyond that provided by the nation. They will be beyond reproach.

13. A single national biometric Unique Identification system will be introduced for all citizens to provide social justice and equality, incorporating finger prints, iris, photo and DNA records.

14. Independent citizen based State Law Enforcement & Security Committees for policies, performance, complaints and direction will be established. These will report to the CM, State Ministers and the Centre.

15. An independent Law Enforcement & Security Board, with cross-state professional law enforcement membership, will be established to decide the selection, promotions and transfers of law enforcement and security officers and other staff.

16. An independent Central Law Enforcement & Security Complaints Authority will be established, with prosecution powers, to inquire into allegations of law enforcement, security and police misconduct.

17. Middle and higher ranking law enforcement and security officers will be in post for a minimum of 2-3 years and will not be transferred more frequently than every two years.

18. Neither state government nor local politicians will ask or influence the law enforcement and security forces to hire, fire, promotion or transfer any individual;nor will they choose the State Chief Police Commissioner. Any breach will be deemed as a criminal offence.

19. There will be separate distinct staff departments within law enforcement and internal security agencies for investigation and for patrolling activities and duties.

*"I will not let anyone walk through my mind with their dirty feet."*
Mohandas Karamchand Gandhi

20. Laws of Confiscation will be introduced to transfer all assets acquired within a period of 10 years prior to the first hearing for all corruption, fraud, drug trafficking, armaments trafficking, people trafficking convicted individuals, their associates and their immediate families. The onus of proof of assets and responsibilities lying with the convicted felons.

21. Additional and appropriate prisons and detention facilities will be built to accommodate the convicted citizens.

22. Anti-social activities and behaviours will lead to a prison sentence removing these individuals from society until they have reformed.

23. A second conviction for corruption or fraud will lead to an automatic no-bail and no parole sentence.

24. A third conviction for corruption or fraud will lead to an automatic full (whole of) life sentence.

25. A second conviction for drugs, armaments or people trafficking will lead to an automatic full-life sentence.

26. No citizen who has any criminal record or conviction of crime within a 10 year period, prior to standing for election, will be allowed to stand for or hold a government or public position, role or office.

27. No citizen with a *pending* case of any nature will be allowed to stand for election or hold a government or public position, role or office.

28. All citizens will have access to view authorised Central and State information and documents, and their own private records and information held by the authorities.

29. All citizens will be able to live in their homes and walk the streets of our villages, towns and cities any time of day or night, without fear for personal security.

*"The law has no compassion. And justice is administered without compassion."*
**Christopher Darden**

30. We will open direct dialogue with all disenfranchised citizens and groups with the aim to resolve all social, healthcare, education, infrastructure and security issues, in a time agreed manner.

31. ........................................................................................

32. ........................................................................................

33. ........................................................................................

34. ........................................................................................

35. ........................................................................................

Etc..............................................................................................

*"The oppressed are allowed once every few years to decide which particular representatives of the oppressing class are to represent and repress them."*

**Karl Marx**

# 5

# NATIONAL SECURITY

*Thus we may know that there are five essentials for victory:*
*1—He will win who knows when to fight and when not to fight*
*2—He will win who knows how to handle both superior and inferior forces*
*3—He will win whose army is animated by the same spirit throughout all its ranks*
*4—He will win who, prepared himself, waits to take the enemy unprepared*
*5—He will win who has military capacity and is not interfered with by the sovereign.*

**Sun Tzu**

The Government of India is responsible for ensuring the defence and security of our nation and its interests wherever in the world they may be. The supreme command of the Armed Forces rests in the President of India, and the responsibility for national and security defence rests with the Cabinet, through the Ministry of Defence, which provides the policy and framework to the Armed Forces to execute their accountabilities for the defence and security of the nation. The Defence Minister is the head of the Ministry of Defence, whose principal task is to obtain policy directions from the Government on all defence and security related matters and to communicate these for implementation to the Armed Services Headquarters, Inter-Services organisations, military production establishments and research and development organisations.

We are a nuclear weapon, ballistic missile and satellite launching nation, making us a regional power, with the 4$^{th}$ largest standing army in the world, with increasing military expenditure

*"People sleep peaceably in their beds at night only because rough men stand ready to do violence on their behalf."*
George Orwell

143

which now ranks us 9th highest military spender in the world (~US$44.28 billion in 2011—excluding nuclear spend, and expected to be the 4th largest spender by 2020), and is currently the world's largest arms importer, accounting for 10% of all global armament sales. Our nation spends ~2% of GDP on the military, which is without accounting for expenditure on defence pensions, paramilitary forces and the defence ministry.[111]

According to Global Firepower Research, in 2011 we had an armed services strength of ~1,325,000 active personnel and ~1,747,000 armed reserve personnel.[112] The responsibility of these individuals is to protect the life and property of every citizen, and these are now being seriously threatened particularly in areas affected by terrorism (Jammu and Kashmir), insurgency (North-Eastern States) and with Naxalite/LWE violence in much of our nation's mainland. These services have the unenviable task of protecting us along some of the harshest and longest land border in the world at ~14,100 km and a coastline of ~7,500 km, with over 14,500 km of rivers and waterways.[112] Until recently, our armed services have had an unblemished record as the most professional and competent of all our government services, with individuals, teams and a culture of the highest integrity and probity, a military culture.

## PRIORITIES

The areas of focus for our Armed Forces in the foreseeable future could be on:

1. Long range precision guided mobile munitions and weapons systems
2. Defensive and offensive asymmetric warfare capabilities
3. Secure networks, communications and information management systems for all services and equipment
4. Singular command capability through fully integrated combat systems across all services for each theatre of operation

*"The soldier is the Army. No army is better than its soldiers. The Soldier is also a citizen. In fact, the highest obligation and privilege of citizenship is that of bearing arms for one's country."*

George S. Patton, Jr.

5.  Stealth, night and all weather condition operability for all services
6.  Three dimensional deep blue water naval capability
7.  Increased indigenous development and manufacture of all critical and technological equipment
8.  Significantly improved military intelligence

It may be time that our armed forces evolved to have a *'Head or Chairman of the Joint Chiefs of Staff'*, or similar role. This would be a non-operational role that is the single point of contact for all armed services. As we move towards a more developed military doctrine for the 21$^{st}$ century, we are seeing the growth in asymmetric warfare and the increased need for combined services operations, with the development of strategies and tactics that involve participation of all services and singular command structures to lead theatres of operation. This requires a seamless structure and operational command throughout each theatre with each armed service understanding, recognising, appreciating and valuing what each is capable of, and who best makes what contribution where etc. This also requires a programme of joint exercises, cross-collaboration and cross-fertilisation of ideas, capabilities and competencies. The Chairman of the Joint Chiefs of Staff would be elected internally by the heads of each of the armed services and the Ministry of Defence and proposed to the Minister of Defence for approval. Prioritisation of military investment must also be made across all services, as the sequencing of development and achievement of operational capabilities will require a holistic and unbiased view of our military requirements.

## OUR CHALLENGES

In general our three million armed forces operate with outdated and insufficient equipment and materials. We have recently been undergoing a major overhaul and updating, another possible example of *'build, neglect, rebuild'*. A surge in spending usually

*"We don't thrive on military acts. We do them because we have to, and thank God we are efficient."*
**Golda Meir**

implies a new threat, better funding availability, poor strategic planning or a belated awakening and realisation that modernisation and indigenisation initiatives have not really worked and have been implemented incomplete, inefficiently and ineffectively. Realisation that our western neighbour, Pakistan, may not change its behaviour in the next decade, and our eastern neighbour, China, with its economic development has quite rightly begun a significant military expansion to protect its global interests, and we were slow in realising the 'string of pearls' being created (China financing development of ports in Pakistan, Sri Lanka, Bangladesh, Myanmar and the Seychelles), and we, in turn were late in trying to create a 'necklace of diamonds' to protect our own economic and geo-political interests.[113] Historically, as a culture we have been an insular and inward looking nation, always invaded, never invading, philosophically content to enjoying and living life as best as available. Depending on the individual citizen's view of history, this may or may not have supported us in the past and in the latter half of the 20th century. Invasion of a foreign land in not advocated, but a more realistic global perspective for national asset and citizen protection in line with the 21st century international and regional threats and environment is required and necessary.

Large numbers of troops are necessary for large offensive of defensive movements, occupations and maintaining control etc. However, as warfare technology progresses our doctrine and approach to warfare should also change; we need to be addressing and resolving a future range of activities and scenarios, and prepare for and equipping ourselves accordingly. Our military doctrine since independence had been focused on our Western neighbour, Pakistan, with a European 'Cold War' view to large-scale military engagements where sheer force of personnel numbers, artillery and tanks would decide the outcomes; the ability to quickly move soldiers and equipment on a large scale to the theatres of conflict, and to occupy land. And quite rightly, this had been proven successful in our last few encounters. Partition had somehow created an unhappy, discontented, disenfranchised and 'anti-Indian' cousin as a neighbour; one which was not

*"Prepare for the unknown by studying how others in the past have coped with the unforeseeable and the unpredictable."*
George S. Patton, Jr.

content in building and managing their own *'house'* for long-term success, but seemed more concerned with the garden boundaries. Following the Kargil conflict in 1999, it has become clear to some citizens that our military and security doctrine has to change; and this has been further reinforced since the 2001 Afghanistan invasion.

Global events in the last 30 years and the experiences from other nations military engagements have shown a significant change and acceleration in the way some conflicts are created, the changes in tactics and philosophies used, and how these are best addressed and resolved. Major multi-nation conflicts include:

- Iran-Iraq War 1980
- The Falkland campaign 1980
- Operation Desert Storm 1990
- Bosnia & Herzegovina 1992
- Ethiopia & Eritrea 1998
- India-Pakistan (Kargil) 1999
- Afghanistan 2001
- Iraq War 2003

Major Internal Conflicts include:

- Sri Lankan Civil War 1983
- Sierra Leone Civil War 1991
- Algerian Civil War 1992
- Burundi Civil War 1993
- Chechen conflict 1994
- Congo conflict 1998
- Liberian Civil War 1999
- Sudan Civil War 2003

There are many other conflicts across the world that we can learn from; Mexico drug wars, conflicts in Central and Southern America, multiple conflicts in Africa, Indonesia, Middle East and the Philippines etc. and even the recent social unrests in Egypt. These include communal and ethnic violence, insurgencies, coups, drugs cartels and many more, all similar issues to what we are experiencing directly or within our neighbourhood.

*"War will exist until that distant day when the conscientious objector enjoys the same reputation and prestige that the warrior does today."*

**John F. Kennedy**

We need to be better planned, prepared and equipped to address these types of engagements. Our troops need to be action ready, and thereby have regular active duty to ensure preparedness. Our involvement in the UN Peacekeeping Force has had mixed but generally positive press; however, it is essential to continue this to ensure our armed forces gain international experience in different types of conflict zones; we are already the world's 3rd largest troop contributor to UN peacekeeping forces.

At an international level, we need to be prepared to successfully engage in a wide variety of conflicts; from contained border engagements, skirmishes, encroachments, surgical strikes to a nuclear stand-off or the use of large or tactical battlefield nuclear strikes prior to a stand-off or all-out war, and everything in between. At a national level, we have to prepare for asymmetric warfare; we need to ensure our borders, seas and land mass are safe, and our citizens can venture into any part of our nation safe and secure, and to doing so, our armed forces need to be actively used and engaged to tackle the insurgencies, terrorist and Maoists/LWE threats across our nation. For this they will require guerrilla, mountain, jungle, desert and Special Forces type of capabilities; given the range of challenges our nation faces, we have all the conditions necessary to provide our armed services with the full range of conflict experience essential to create and maintain a great soldier.

We need to prepare for, and have the capability and competence to successfully engage in at least two simultaneous theatres of conflict on land, on the Eastern and Western land borders, which involves our land Army and Air Force, in parallel to maintaining our maritime trade sea lanes open and coastal borders secure, which would have to cover the Arabian seas to the Middle East, Bay of Bengal, Andaman Sea, Celebes and Banda Seas, Gulf of Thailand, parts of the South China Sea and Philippines Sea and across the Southern Indian ocean, involving our Navy. We need to be able to have a co-ordinated singular command capability, fully integrated combat system, for our land, sea and air forces, and across all our other armed services

*"War is an ugly thing, but not the ugliest of things. The decayed and degraded state of moral and patriotic feeling which thinks that nothing is worth war is much worse."*
**John Stuart Mill**

to execute this effectively and efficiently; to retaliate against a concerted and combine strong conventional fire-power with high-intensity cyber-attacks and internal security threats and civil unrest in parallel. We must not focus on either the East or the West, we have to be prepared for both, with the intention that neither materialise.

We are deemed to be the 4th most powerful armed nation on Earth, by global fire-power comparisons, using a range of metrics based on equipment and personnel numbers. This may or may not be the case in reality, as focusing on the effectiveness and efficiency of the personnel and the equipment rather than absolute numbers, may be a better, but difficult benchmark, as absolute numbers mask a variety of ills and errors (old and poor quality equipment and ammunitions, poorly trained personnel etc.). By the *fire-power* definition, we are behind the USA, Russian and China, and ahead of the UK, Turkey, South Korea and France. Simplistically, even by 2011 figures, we are by far the lowest military spender per active armed personnel, amongst the top 10 nations, (Japan spent US$44,100, South Korea spent US$13,500 and Taiwan US$9,600, India and China at similar levels in between these two. By comparison, European nations spent on average US$140,400 per service member in 2010 and the United States US$504,800 in 2011) which is a telling statistic.[114] As we draft our 15-20 year military plans, we should consider the appropriateness of leveraging our service personnel to be more effective and efficient, armed and supported with the most appropriate tools and technologies for them to execute their tasks, rather than sheer force of numbers. A platoon of highly trained and well-armed troops can overrun a company of enemy, as can a flight of aircraft defeat a squadron and a task unit of ships defeat a task group; it is the quality and training of the personnel and the effectiveness of the equipment that is the winning formula.

In general, our military development and preparedness has moved at the pace of our civilian government processes and procedures, at an alarmingly slow rate. We may then seem to be in a hurry to try to *catch-up*, and in the process, we are more

*"We have war when at least one of the parties to a conflict wants something more than it wants peace."*
Jeane Kirkpatrick

liable to make mistakes, both in the selection and the agreements for the procurement of equipment.

As quoted by the DNA newspaper on 28 March 2012, the leaked letter Army Chief Vijay Kumar Singh sent to Prime Minister Manmohan Singh in March 2012, stated that India's entire tank fleet did not have sufficient ammunitions, air defences are *"97 per cent obsolete"* and the elite forces are *"woefully short"* of *"essential weapons"* . . . *"The state of the major (fighting) arms i.e. mechanized forces, artillery, air defence, infantry and special forces, as well as the engineers and signals, is indeed alarming."* There were also major gaps in the army's ability to conduct surveillance, including an inability to fight at night. The *"hollowness"* of the 3rd largest army in the world, according to the General, lies with the slow procurement process and lack of urgency among bureaucrats.

Understandably, after the infamous Bofors scandal potentially implicating a past Prime Minister, and the most recent 12 VVIP Agusta Westland helicopters deal, all nations would have directed weapons purchases to have stricter controls, with procurement rules rewritten several times to avoid corruption. However, as with many other things Indian, we may have over complicated the processes and procedures and further enveloped them with our own brand of bureaucracy; adding to this, very poor decision making processes, visioning and long-term planning processes which seem incapable of identifying, agreeing and executing asset requirements for our longer-term needs. This then strangles and stretches the process.

Could it be that plain indifference to the needs of our armed forces coupled with corruption rather than the scrutiny of deals, which are the reasons and excuses for decision delays? We need a strong Centre and stronger Central leadership that is credible, authoritative and forward thinking to ensure our armed forces are capable and able to protect us. This creates the mutual respect necessary for the healthy military-civil leadership and relationship required.

*"The best weapon against an enemy is another enemy."*
**Friedrich Nietzsche**

# INDIAN ARMY

The Army forms the bulk of our armed forces, and has historically been the reason why our nation has had secure borders, repelled invaders and we have maintained a secular and democratic government since independence. Published information as of 2011 estimates that we have ~3,500+ battle tanks and ~66,300+ land based artillery and weapons, ~980,000 active soldiers with ~300,000 front-line reserves and ~500,000 second line reserves; and we can call upon a further ~200,000 in the territorial army. This all sound very powerful as big numbers indicate a large and powerful force; however, secondary and tertiary analysis provides a disturbing picture, especially in a new era of warfare, it is not the numbers that count, it is the *firepower'*, and the effectiveness and efficiency at which you are able to apply that upon the enemy.

In January 2010, General Deepak Kapoor, the then Army Chief had affirmed that 80% of our tanks were night blind, which effectively means unfit for war, further reconfirming the March 2012 letter.[115] Post the 26/11 Mumbai attacks, all three Services Chiefs had apparently sent a list of equipment deficiencies to the Defence Minister to ensure they were able to address these types of events. The April 2012 information that Army Chief General V. K. Singh had written to Prime Minister Manmohan Singh, telling him essentially that the army was unfit for war did not come as a surprise to many; albeit shocking, the absence of surprise is disturbing and concerning. Apparently, the General had also written to the Defence Minister a week earlier and in greater detail. It leads to a possible recognition that the armed services and the bureaucracy that supports it is now as ineffective as the Central and some State governments.

There is a litany of examples which also causes concern to the effect on the moral, well-being and management of our armed forces, apparently:

- New assault rifles will take at least another three to four years before they are acquired.

*"There is no avoiding war; it can only be postponed to the advantage of others."*
Niccolò Machiavelli

"Every gun that is made, every warship launched, every rocket fired, signifies in the final sense a theft from those who hunger and are not fed, those who are cold and are not clothed."
Dwight D. Eisenhower

- The army had not fired a single 9 mm carbine for the last three years because it does not have the ammunition.
- The army has not conducted practice firing on its tanks, as it does not have ammunition.
- Artillery rounds are in short supply.
- Artillery rounds are of poor quality as the current range for the munitions is between 35-37 km, whereas the range of the artillery of Pakistan and China is 40+km.
- Army Aviation helicopters are assets from the 1960s which have been upgraded, whilst the acquisition of 197 light observation helicopters has been delayed by 10 years. The last tender was cancelled in 2007 and was re-tendered, but it is still under process.
- We only have ~800 T-90S and 124 Arjun tanks in service with night fighting capability.
- We have ~2,400 T-72 tanks, a 1960s Soviet design which is night blind. Purchase of 'add-on' night sights for the T-72 has not be completed.
- We do not have sufficient armour piercing tank ammunition; however, we do hold considerable quantities of training ammunition that is incapable of penetrating an actual tank.
- We have ~220 artillery regiments (3,960 guns as there are 18 guns per regiment) using equipment that is at least 25 years old, and it is claimed there has been no artillery procurement since 1987.
- The 'Artillery Rationalisation Plan' proposed acquiring 3,000-3,600 155mm, 45 calibre ultralight and 155mm 52 calibre towed, mounted and self-propelled guns in the next decade for about 180 of our 220 artillery regiments. This does not seem to be progressing.
- The radar network across the length of the border has huge holes, and the development and production of new radar by Bharat Electronics Limited is significantly delayed.
- Some air defence equipment is 40-50 years old; the L-70 and ZU-23 guns are from the 1960s and 1970s, while

programmes to upgrade them, by integrating these to modern radar, are yet to be implemented.

- Missile systems like the SAM-2 Pichora are repeatedly given life extensions, and are claimed to be incapable of bringing down a modern, high-performance fighter jets.

- Mechanised forces' mobile air defence equipment like the ZSU-23 Schillka and the OSA-AK (SAM-8) date back to the 1970s.

- Primary infantry weapon, the 5.62mm INSAS rifle and light machine gun, fabricated by the Indian Ordnance Factories is claimed not to have met modern army standards and needs.

- Majority of the 30,000 night vision devices from Bharat Electronics Ltd. remain undelivered.

- Short range radio communications devices used are of poor quality. Senior officers claim that Pakistani terrorists who infiltrate into Jammu & Kashmir often have better night vision and radio communication devices than the Indian Army.

In such a large army, which is still developing, this could be expected to happen. The MoD together with the Armed Forces are beginning to make a concerted effort to improve the procurement procedures and structures in order to build a comprehensive defensive capability; however, as the average procurement contract lead time will take anywhere between 2-7 years from concept, requirements through to agreement and then delivery, we will have to pass through a *transition period* over the next 5-10 years.

The leadership of the Indian army is assumed to be well aware of the challenges they will face, and the improvements and changes that need to be executed, for them to do their job.

*"In peace prepare for war; in war prepare for peace. The art of war is of vital importance to the state. It is matter of life and death, a road either to safety or to ruin. Hence under no circumstances can it be neglected."*

Sun Tzu

# INDIAN NAVY

Few may know that we have a maritime history dating back to the first recorded events, with shipping, trade and docks built at Lothal around 2300 BC during the Indus Valley Civilization, near the present day Mangrol harbour on the Gujarat coast, where there is tangible evidence of the sea-faring skills the nation possessed in the days of sail. The Cholas and Southern Indian States extended their influence across South East Asia and had trade links with China and the Middle East. During the 17th and 18th centuries, the Maratha and Kerala fleets were formidable and became the most powerful navy on the subcontinent, defeating European navies at various times.

We have never really been a naval nation, as were some of the Europeans, Japanese, Chinese and now the Americans; however, as we entered the 21st century, with our growing trade interests and the movement of global trade through the Indian Ocean, we have had to revisit this view. Our future security and national interests need to be protected by us projecting support and capabilities to protect those interests far beyond our land borders. To that end, we will have to continue to expand and accelerate our three dimensions marine warfare and defensive capabilities to have a truly blue-water navy.

We need to project and maintain our influence in India's maritime area of interest, to further the nation's political, economic and security objectives; and in conjunction with the Indian Coast Guard, ensure stability and security in India's maritime zones of responsibility.

Monitoring the Indian Ocean is a challenge as at least 34 nations border this Ocean, and predominantly all are developing or less industrialised nations; Vice Admiral (Retd) G. M Hiranandani in his book states that the Indian Ocean contains half the world's seabed minerals, and that by 2020, two thirds of the world's trade is likely to be passing through it. Some European countries and America still have *'ownership'* or a historic special relationship with some of the islands, and China

*"A man's country is not a certain area of land, of mountains, rivers, and woods, but it is a principle and patriotism is loyalty to that principle."*
**George William Curtis**

has begun to patrol this Ocean and build ports and potential naval bases.

Albeit, we have had some experiences with frigates and destroyers, we need to increase the range of capabilities of these types of vessels and thereby also increase the numbers we have in operation, together with the necessary reconnaissance, supply and support ships.

Protection of national interests will also require us to expand our submarine and aircraft carrier fleets. We have begun joint ventures, partnered with suppliers and have also begun to develop our own indigenous design and technology. This is excellent; however, we are significantly behind in our capability and competence to design and build our own nuclear powered aircraft carriers and submarines; we have to bridge this gap very quickly. We have had the significantly delayed refit of the aircraft carrier Admiral Gorshkov (INS Vikramaditya), and also the delayed K-152 Nerpa Akula-II nuclear submarine (INS Chakra).

Stealth, surprise and firepower are usually the characteristics of successful naval warfare, whilst defence involves overwhelming superiority of force to eliminate the aggressor or his will to continue to fight (which is applicable to all armed forces). Our nation's 'Maritime capability perspective plan for 2012-2027' aims to have 150 major warships, at least six additional submarines and seven stealth frigates. In the short-term, this will require the number of sailors to increase from 48,000 to over 60,000 and officers from 8,200 to over 11,000 by 2015. We will have a competence gap of semi-skilled and skilled servicemen as we expand our armed forces; we can only deliver this through increased education. We are currently a relatively small navy compared to our nation's requirements; however, we must achieve true blue-water navy capability. We are only one of six countries in the world to operate aircraft carriers and submarines; however, we need to be one who also design and build them.

*"Patriotism is when love of your own people comes first; nationalism, when hate for people other than your own comes first."*
**Charles de Gaulle**

# INDIAN AIR FORCE

Indian fighter pilots have been stated by some of their foreign peers to be among the best in the world, with fast reactions and good hand-eye co-ordination, which is essential in aerial combat. This is a credit to the Indian Air Force and their work over the last 50 years.

Similar to the changes the Army needs to make for the new types of threats, the Air Force will also have to re-write its strategies, tactics and training manuals as we move towards $5^{th}$ generation stealth aircraft, unmanned aerial vehicles (UAVs), lasers, higher altitude mountain aerial combat, and surgical strike scenarios etc. on both borders as against the mass 'Cold War' model, and our last encounters and experiences with the Pakistani Air Force.

We operate ~2,500 aircraft and ~850 helicopters, and currently have a shortfall of aircraft as we are operating with 33 squadrons against a target of 45. By the time all the Rafale's are delivered, under the new agreement with France, more MiG's will have been decommissioned.

We are witnessing a major re-equipment programme to raise the Indian Air Force to world-class standards, as the aging Sukhoi, MiG and Mirage fighter jets formed the bedrock of our nation's air strike capabilities, our military planners are now focused on the Indo-Russian T50 Fifth Generation Fighter Aircraft (FGFA), a stealth jet, and our indigenous Advanced Medium Combat Aircraft aimed to match the capabilities of China's J-20 fighter and the American F-22 Raptor and the F-35.

Fifth generation aircraft are designed to incorporate numerous technological advances over the class termed $4^{th}$ generation. The exact characteristics of $5^{th}$ generation jet fighters are controversial, with Lockheed Martin defining them as having all-aspect stealth even when armed, low probability of intercept radar, high-performance air frames, advanced avionics features, and highly integrated computer systems capable of networking with other elements within the theatre of war to achieve an advantage in situational awareness. The only currently

*"We can easily forgive a child who is afraid of the dark; the real tragedy of life is when men are afraid of the light."*

Plato

combat-ready 5<sup>th</sup> generation fighter, the Lockheed Martin F-22 Raptor, entered service with the US Air Force in 2005.

We have agreed with the Russians to build up to 300 FGFAs (T50s) over 10 years in a deal estimated to be worth US$35 billion. The T50 is marketed to be the equivalent of the US F-35 and the Joint Strike Fighter, and is expected to join the Russian air force in operational trials by 2016, and with us four years later.

Bangalore-based Hindustan Aeronautics Limited (HAL), which already assembles MiGs, Sukhoi's and BAE Systems Hawk jets, has sought at least a 25% share in the production of a two-seat version of the FGFA. The fighter would also be equipped with BrahMos cruise missiles, which have also been jointly developed and tested by Russian and India. Ashok Nayak, a former chairman of HAL, described the project as *"more daunting"* than any of the initiatives India's aeronautics industry has embarked on, including the indigenous development of aircraft such as the Teja, Kiran or Marut.[116]

Fighter Jets always capture the public imagination; however, we need to also develop our own capabilities in heavy bombers, helicopters, gunships, transport and reconnaissance, eavesdropping, radar, communications and military vehicles; the full range of aerial combat and defence vehicles. The multi-role transport aircraft (MTA) is a step in the right direction.

Notwithstanding the continued need of humans in military aircraft in the near future, the future in aerial defence and offensive action will move towards greater use and application of UAVs, which have proven to be extremely effective and efficient in the Afghanistan and Iraq conflicts. We are currently using Israeli designed and built UAVs and are also developing our own *'Rustom'* range. The range of capabilities of these machines continues to expand; whilst, the cost and risks of loss of lives of highly trained pilots is removed all together. These UAVs allow *'pilots'* to command these vehicles in a secure and reduced stress environment, for much longer periods of time, thousands of miles away from the conflict zone through *'remote split operations'*. There are no concerns with retrieving downed pilots nor having these expensively trained and valuable individuals at bases close to the

*"Those who live for others really live; those who live only for themselves are more dead than alive."*
Swami Vivekananda

combat zones, and with all the cost and support that entails. A large part of the restrictions in performance of military strike aircraft is the requirement of having a human inside it, leading to performance limitations; taking the human away enables these vehicles to be designed to perform at much higher performance levels and tolerances. The issue then becomes the communication and response speeds of instruction to, and reaction of, the UAVs. UAVs are evolving to become stand-alone aerial reconnaissance and combat vehicles which would eventually patrol areas and borders and take action against those transgressing these borders or launching attacks on us from either side of our borders. We could establish sustainable regional sphere of influence through connected, multi-mission UAV systems, providing us a leaner more adaptable and efficient secondary air force. This is a major opportunity for our nation.

Medium and high altitude airships are also being potentially considered in other nations for surveillance and reconnaissance, cargo lift for transportation and logistics support for high altitude and difficult terrain. They are operable for long-durations and can support coastal, border and mountain regions. There are many other ideas that nations around the world are considering, and we should also focus our procurement and indigenisation efforts on those we prioritise as being applicable and beneficial to our nation.

# NUCLEAR AND NON-NUCLEAR MISSILE DEFENCE

We have a proud and enviable record of being a nation that has developed its own indigenous missile designs and technologies. The continuing success of BrahMos Aerospace with its multi-purpose missiles is an excellent example of what we can achieve. These 50:50 joint-ventures seem to be operating well, and there are a number of others in the pipeline, bringing in other Indian government and private enterprises.

*"If you can dream it, you can do it."*
Walt Disney

The recent successful launch of the Agni-V rocket makes us only the sixth nation with an intercontinental ballistic missile capability. These developments are more to deter a pre-emptive attack as against planning for one, and to show China and Pakistan our capabilities. The April 19, 2012 test, albeit, a great first success for us was a low risk test, to ensure success, further tests and performance developments will be needed. The range, combined with road mobility and multiple warheads on each missile, will make Agni-V a potent deterrent system. It may be an unsettling prospect for Chinese leaders to realise their biggest cities are vulnerable to Indian attack, but the problem we face is that we lack reliable defences against a Chinese nuclear attack, and we therefore need a credible retaliatory capability to dissuade Beijing from ever contemplating such aggression. The mobility of the missiles means that the Chinese would not be able to target them pre-emptively in a crisis, so in the peculiar logic of nuclear strategy they are not deemed *"destabilising"*, meaning they present aggressors with no incentive to strike first.

Pakistan's test of a new ballistic missile the following week was evidence that they wish to maintain the credibility of their own nuclear deterrent as Indian capabilities expand. This follows a pattern that began in 1998, when Pakistan conducted its first detonations of nuclear devices two weeks after we carried out our second test, and they are maintaining a minimal force of 100-110 warheads to potentially dissuade aggressors from nuclear or other forms of aggression.[117] A key difference between the Indian and the Pakistani ballistic missile programmes is the degree to which technology is imported from abroad. We have focused our own efforts on indigenous development, whereas our neighbour seems to have secured much of its missile technology from North Korea and some of its nuclear warhead technology from China. The increasing global concern is what would happen to their ~110 nuclear warheads in a continuing destabilisation of Pakistan, or the increase of radicalisation and extremism within its armed forces. How secure are these warheads? What options are available to the global community to ensure these do not fall into the wrong hands?

*"If you practice it now, you can call on it later."*
Unknown

159

Indigenously, we have developed a range of short and medium range missiles such as the super-sonic, mach 7.5 Shaurya, a canister based single vehicle missile, the nuclear-capable submarine-launched Sagarika ballistic missile and laser guided Sudarshan and the solid-fuelled surface-to-surface Prahaar tactical ballistic missile. All these provide slow but sound progress.

We need to work with both our neighbours to begin to reduce our nuclear arsenals, and especially Pakistan as their *'anti-Indian'* focus coupled with further potential national instability could pose greater risks to the whole region, and far beyond.

# NUCLEAR DETERRENT

Our nation's defence plans call for a *'nuclear triad'* in which nuclear weapons could be launched, as a defensive measure, from land, sea and air, and we are in the process of learning and knowledge transfer through testing to improve the accuracy and range of each of these systems.

# ANTI-BALLISTIC MISSILE (ABM) DEFENCE AND ANTI-SATELLITE WEAPONS

The ABM project has two missiles, the Advanced Air Defence (AAD) and Prithvi Air Defence (PAD) missiles. The AAD is an endo-atmospheric interceptor, which can intercept targets to an altitude of 30 km, and the PAD is an exo-atmospheric interceptor with a dedicated second stage kill vehicle for ballistic missile interception, up to an altitude of 80 km. All nations face a similar challenge when creating an effective ABM as this is in affect trying to hit a bullet with a bullet, where the incoming bullet can be moving at supersonic speeds.

China, recently tested a laser based anti-satellite weapon, and hunter-killer satellites have been rumoured to already

*"Lunacy is to continue to do the same thing and expect a different result."*
Unknown

exist. As warfare and national defence becomes increasingly technologically driven and dependent, where theatres of conflict are centrally co-ordinated and networked across all participating humans and equipment, communications will need to be better managed through secure satellites, aerial or earth bound transmitters and these will have to be defended to maintain integrity of the whole warfare network and systems. We need to be able to create and operate our own secure and protected networked communications systems, supporting hardware, software and human communications. This is not an insignificant task.

# INDIGENISATION

While self-reliance has been our nation's long stated goal for defence procurement, we still import ~70% of our weapons, and domestic production facilities are still relatively very basic, simple and inefficient.

As our indigenisation process has been slower than one would have wished, again, we are possibly following our civilian capability and competence in delivering something of quality on time, as we are now the largest global importer of weapons and military equipment, at 10% of all global sales. This has given rise to many concerns of corruption and competence in the selection and procurement processes. The infamous Bofors scandal, bullet proof jackets, night vision goggles, army fuel, army land, aircraft parts, UN mission purchases etc. And the recent Tatra trucks affair bring into question how US$100 billion would be best spent in the next 10 years. In March 2012 alone, six armament companies were barred by the Defence Ministry for 10 years for alleged corruption, and in all cases involving a former Director General of Ordnance Factories. The sanctioned companies include producers from Israel, Switzerland, Singapore, Russia and two local facilities. Some activities have bought shame upon those wearing our nation's military uniforms.

*"There is no try. Do, or do not."*
George Lucas

Most officials agree that our nation's weapons procurement system is marked by bureaucratic delays, corruption and poor long-term planning. In the 2011-12 Defence Services and Ordnance review, the Comptroller and Auditor General of India found that the army had failed to decide on what features it wanted in its artillery for four years. In another report from 2007, they found that the army had created a set of unrealistic and inconsistent requirements that could not be met by the technology available at the time.

There is usually no one wrong party, both the armed forces and the civilian bureaucracy would be at fault. The army is unable to decide on the equipment it wants, and is incapable of submitting accurate specifications for the equipment it wishes to have, and a significant amount of effort and time is expended, and lost, in finalising and agreeing the specifications and qualitative requirements. It is claimed that many times the specifications and qualitative requirements are too ambitious for suppliers to achieve, which, results in tenders issued, withdrawn and then re-issued, leading to chaos, confusion, frustration and additional costs and therefore price.

Another case highlighted was that of 155-millimetre ammunition that was to be produced at an Indian facility. The project was delayed by more than a decade because the Ministry of Defence banned the two international firms that were supposed to provide equipment and technology for the project because of allegations of bribery. This is the correct action; however, we should have executed a *'Plan B'*, an alternative.

Some estimate that during the past decade, the Indian Armed Forces have returned about US$5.5 billion allocated to it by the government because it did not, or could not spend the money. This is the correct action. It is better to have taken decisions to return these funds rather than spend these without a clear vision and opportunity, and then have unnecessary and ill-equipped service personnel. The Army then may have also been accused of incompetence and waste.

Guy Anderson, chief analyst for IHS Jane's Defence Industry said, *"Allegations of corruption have long been endemic in India and have derailed many defence programs in the past,"* . . . *"For potential defence exporters to India there are still a number of challenges"* . . . *"There are concerns about economy, the notorious project delays and almost habitual cancellations-not to mention the corruption.",* blaming bureaucracy and corruption for these situations.

China has successfully acquired credible indigenous design and production capabilities in the defence and military arena; albeit, maybe like the early Soviet Union and some other nations, it may have used some indirect means to access some highly sensitive secrets from other nations. It has also successfully reverse engineered advanced technologies, through developing and utilising its domestic industrial base to its advantage.

Our nation on the other hand, has the dubious distinction of becoming the world's leading arms importer over the last decade. Much of this funding goes to foreign suppliers and over the last 20 years, Indian funding has proved crucial to the potential survival of defence industries in Russia, our largest supplier, and now maybe in France.

As a nation, we may not have taken a path to acquire highly sensitive and secret technologies; however, we should have better utilised our human resources, talent, capability and competencies to develop new and leading edge technologies; many engineers and scientists across the world are of Indian origin, so we do have an existing national talent pool that is capable of achieving this; the challenge is in creating, managing and maintaining an environment (working conditions, apparatus, colleagues, values, ethics, behaviours and 'ways of working') in which they will thrive; creating and developing tools, technologies, capabilities and competencies to help the nation achieve its objectives. We also have an opportunity to reverse our capability and competence brain drain, and seek our émigrés and NRIs to return.

Since 1948, in our first Industry Policy Resolution, and validated in an Act of Parliament in 1951, production of defence equipment has always been under the control of the government

*"The ability to convert visions to things is the secret of success."*
Henry Ward Beecher

163

and in the public sector. As a consequence, the complete defence infrastructure is in Central government and Civil Service control. We currently have:

- 8 defence Public Sector Undertakings (PSUs)
- 39 ordnance factories with two more planned
- 50 Research & Development (R&D) units, under the Defence Research and Development Organisation (DRDO)

Government enterprises in any nation operate at the speed which the government operates, and the majority of governments operate at an exceedingly slow pace. These entities have a monopoly and do not operate in a competitive environment, so they are inefficient and ineffective, and individuals are usually unaccountable. There is no motive for them to be productive, lean or agile in their design, supply or maintenance of goods and services, quality generally is suspect, and costs are uncompetitive. This does not have to be the case. Some nations have moved their government-owned operations into clear profit centres generating revenue and returning profits to the nation or re-investing for expansion. It is an option our nation and the leaders of these entities should consider. Generally, it is *evolve and adapt, or die*, maybe not tomorrow, nor next year, but in 10-20 years, it could be a possibility.

Many of these PSU led projects have fared poorly, leaving India with significant gaps in critical defence capabilities that have had to be filled by buying foreign equipment as a temporary measure, which as time passes, frequently become permanent supplies for our armed forces.

Due to sensitivity security issues and the nature of defence projects, private firms had generally been limited to only undertake roles as sub-contractors and ancillary support; by mid-2007, there were about 5,200 companies supplying between 20-25% of defence needs,[118] although significant, this was generally restricted to the supply of raw materials, parts, components and semi-finished products to: army base workshops air force base repair depots navy dockyards defence PSUs ordnance factories

As our nation's stated objective for self-reliance in defence is critical, in May 2001 the Central government decided to open the defence industry for private sector participation with up to 100% equity, with foreign direct investment (FDI) of up to 26%.

From being suppliers of raw materials, components and sub-systems, private sector companies have now become partners in the manufacture of complete advanced equipment and systems. It was hoped that the involvement of these companies would bring world-class expertise, scientific and high technology skills, competent management, and their ability to raise resources to supplement the indigenous defence production capability. Many large corporations have shown interest in being *system integrators* by investing both in R&D and infrastructure to develop capabilities in defence production. Leading corporates such as Tata Group, Mahindra Group, Kirloskar Brothers Ltd., Larsen & Toubro Ltd. and many others are now involved in the domestic defence equipment sector.[119]

The MoD has introduced a policy to designate approved private companies with the status of *'Raksha Udyog Ratna'* (RUR)—champions of defence production. These RURs are platform producers and system integrators, at a peer level with the defence PSUs; having similar access and rights to bid for defence contracts, with options to collaborate with foreign technology partners, and able to leverage FDIs.

Indigenisation is critical and essential. It may be disappointing that we have lost ~20 years due to failures and delays in our own progress, this is the right strategy; however, we need to change our approach. Would we have moved to only procure equipment then we would have been locked into technologies we have no control over or real experience of, and the repair and renewal cost can be much more significant than initially envisioned. It is frightening to know that *'circuit boxes'* in high technology equipment and machinery would have to be transported back to the host country, each time they fail or malfunction, and the costs can be exorbitant. The initial capital

*"No army can withstand the strength of an idea whose time has come."*
Victor-Marie Hugo

165

costs may be low; however the maintenance, repair and operation costs can be crippling.

# INTERNATIONAL COOPERATION

Our government's objective is to have a proactive leading edge defence industry. For foreign companies, the benefits are in having an equity investment in an Indian defence company which will appreciate with the growth in the sector, while the Indian partner can be the cost-effective high-quality manufacturing supplier, with export potential. This also supports the government PPP model to deliver critical defence capability to the nation whilst building a sustainable domestic industrial base.

We have defence cooperation projects with many other nations:

**Russia**—An India-Russia Inter-governmental Commission on Military Technical Co-operation (IRIGC-MTC), with an agreement in 2007 for Hindustan Aeronautic Ltd (HAL) to produce precision Aero engine components. We have a long history of cooperation with Russia, and the FGFA/T50 project begins to put us at the forefront of military aircraft design and upholds a longstanding Russian promise to share the most advanced technology, something other nations have not been ready to do.

**France/Europe**—European Aeronautic Defence and Space Company (EADS) announced in 2006 that it was going to invest US$1.5 billion over 15 years, in production and R&D facilities. Indian defence production units are currently involved with a joint venture with companies in France on Scorpene submarines. Thales International put in a formal bid for upgrading the Mirage 2000 fighters of the Indian Air Force.

*"The key to success is never to follow the others."*
Masaru Ibuka

**Israel**—An agreement on joint production of various types of ammunition and other items at India's Ordnance Factories, had led to the first defence FDI project in 2006.

**UK** BAE Systems agreed to supply 66 Hawk advanced jet trainers, of which 24 are to be made in the UK and 42 to be manufactured under licence by HAL.

**America**—A 2005 New Framework Agreement for a US-India Defence Relationship outlined a strategic relationship in the field of defence production, co-production and technology collaboration arrangements. Lockheed Martin is 'putting meaningful work' in India, independently of any sales contracts to leverage our growing engineering competence.

We have succeeded in many indigenous ventures, as we have launched our own satellites and ballistic missiles etc. And some of our indigenous aircraft such as the Tejas, Kiran and Marut have been good learning experiences.

Our predicament of a potential 'triple trap' of relying on foreign defence procurement is succinctly described by the Shri M. Natarajan, Scientific Adviser to the Defence Minister as:

1. What is developed abroad may not suit local requirements
2. What is suitable may be denied
3. What is not denied could be unaffordable

This confirms the position that our defence industry must change faster and evolve to retain and increasingly build local capabilities to meet our needs.

We are building the Sukhoi-30MKIs, Hawk trainers, battle tanks, Scorpene submarines and many other armaments and equipment under license; however, recent experiences with the main battle tank, aero engines and light combat aircraft show how we took an inordinate time to develop something of our own. We need to show greater determination and relentless in support of indigenisation programmes and its progress and

*"Alone we can do so little; together we can do so much."*
**Helen Keller**

outcomes. In the short span of 20 years, Brazil emerged from relative technological backwardness to become a major exporter of tanks, rockets and aircraft. Many nations including Israel and South Africa have created their own defence industry through developing leading edge tools, techniques, technologies and equipment through practice, trial and error, and learning from application and use. The environment of necessity and restriction had led to creativity through determination. What stops us from doing this? Why are we not doing this? Why have we not succeeded? We need to better understand ourselves, our limitations and our own barriers, and begin to remove these hurdles one-by-one. We can do it too.

# PROCUREMENT

Apparently it took 11 years to select France's Rafale as the favoured candidate for a US$15 billion purchase of 126 combat jets to replace ageing Soviet MiGs which we have had since the 1970s; dubbed the *'flying coffins'* for their high crash rate, over half the Indian MiG-21s purchases have crashed since the 1960s, raising questions whether defence procurement procedures can come up with new hardware faster than old equipment is naturally scrapped, at the additional cost of the lives of the highly trained aircrew.

Some individuals will argue that suspending procurement cases pending the investigation, or blacklisting of firms, does more harm to the country's defence preparedness than the economic woes it inflicts upon the concerned firms. This approach is tantamount to supporting and encouraging corruption. We have to draw the line on corruption on all forms and live by our principles, first and foremost. We have to find alternatives and create our own technologies more rapidly and in parallel. We must also remove the corrupt bureaucrats and armed services personnel out of the system. Once they operate in a corrupt fashion, unless they have reformed, they will be corrupt

*"There is a no right way to do a wrong thing."*
Unknown

again, just that the second time, they will be better practiced to avoid getting caught.

While the procurement systems may be sufficiently robust enough to make a wide range of standard armament purchases, and thereby maintain the call-down processes for replacements, the questions asked are if we could have done better with the same amount of monies spent. Did we get value-for-money? Many cases coming to light in the press and television media highlight how the cultural endemic corruption of our nation has blighted the armed services. Regardless of motives and repercussions, it is a brave move by the Chief of Army Staff to address the issues directly to the Prime Minister; however, it is also disappointing that we have got to a position in our re-armament process that the Prime Minister has to be informed of replacement parts by the Chief of Army Staff. Something is fundamentally wrong. Spending US$100 billion in the next ten years will not solve this: we need to resolve this before the majority of these monies are spend, we have the window of opportunity to do this now, or we will look back in a decade's time and say, *"What did we get for it? . . . Was it just this? . . . Where did all that money go?"*

We need to have an independent view on the procurement and indigenisation processes, and to ensure that these are initially both efficient and effective to meet the needs of the armed services, and that the input requirements and outcomes of the purchases are to the contractual agreement, of performance, time, quality, value and price. There is no nation on earth where defence procurement is a smooth process; there are inevitable delays and redesigns, especially when working on leading edge technology; however, for the standard artillery and military armaments, this should be much simpler.

Some of our armed forces are using very old and out-dated rifles and other weapons, single or multiple shot with manual loading; however, whilst updating our equipment we should take a leap forward rather than an incremental step. We will continue to get left behind, and killed, by those that wish to harm us. We recently purchased AK47s (unless there is a significant

*"Our greatest glory consists not in never falling, but in rising every time we fall."*
Oliver Goldsmith

169

cost-performance benefit) for some of our armed forces; this is a weapon designed in 1945 that came into use in 1949 and has had several revisions; albeit the weapon of choice for many groups and nations and probably the most widely produced and used rifle since the second world war, we should be procuring more advanced and effective equipment for our armed services. Indian Ordnance Factories are licensed to produce the AK-47; a form of old indigenisation, but our Ordnance factories need to evolve, and our armed services need to potentially have wider experience of rifles. It is like our police and security forces still driving around in the Hindustan Motors Ambassador, a little altered 1956 Morris Oxford III model from the United Kingdom. Wider experience of other motor cars and understanding of true performance and capabilities would lead to better decisions, faster responses, with more lives saved and better service.

At the time of writing this book, a typical challenge we will continue to face in our international armaments decision making, is the example of the USA now wishing to potentially provide technical information to us on the F-35 Lightning II (produced by Lockheed Martin which is viewed as a heavier, cheaper version of the F-22), and has indicated that it would supply the aircraft at a heavily discounted price of $65 million per aircraft with deliveries beginning by 2015. Some defence correspondents and others have therefore, suggested that the Ministry of Defence abandon the purchase of *'overpriced'* fourth generation Rafale fighters and immediately leap to the stealth capabilities offered by the F-35 in a single-vendor contract.[120] Others, including Indian defence analysts say that the procurement process to choose the medium multi-role combat aircraft is too far advanced for a U-turn, and current needs are too pressing, whilst the American offer of stealth technology also puts the T50/FGFA partnership at risk, and why would we want two stealth fighters? A sudden departure from the process would dent India's credibility, they say, at a time when the conduct of its bureaucracy is under greater scrutiny after a number of corruption scandals. So, the process may or may not be complete

*"When a gifted team dedicates itself to unselfish trust and combines instinct with boldness and effort, it is ready to climb."*
Pat Riley

The Defense Procurement Procedure (DPP) also allows for a *fast-track procedure* where immediate operational requirement for weapons or weapon systems can be acquired via a *fast-track* route. Under this provision, the armed forces can go to one vendor, negotiate and procure the required equipment. It has been claimed that in at least four cases, the Infantry and Special Forces have used the *fast-track* procedures; however, this too has taken 4 years and are nowhere near finalisation. In November 2011, the army had to make an *emergency purchase* of 66,000 125mm rounds from Russia, at a significant premium as we were forced to waive the offset clause mandatory for all purchases above $60 million (INR 306 crore), and this *emergency purchase* was significantly above this value.[121]

This further validates the need for an independent review, assessment and redesign of the DPP and indigenisation programmes, plans, processes and procedures. This should also look at the military supply chains and their parameters as this has a major implication on the draw-down and re-ordering processes. Given the size of our military, the range of applications we need, we should be a creator and exporter of weapons and technology, and not an importer.

# RESEARCH & DEVELOPMENT

The Defence Research & Development Organisation (DRDO) has been the primary government body supporting our nation develop some of the leading tools, technologies and equipment that have made us an indigenous arms producer.

It has had many successes given its limitations and the government environment it has had to operate in. However, as the military and armaments environment has significantly changed and is further accelerating, the DRDO is experiencing difficulties in maintaining the pace, agility, capabilities and competencies required to meet the needs of the nation. There have been many programmes that have failed to deliver, been

*"Unless you try to do something beyond what you have already mastered, you will never grow."*
Ralph Waldo Emerson

'*semi-successful*', or have had significant delays; Kaveri jet engine, Rustom missiles, Arjun tanks, Integrated Guided Missile Development Programme, Weapon Locating Radar, UAV Nishant, Light Combat Aircraft Tejas, INSAS rifles. There seems to be a lack of accountability, inefficiency, ineffectiveness and an environment averse to being bold, courageous, taking risks and making rapid decisions, where paperwork and duplication is seen as more important than output and production, as in all government PSUs.

There have been many reviews, studies and recommendations, which the MoD and the Defence Minister will implement at their discretion; however, the challenge will be to support the DRDO professional staff to create a niche within their operations to be able to prove themselves as worthy participants and leaders in the armaments industry. An organisational change alone will not solve anything. It will be like '*moving the deck chairs on the Titanic*'.

We need the DRDO and its capabilities and competencies, and we need to enhance and build these. The organisation, like many PSUs, needs to move out of their civil service, bureaucratic government, jobs-for-life mindset, and transform themselves to commercial type operations with clear accountability, focus, deadlines, development plans, and outputs. This would require a change in some key leadership, management staff and a new organisational ethos.

To achieve our goals we will also need to increase higher-end university and industry based research & development, we need to refocus on the primary sciences, technologies and development of world-class leading edge thinking and application, where these institutions can work with the government and form commercial joint ventures to provide practical applications.

Qinetq, the former Defence Evaluation and Research Agency (DERA) of the UK could be an interesting case study for the MoD and DRDO to review and may be apply a few of their lessons learned.

*"None of us is as smart as all of us."*
Kenneth Blanchard

# MOVING FORWARD

Conventional weapons now need to be paired and merged with cutting-edge technology systems; these have to be engineered and created to be specific to the nation itself, and not bought off-the-shelf or designed by another nation. To do this we need our own source codes, computer operating systems, hardware and dedicated military networks combining artillery, tanks, infantry, ships, airplanes etc. Connecting all the men and equipment in the theatres of operation, to operate robustly without interference both in peace and war-time conditions. Our future engagements will have us and our enemies use satellites, hi-tech electronic surveillance, lasers, UAVs, stealth, special forces, surgical pre-emptive strikes, cyber warfare, etc. China recently tested technology to destroy satellites; and we need to stay in parallel or one step ahead. It is hoped that the Indian 15-year Long-Term Integrated Perspective Plan will provide both the vision and an effective implementation plan, that is executed on-time and in-full.

# HUMAN RESOURCES

The Indian volunteer professional armed forces are an exceptional organisation that owes its abilities to the individuals that serve within it, and form the essential back-bone of the national security apparatus. Given some of its challenges and short-comings, there is now a high staff turnover and increased resignations; highly trained staff leaving for work in the private sector, or just changing profession.[122] The Indian Army, Air Force, and maybe the Navy too, seem to have followed the pre-war British colonial model of operating distinctions between officers and enlisted staff, practices and customs that are from the 19th century, which the British had maintained but very rapidly discarded post the Second World War, and which we, as with their bureaucracy and legal system, built on it further. Potential *gentlemen's type agreements* on border control processes

*"Don't be afraid to take a big step if one is indicated. You can't cross a chasm in two small jumps."*
David Lloyd George

that may have led to Kargil, commissioned soldiers doing errands for senior staff and their families all need to be expunged. The armed forces operate on building clear leadership qualities, and I fear that as the services are expanded, and we move to a new phase of development with different scenarios, that the quality of leadership may weaken; hastening the exit of our higher calibre individuals. We need to also ensure that senior military staff are in post for 3-5 years as part of their normal rotational assignments; this would give sufficient time for these professionals to ensure that they can make a positive difference and visible contribution in each of their roles. We need to take a concerted review of our Armed Forces organisations and Human Resources processes to ensure we recruit and retain the talent required, and begin to retire and redeploy individuals that may not be able to operate the new processes and procedures necessary. This would equally apply to the military PSUs, R&D and support organisations

# BORDER CONTROL

Our armed forces are doing an excellent job securing our national borders as best they can with the tools and equipment we have provided to them. Their passion and commitment cannot be questioned. However, we need to better secure these borders, as fencing and flood lights are insufficient to deter committed terrorists, drug and people traffickers, money launderers and arms smugglers. We need to begin to apply and use more relevant methods and approaches to seal and secure these borders, such as securing *'no-man's land'* zones on our side of the border, and use of unreasonably excessive lethal force to all that transgress that zone. Clear multi-lingual and pictorial warning signs would ensure adequate warning of certain death. We need to develop and use more relevant technology and equipment to support surveillance and monitoring, such as pilotless UAVs, airships that can hover for months, 24 hour visual and audio monitoring, and

*"The love of one's country is a splendid thing. But why should love stop at the border?"*
Pablo Casals

automated defences. These devises should be used for both land and coastal border control.

We need to be able to cover a long border and large surface area remotely, whilst being able to focus our armed human resources to take quick and decisive action on specific identified threats. Artillery or weapons fire from across any of our borders should be responded to with immediate, focused, unreasonably excessive lethal force to prevent further action. This would be in the interest of both nations across the border as third party organisations, entities and groups are potentially interested in increased conflict and tensions. This would ensure the nations on both sides of the border maintained control of their side.

Terrorism is one of the greatest threats to our internal security; this could be supported from elements outside our borders. Our nation suffers from both state-sponsored terrorism and organisational terrorism. We have legislated several laws to comprehensively manage terrorism including the Unlawful Activities (Prevention) Act, we have also several counter terrorism law enforcement agencies at both the local level, like the Anti-Terrorist Squad of Mumbai, and the national level, like the National Security Guards; however, in some instances, our Special Forces and other land and air armed units could be better utilised to support these internal efforts. We need to apply the instruments of law, forces of democracy, development and social cohesion to defeat the elements of terror, insurgency and Maoist/LWE violence.

*"When patterns are broken, new worlds can emerge."*
**Tuli Kupferberg**

## INDO-PAK BORDER

Our Indo-Pak border security needs to be further enhanced to seal the border against terrorist incursions, arms, drugs, counterfeit money and goods transfers. Albeit recently fenced, it is an example of an incomplete and part-solution as this is a porous border; we need to take further steps to increase security and use of unreasonably excessive lethal force to protect our border; there have been too many successful attempts of undesirable individuals and goods crossing into our nation, which is beginning to successfully destabilise some parts of our nation. The collateral damage and longer-term consequences from these individuals and goods coming into our nation is far greater than the cost of prevention.

As NATO forces leave Afghanistan, the Afghanistan-Pakistan (Af-Pak) border and other internal security issues will increase for our neighbour, which could have a grave and potentially catastrophic impact on the operation and survival of their current national institutions and structures. Given past performance, and the potential consequences, a scenario could be that these armed individuals and groups could be 'redeployed' towards the Indian border to alleviate the Af-Pak and internal issues. The hawkish military neighbour and the majority of its citizens have an 'Indian arch enemy' indoctrination, which will require a multi-generational change of internal soul-searching and 'de-indoctrination' to resolve. National instability and economic crisis in a nation armed with significant nuclear warheads aimed at us requires us to take more firm action and steps, in parallel with economic and other humanitarian support, to help our neighbour improve the quality of the neighbourhood we both live in.

Border fencing, floodlights and patrols are insufficient. We need to secure an area from the border that is 'no-man's land', to literally be 'no-man's land', similar to the North-South Korea border, providing clearer points of entry and exit to help improve trade, commerce and community links and relationships. These entry and exit points can then be reviewed on a periodic basis as trade, commerce and community relations continue to improve. It is recognised that Actual Ground Position Line and Line of Control (LoC) across the higher mountain terrain is more difficult to seal; however, we need to begin to develop and use the newer technologies and tools to help us seal these borders too. Any trespass, from either side of the border, within these zones, would be met with unreasonably excessive lethal force.

We could not have asked for more from the performance and sacrifice of our armed forces during the Kargil incursions;

"I come bearing an olive branch in one hand, and the freedom fighter's gun in the other. Do not let the olive branch fall from my hand."

Yasser Arafat

however, questions still remain as to the intelligence, processes, procedures and events that led to incursions and the actions taken in the immediate aftermath. These lessons learned are now more applicable to the Eastern borders.

## EASTERN BORDER

The Indo-Bangladesh border faces the same issues as the Western Indo-Pak border. The solution has to be the same, and at least here after 60 years of independence we have a clear demarcation of the border.

## NORTH EASTERN BORDER

Some parts of the North-Eastern border seem to still be in dispute. This is disappointing. We face a combination of challenges across the Eastern States and territories (Manipur, Mizoram, Meghalaya, Assam, Tripura, Nagaland and Arunachal Pradesh); insurgence, ethnic conflict, independence demands, and local power factions. At a larger level, better governance, infrastructure, education, healthcare and security will significantly resolve many of the tensions and their extended consequences. The Central government has used dialogue, discussion and come to agreements in many of these regions; investment and spending has also increased, however, as always, more still needs to be done: Civil government in these regions need to significantly improve their performance in management and control of the region, or be enhanced by Central support.

China's territorial claim on Arunachal Pradesh has been a long-standing issue of concern for our foreign policy. While both countries signed a framework agreement to resolve the issue in 2005, not much progress has been made towards a final resolution. We need to further bolster our Armed and Special Forces to strengthen our defence posture in the Eastern regions. As parts of this border are in potential dispute and in difficult

*"The true measure of a man is not how he behaves in moments of comfort and convenience but how he stands at times of controversy and challenge."*
Dr. Martin Luther King, Jnr.

terrain, we need to take more urgent and concerted effort to secure and seal these borders.

# THE INDO-TIBETAN & SINO-INDIA BORDER

Tensions have remained high since the 1962 border conflict, and over the last few years, this has increased. As China quite rightly reinforces a 3,500 km (2,200 mile) shared but disputed border through the Himalayas, they are building infrastructure to protect their interests.[123] We have again possibly been late in both realising that this was going to happen, and finding out after it has happened. Déjà vu 1960's; when we only realised border outposts had been built after the event. We have only just begun, as of ~2009, to better secure this border region, support regional economic development and now begin to accelerate the recent road, rail, air and power infrastructure as a matter of urgency. Will our infrastructure be robust enough to do the job? Or will we follow the *'build-neglect-rebuild'* syndrome and have to redo all this after a few severe winters?

# COSTAL BORDER

Coastal border security is perceived to be weak. Smuggling is common, and defences weak, as was clearly illustrated by the terrorists who landed in Mumbai, the commercial capital of our nation, before 26/11/2008.

We have a long and porous coastal border and control must be significantly improved. We have only recently begun to strengthen coastal security, through an additional 204 interceptor boats and constructed an additional 109 of the approved 131 Coastal Police Stations.[124] Further measures will be required to protect our nation and interests.

# COUNTER TERRORISM

We need send a message to those that wish to harm us, and have a proven record to say: "You *can run, you can hide, but we will find you, we will hunt you down and we will bring you to justice*". Our citizens need to know and have confidence that the nation and its security forces will look after their citizens, at home and aboard, and will not accept individuals, groups and nations who wish to harm them. Radial extremism at home and abroad that aim to harm our citizens cannot, and will not, be tolerated or allowed to operate.

Recent history has clearly proven that individual terrorist leaders and nascent organisations should not be allowed the time and space to grow and infect the environment in which they operate, or wish to operate, which would then provide them the platform, capacity and capability to bring fear, death and destruction to our citizens, anywhere in the world. Bad men have to be stopped before they become evil. Protecting individual liberty has to be balanced with the democratic processes of government, and the priorities for securing the safety of the citizens and the nation.

Our intelligence gathering has to be reliable and world class in its timeliness and quality; human feet on the ground through to eavesdropping and electronic and visual information.

# SINO-INDIA RELATIONS

The relationship between India and China goes back many millennia, it is of mutual cultural respect and admiration, and it is also complex, involving as much cooperation as competition. The greatest threat to both nations is the lack of understanding, communication and misunderstandings between our two great nations. We have much more in common than our differences, and we both have long and proud histories and cultures, and have increasing commerce and trade between our nations and common trading partners. Increasingly, our national economies

*"If we open a quarrel between past and present, we shall find that we have lost the future."*
Winston S. Churchill

179

find themselves competing across the world for investors, investments, partners, resources and technologies. We will compete and therefore, we need to have more deeper and meaningful engagement, communication and friendly cultural and philosophical exchanges.

This lack of understanding, poor communication and misunderstanding could in some way have led to the 1962 conflict, and that humiliating experience for us, still in some way, represents a fear of not letting that happen again, at any cost. Many in China may not view India as an enemy, and China may not have any intention to take part in a military conflict with India; however, as China aims to secure it sphere of influence, it will overlap with the Indian sphere of influence, and this is where both nations will need to jointly work together.

We need to engage China on the Sino-India border, and on the open seas, to improve friendly relations and engagement for mutual benefit; Indonesia who has a smaller Navy than ours faced-off with China in the South China Sea. We need to work with China to secure our mutual and joint interests in both the South China Sea and the Indian Ocean. There needs to be much more communication, especially navy-to-navy, and army-to-army.

## MILITARY INTELLIGENCE

Military intelligence can be defined as strategic and tactical information that is pertinent to a nation in the defence of its national interests at home and aboard. The 1962 border conflict, the 1999 Kargil Operation, and the National Parliament attack in 2001 were all as a result of our neighbours or their representatives crossing our national border. In 1999 we lost the strategic vantage points, and were successfully deceived into a sense of 'business as usual' and then 'surprise'. Our soldiers having to sacrifice lives in excess of what would ordinarily be required; coupled with the 2008 landing of a boat full of armed terrorists in a key district of Mumbai, the commercial capital of

*"If you know the enemy and know yourself, you need not fear the result of a hundred battles. If you know yourself but not the enemy, for every victory gained you will also suffer a defeat."*

Sun Tzu

the nation, would point to a lack of military preparedness due to poor and insufficient strategic, tactical and operational military intelligence information. Some information and events cannot be intercepted by our armed services, and other more prepared and advanced military nations have also failed in spotting the signs of invasion and conflict; however, in the last ten years, the increase of global terrorism has significantly focused national energies on vigilance, surveillance, monitoring and tracking of individuals and groups. This has also led to pre-emptive surgical strikes to prevent attacks and expansion of terror networks.

Some could claim that systematic military intelligence analysis may be better in Rawalpindi and Beijing. Kargil in 1999, Indian Parliament in 2001 and Mumbai in 2008 could lead us to believe that our neighbours may be better aware of our own limitations than we are. Do we have a cultural bias towards self-confidence and self-belief?

We need to ensure excellence in internal and external, strategic, tactical and operational intelligence gathering; in the collection, categorisation, analysis, prioritisation and dissemination of military intelligence information. We need to use this to take bold action when required, and pre-emptive covert action when necessary to ensure the defence and safety of our citizens and nation.

There is nothing that prevents us from building and developing our intelligence gathering through overt and covert Human, Communications, Signal, Imagery and Electronic Intelligence, and bringing all these together under a single command and control umbrella that includes the three major armed forces and the internal armed security and law enforcement services. Taking as examples of the changes that have been made in the last 15 years in America, UK, Russia and many other nations, they are moving towards a singular, better co-ordinated and all-encompassing intelligence networks. Internal corruption and national security activities would be a separate arm within this umbrella organisation to ensure a degree of *'independence'* to carry-out its necessary duties.

*"Integrity without knowledge is weak and useless, and knowledge without integrity is dangerous and dreadful."*

**Samuel Johnson**

It is inappropriate that we have multiple intelligence organisations and agencies focused on their own sphere of interest or influence. This approach inevitably leads to gaps or overlaps between the agencies, use of different operating protocols, definitions, approaches, and priorities, which lead to conflict, poor information sharing and inevitably poor performance and failures.

# CYBER WARFARE

We have observed a seismic shift on the affect and impact of technology and computerised systems in, on and off the battlefield, resulting in a potential paradigm shift on how the broader warfare arena needs to be managed, and the range of new accompanying military strategies and ideologies. We are seeing, in real time, a move to a new type of warfare.

Cyber warfare is becoming a reality, moving from small commercial espionage type activities to a weapon and tool to be used as a potential force multiplier in military operations, as a pre-emptive weapon, and for continued application during the conflict. This is a weapon in its infancy and its application can range from adversely affecting the enemies military architecture and warfare systems through to damaging civilian life, governance and commercial activities. These could include water and electricity supply, banking, commerce, telecommunications and all other essential services. Potentially anything that is connected to a computer, telecommunications and with use of micro-chips and programming can be targeted. In our more technologically dependent world, its uses and applications can be endless and devastating.

We see this as web-site hacking, virus attacks, government computer departments and law enforcement agencies being hacked; these are either independent or State sponsored activities. As we become more technologically dependent, we need to have our best minds working on defending our national and military infrastructures. We should be a world leader in this arena, as a defensive player, given our IT and technology systems capabilities as a nation.

*"A nation that continues year after year to spend more money on military defence than on programs of social uplift is approaching spiritual death."*
Dr. Martin Luther King, Jnr.

# CONCLUDING COMMENTS

A perception can be formed of a volunteer armed services that is professional, dedicated and has a proven track record of excellence in the face of the enemy; however, over a period of time, it has been influenced by the bureaucracy it works with, and by the society in which it lives and operates; usually a military culture is distinct and stand-alone, and a culture unto itself be it the Army, Air Force, Navy, or Special Forces. We need to move away from any post-independence type, pre-independence types of behaviours, processes and procedures within the armed forces that do not align with a professional meritocracy-based fighting force for the 21$^{st}$ century.

Indian Armed Forces have a decorated history of professional excellence; bravery is never questioned and our soldiers and officers have done great work to operate with what they have been provided. We will always need the infantry men and front-line soldiers, artillery and tanks. However, future conflicts and wars may not be heavily personnel number driven or dependant; they will be information, technology, machine, network system dependant, and as we invest in re-armament with new technologies and equipment, it could be an opportune time to up-skill our armed forces to begin to focus on higher capabilities and competencies, and thereby increase its overall 'fire-power' rather than number of personnel.

We need to build network centric indigenously-equipped armed forces, with dedicated closed systems. This will take time to develop and establish, but it is essential for our defence independence and autonomy.

As a nation we should spend more on civil and individual citizen development than the military, and for our neighbourhood to be safe. For this we need to further educate our citizens and ensure greater communication and collaboration with our neighbours, to increase the cross-border exchanges and commerce. We have more in common than our differences. We all have more to gain by peaceful cultural and commercial exchanges, communication and awareness, and have more to lose by conflict.

*"Action expresses priorities."*
Mohandas Karamchand Gandhi

183

The 'Foundation Pillar for National Security' could read that we will:

1. Prioritise and develop our long-term national defence needs whilst maintaining our short and medium-term readiness.

2. Maintain and expand our national capabilities and competencies in indigenisation of all major armaments, equipment, technology and networked systems.

3. Maintain and expand our UN Peace-keeping activities to support global peace.

4. Develop fully integrated networked battlefield systems.

5. Continue to transform the Armed Services into a meritocracy with these professional services being an international benchmark and examples of integrity, valour and patriotism.

6. Build better communication and cultural exchanges with our neighbours and regional nations to improve mutual understanding, respect and appreciation.

7. Work with our neighbours and regional nations to ensure protection and recognition of our spheres of interest and influence.

8. Maintain a singular command structure for all battle field and combat theatres under fully integrated combat systems.

9. Support the Indian Army to realise its strategic plans and to increase the *fire-power* through effectiveness and efficiency of its combat troops and equipment.

10. Support the Indian Navy to realise its three dimensional true blue-water capabilities.

11. Support the Indian Air Force to realise its strategic plans to ensure dominance over Indian air-space and its sphere of interest and influence.

12. Support our Missile and Satellite Defence operations to ensure safety of the Indian mainland and its territories from attack.

"Duty is the most sublime word in our language. Do your duty in all things. You cannot do more. You should never wish to do less."

Robert E. Lee

13. Establish greater *'fire-power'* per armed services personnel through focusing on higher capabilities and competencies in their effectiveness and efficiency of brining this to bear onto the points of intended contact.

14. Continue to redesign the armed forces Procurement Purchasing Processes from initial preparation of *'specifications of performance requirements'* through development, installation and post-application efficacy.

15. Continue to redesign the indigenisation processes from initial preparation of *'specifications of development'*, *'specifications of performance'* and *'specification of production'* requirements through development, production, installation and post application efficacy.

16. Ensure agile armed forces adaptable to changes in military doctrine and fully prepared for the range of expected operational environments from asymmetric and cyber warfare through to Special Forces operations etc.

17. Work to improve the operational culture of our Military PSUs, ordnance factories, depots and dockyards, associated and support organisations to be more commercially focused and prioritised to deliver outcomes in an effective and efficient manner.

18. Promote a Military R&D and national science R&D culture that is creative, radical and productive, where licensing with universities, independent research institutions and commercial organisations leads to development of leading edge solutions and applications.

19. Support local independent commercial military suppliers to partner with international companies to create joint ventures to supply the nation's Armed Services.

20. Ensure senior Armed Services staff have at least a 3-5 year assignment and role rotation to ensure officers are able to positively contribute to performance improvement and their own personnel development.

21. Ensure all our land and sea borders are secure and sealed from trespass, from both sides, through monitoring and patrol.

*"You do not want to be considered just the best of the best. You want to be considered the only ones who do what you do."*
Jerry Garcia

FOUNDATION PILLARS FOR CHANGE

"Trust may be risky, but nothing is so risky as mistrust."
Unknown

22. Support the Ministry of Home Affairs and the Internal security armed forces to ensure all internal terrorism, insurgency and Maoist/LWE type activities are eliminated from all Indian territory; initially through discussion, dialogue and provision of education, healthcare, governance, security and infrastructure.

23. Employ a more focused international anti-terrorist doctrine to remove the threats from home grown or foreign individuals and organisations that wish to harm our citizens and national interests.

24. Establish organisations to create and build preventative tools and technologies, capabilities and competencies, to maintain the integrity and independence of all Indian civilian, commercial and military electronic communications, applications and devices within our sphere of influence and interest.

25. Significantly improve the Military Intelligence operations at home and aboard to ensure national security and defence.

26. Create a command, control and co-ordination organisation to gather and make available all national security information for use by our Armed Forces for internal and external security.

27. ...........................................................................................

28. ...........................................................................................

29. ...........................................................................................

30. ...........................................................................................

31. ...........................................................................................

Etc ........................................................................................

186

# 6

# INFRASTRUCTURE

*"There is a sufficiency in the world for man's need but not for man's greed."*

**Mohandas Karamchand Gandhi**

Infrastructure has been described as the economic arteries and veins of a nation; its roads, railways, sea and airports, power lines, canals, pipes and wires that enable people, goods, services, commodities, water, energy and information to move efficiently and effectively. Agriculture and Environment need to be added to this mix as these three are inexorably intertwined and linked. One significantly affects the others two. As individual citizens, and as a nation, we need to ensure that all three are prioritised equally to ensure we realise the sustainable benefits for the longer-term, as short-term decision making and behaviours will irreparably damage the nation for our future generations. We need to set the expectations, standards and targets now, and work diligently towards achieving these.

When we look at other nations and how they have developed and moved from a predominantly agrarian to an industrial society, there are a list of positives and negatives. Our nation is a predominant agrarian society with a rich and diverse ecology, and given the size of our land mass and the projected population growth, our national survival, competitiveness and distinctiveness will be in maintaining and further developing our agrarian society and ecology with industrial development.

Our economy has undergone fundamental changes in the last thirty years, and will so in the next thirty; however, we have to plan till at least 2050. Recent growth in investor interest had been driven by strong economic growth, rising foreign exchange

*"Respect the past in the full measure of its desserts, but do not make the mistake of confusing it with the present nor seek in it the ideals of the future."*

**José Ingenieros**

reserves, quality and cost competitiveness and investor friendly Government policies. This economic growth had led to an expansion of industry, commerce and per capita income, which in-turn demand an increase in robustness of infrastructure services including energy, transportation, telecom, water and urban infrastructure; increased affluence and activity also increased the demand for food items. However, these economic benefits do not have as sound a set of fundamentals as we would wish to have to ensure sustainable development. Our national economic and fiscal performance needs to be significantly better. We are affected by the global economy and need to operate in this on a competitive basis across all industry sectors. Investment in Indian Infrastructure has increased from 4.9% of GDP in 2002-03 to 7.18% in 2008-09, and is expected to increase to over 8% by the end of 2010-11, and needs to reach 10% of GDP in 2012-17 to deliver the growth necessary in our economy.[125] With increasing investment, the share of the private sector in the total investment in infrastructure has also increased rapidly. The contribution of private companies in total infrastructure investment in each of the first two years of Eleventh Plan (2007-2012) was around 34%, this was higher than the Eleventh Plan target of 30%, and 25% achieved in Tenth Plan period. It is expected to rise to 36% by end of Eleventh Plan and 50% during the Twelfth Plan (2012-2017). Addressing the Asian Development Bank in Manila, in May 2012, the then Finance Minister Pranab Mukherjee said India needed about US$1 trillion in the next five years for infrastructure development; half of which had to come from the private sector, and that India had made provisions for creating an infrastructure debt fund to attract investment in this sector, making it a sound investment.

Increasingly, infrastructure is regarded as a crucial source of economic competitiveness. Our citizens need to be able to move safely and rapidly to and from their areas of leisure, work and living; we need to move goods and services effectively and efficiently across the nation, and to and from our sea and air ports to ensure they arrive without delay or damage to ensure productivity and competitiveness. Infosys Chairman N.R.

*"The only real failure in life is not to be true to the best one knows."*
**Siddhārtha Gautama Buddha**

Narayana Murthy is claimed to have stated in the Bloomberg Business Magazine: *"If our infrastructure gets delayed, our economic development, job creation, and foreign investment get delayed. Our economic agenda gets delayed, if not derailed."*

China and India are often compared by Western executives weighing sites for expansion or outsourcing; but the reality of the situation is that in terms of infrastructure, China is decades ahead of us, an important consideration for industries reliant on strong power, water, transport or information infrastructure. While the list of problems is extensive, however, all investors should be reminded that our nation has just as many other advantages.

We are today where China was probably 10-15 years ago. Beijing launched an initiative to build more than 25,000 miles of expressways, which criss-cross their nation and are as good as the best roads in the world. We by contrast, have only 3,700 miles of such highways. Beijing invests ~9% of its GDP into public works, compared with New Delhi's ~4%. It is true that an authoritarian regime gets faster results, and nothing should stop our nation having stronger Central control to support the States build infrastructure for the long-term benefits of our citizens and nation. Daniel Vasella, Chief Executive Officer of Swiss pharmaceutical Novartis is claimed to have said, *"If you have to build a road in China, just a handful of people need to make a decision . . . If you want to build a road in India, it'll take 10 years of discussion before you get a decision."*

Rural Development agencies estimate 25% of Infrastructure investment gets siphoned off by corrupt officials and many public works projects either go over budget or are part or never completed. Political infighting and poor decision making has led to decisions not in the best interest of our citizens or nation. Unless our nation shakes off its legacy of bureaucracy, criminalised politics and corruption, its ability to build adequate infrastructure will remain in doubt, and so will the economic destiny of our future generations.

We have seen an increase in Foreign Direct Investments (FDI) in India; however, as infrastructure has not kept pace with growth, these businesses are building their new plants in other

*"Justice is the infrastructure of proprietorship."*
**Kemal Ataturk**

South-East Asian nations and China. We are only getting a disproportionately small fraction of what is invested in Asia. We will continue to have an increase in FDI from businesses, which aim to leverage our intellectual capital base of cheaper graduates and skilled labour, or those that wish to provide a service to Indian citizens; however, we are and will continue to miss out on the more valuable and longer-term manufacturing investments which are key to employing our skilled, semi-skilled and unskilled citizens coming into the job market, helping our balance of payments and supporting businesses and citizens across the whole value chain.

At the current rate of progress, policy development and execution our nation will not be able to deliver either the Infrastructure required or the food and water needed to sustain our population by 2050. The consequences of this are catastrophic.

By 2050, our population is expected to reach 1.6-1.7 billion citizens, from the current 1.2 billion (which was a 60% increase from 2000). The urban population is expected to grow from ~325 million in 2005, to ~575 million by 2030, and reach ~875 million by 2050. Our nation's geographical area will be constant at ~3.29 million sq. km. (2.93 million sq. km.of land mass); the 2001 census indicated an average population density of 325 persons per sq. km., this increased to 382 in the 2011 census, and will reach 571 by 2050, and be significantly more in the urban areas; this also significantly reduces the per capita agricultural land and water availability.[126] Our nation accounts for ~2.4% of the world surface area yet it needs to support and sustain ~17% of the world's population.

Natural resources and sustainability are issues that need to be urgently addressed across our nation. According to Dr. Cline, a pioneer environmentalist and international economist in a World Bank Report on Climatic Changes Impact on South Asia, 2009: *"India is among the most adversely affected with losses of 30-40% (in agriculture productivity) depending upon whether higher carbon dioxide provides a significant fertilization effect . . . Studies have shown that even a one degree rise in temperature can cause a 10%*

*reduction in crop yield. And we are talking about three degrees change expected in future in India."* Warnings about Global warming and its impact on agriculture also project a decline in global rice production of 3.8% by the end of 21st century according to a 2009 report by Asian Development Bank on the Environment.

It is claimed that the bitterest conflicts in the next fifty years will not be over oil but water. The sustainability of human development is being threatened by the growing scarcity of water. Climate change is likely to worsen the situation with water increasingly dominating national and international politics and power. It is this thirst for water that may become critical for ensuring political, social and economic stability. How we manage this valuable resource is therefore crucial for our future. We need an effective and fair policy that is implementable.

Our nation already faces water stress that is likely to exacerbate in the future. Unsustainable agricultural practices, industrial pollution and poor civic planning have further decreased the per capita availability of useable water. Water shortages will not only severely restrain the nation's ability to sustain its economic growth but also lead to food shortages and more conflicts, with negative social and political consequences.

Without major urban land reforms, our cities will not be able to support the inevitable urbanisation, nor sustain the existing population expansion. Without rural land and agricultural reforms we will not be able to productivity use our agricultural land, and without the appropriate infrastructure we will continue to further waste the food produced from our fields before it gets to our kitchens; and without protection of our land, rivers, mountains and forests and their inhabitants, we will damage and irrevocably lose the environment and ecology of our nation and its heritage, and reap its combined catastrophic consequences.

The World Economic Forum, in its 2012-13 Global Competitiveness Report, ranked Indian infrastructure at 84th position amongst 144 nations, compared to 76th position amongst 133 nations in 2010, and our overall competitiveness reduced from 51st position to 59th. This again implies we are falling behind on this *'Foundation Pillar'* too. This fall was largely

*"Economy and environment are the same thing. That is the rule of nature."*
**Mollie Beattie**

attributable to the poor quality of roads, sea and air ports, water and electricity supply.

Progress across the Infrastructure sector during 2010-11, and to mid-2012, has been poor, both in terms of physical progress, policy and regulatory developments. While 2009-10 saw policy and regulatory changes, attempts at improving the pace of award and execution of infrastructure projects, revival of investor interest and more definitive future plans; 2010-11 saw a slower pace of reform as well as development activity in almost all the sectors; a step backwards as we lost focus.

The roads sector saw concerns raised about the performance of the National Highways Authority of India (NHAI). The Sea and Air Ports sector did not see significant capacity addition, and according to the Power Finance Corporation Limited in 2011, finances of the power distribution utilities worsened, with utilities starting to resort to higher load shedding to avoid the burden of extra power purchase costs, and the Central Electricity Authority stated that in 2011 peak deficit of power continuing to be over 10%. The Rail network capacity and infrastructure of Indian Railways saw a negligible increase and the Railways were behind schedule in achieving their 2007-12 targets set for the Eleventh Five Year Plan.[127] The telecom sector was mired in controversies associated with licences and the process followed for the 2G spectrum auction, whilst the water sector continued its deterioration. There is a consistent theme across almost all the sectors is the poor level of monitoring and accountability for completing programmes and projects. Consequently, the targets for physical infrastructure development were not met, and this will prolong the lack of infrastructure.

Japan is an archipelago of over 3,000 islands, with the world's 10th largest population. Its population density of ~343 per sq. km is comparable to that of our nation at ~345 per sq. km. Land use patterns in Japan show a high level of urban concentration. About 45% of Japan's population live in the largest three metropolitan areas of Tokyo, Osaka and Nagoya. Tokyo has a population density of 5,751 per sq. km. In terms of infrastructure, Japan has 23,474 km of railways, 1,183 million km of highways, and 176

*"The fishermen know that the sea is dangerous and the storm terrible, but they have never found these dangers sufficient reason for remaining ashore."*
Vincent Willem van Gogh

airports. Land constraints do not appear to have hindered infrastructure growth. Indeed, in spite of high levels of infrastructural growth and development, Japan has maintained ~70% of its land area under forest cover and open space.[128] No one hurdle besides ourselves and our behaviours, values, ethics, *ways of working* and *ways of living* can also stop us from achieving our balanced development objectivs.

## ISSUES IN INFRASTRUCTURE DEVELOPMENT

With the expected rise in population density, the demand for new development projects, land acquisition proposals for private or public use are likely to increase; so will the resistance to approve these demands. Stronger and wider resistance could be caused not only because more land will be demanded, but also more people have to be displaced for the same area of land. Rural resistance in particular will rise because land is not only an empowering tool for its owners, but also an asset that has the ability to provide a sustainable generational livelihood for tens of millions of rural citizens.

Developers are beginning to acknowledge that *'Land'* is the single biggest constraint to speedy execution of infrastructure projects. Review of delayed projects indicated that 70% of the 190 delayed projects weredue to land acquisition problems; these included 60 Indian Railways, 40 NHAI, and 28 Power projects. However, this is not the only issue—there is a long list which includes law & order and shortfalls in capabilities, skills and competencies. 42% of all projects are delayed, with a further 31% yet to finalise dates; making only 27% on schedule and 1% ahead of schedule.[129] This cannot be allowed to continue.

Governments across the world legally possess *'eminent domain'* powers, by which the State can acquire land for public purposes without the landholders' consent. There is a growing perception, supported by examples, across our nation where these powers are frequently abused, by corrupt politicians, civil servants and

*"We are what we repeatedly do.Excellence, then, is not an act, but a habit."*
**Aristotle**

commercial organisations working in concert, using *'eminent domain'* powers to pay compensation provided by the law, which are not at market rates and is therefore inadequate. This has led to protests against development projects, caused uncertainties and delays in project delivery, and some of these *'land acquisition processes'* in the Tribal and minority regions has led to armed resistance and insurgencies (In some Orissa districts, 56% of the total tribal land was lost to non-tribals over a 25-30 year period, and also in Andhra Pradesh) as reported in a 2005 Wold Bank study. The deficiencies lie not only in the legal and policy framework but also in communication, management of expectations, and as always, implementation.

There are also issues and problems with Land Records and Registry. The primary aim of land administration pre-Independence was to boost land revenue, which was a major source of revenue generation; the focus was on land use rather than on individual ownership. Records were prepared for agricultural land and not residential lands in the villages or urban area and map type records were neglected. In the post-independence period, land revenue declined in importance; sometimes the cost of revenue collection exceeded the revenue, and therefore Revenue staff gave low priority to the maintenance of land records. There are also multiple agencies handling land records (Revenue Department, Survey Department, Panchayats, Stamps and Registration Department, etc.) and there is no interconnectivity among these agencies, and as a result, when one agency updates its records, the others become outdated. We need to implement an integrated approach to land registration:

- Registration (land registration processes)
- Records (survey, settlements and revenue)
- Rights (land rights and security of titles)

Our nation's infrastructure industry has enjoyed a number of years of buoyant business. The future is not so buoyant; the balance-sheets of many Indian infrastructure firms are weak with large debts; and a slowing economy and slow government decision-making causes more problems. There are three major

*"An idea isn't worth much until a man is found who has the energy and ability to make it work."*
**William Feather**

issues: Firstly, new business has significantly reduced prior to the 2014 election; secondly, cash flows are under strain as businesses get paid when they reach milestones towards finishing a project and banks and investors are reluctant to release funds in a credit crunch market, and finally there are worries about long-term profits due to the impact of high Indian interest rates, inflation and a weak Rupee.

Six large listed infrastructure firms' annual reports list 531 subsidiaries, joint ventures or associated entities; these firms often use *'Special Purpose Vehicles'* for contracts and this type of complex financial engineering make it difficult to figure out exactly what is going on; either entities are consolidated in their balance-sheet, or, if not controlled, treated as investments. The warning lights are flashing. We need to maintain the progress and increase the pace of Infrastructure investment; these local businesses will need the government to ensure projects are maintained; however, in return, these businesses will need to raise equity, at a sensible market price, rather than creative debt to fund their balance sheet and expansion.

*"Information is the currency of democracy."*
Thomas Jefferson

# Transportation & Telecommunication

*"You and I come by road or rail, but economists travel on infrastructure."*

**Margaret Thatcher**

## ROAD TRANSPORTATION

Our road transportation network spans over 3.3 million kilometres of tarmacadam and non-tarmac roads. This is insufficient for our future development needs, and the widening and building of new roads will require additional land. The National Highways represent less than ~1.7% of the overall road network of the country; however, these highways ensure 40% of the carriage of commodities and transportation of commuters in the country. 95 projects being implemented by the NHAI and 126 projects by various state Public Works Departments and Border Roads Organisation, have been delayed due to a variety of reasons including delays in land acquisition, moving utilities, obtaining environment, forest clearance and railway approvals, poor performance of contractors and law and order issues within states.

NHAI planned to build 20 kilometres of roads per day; it was however only in June 2010 that it geared itself towards achieving this target after taking steps to meet the recommendations of the BK Chaturvedi Committee. However, a review of developments during 2010-11 indicated that after the initial momentum, there had been a significant slowdown in the execution of this plan. By 31st December 2010, only 678 km of highways were completed of the 3,489 km approved

*"Only now did I recognise the reciprocal relationship which exists between manufacturing power and the national system of transportation, and that the one can never develop to its fullest without the other."*

**Friedrich List**

since 2006. Completion of roads has been only about 10 kilometres a day, much lower than the target. By January 2013, ~800 km of contracts were awarded against an original target of 9,500 km. Over 50% of the total road length under this programme was yet to be awarded for development.[129] There is an urgent need to simplify the governance, management and biding processes of the NHAI; and as almost 90% of the projects were being undertaken through PPPs, under a Build-Operate-Transfer *'Toll'* or *'Annuity'* basis, there is also a major concern on the high level of grants provided to these contractors.

An example of large road development is the work on the Golden Quadrilateral, a US$12 billion initiative spanning more than 4,800 kilometres of four-lane expressways connecting Mumbai, Delhi, Kolkata and Chennai. The 1,483 kilometre Delhi-Mumbai Industrial Corridor (DMIC) is where road development meets industrial infrastructure, which coupled with similar corridors across the nation, has the potential of increasing industrial development. The DMIC is a significant programme of US$90 billion with financial and technical assistance from Japan. This programme incorporates nine large industrial zones of about 200-250 sq. km, high-speed freight line, three ports, six airports, a six-lane intersection-free expressway connecting ournation's political and financial capitals and a 4GW power plant. Several industrial estates with world class infrastructure may be developed along this corridor to attract more foreign investment.

Motor transport is the most common means of local transport across our nation, and bus services account for more than 90% of the public transportation in our cities; the biggest bus terminus in Asia is situated in Chennai. Our road network accommodates both traditional means of transportation included bullock-carts, horse carriages, bicycles, hand-pulled and cycle rickshaw and trams, with contemporary modes driven by engines; this mixture makes our roads the most dangerous in the world. National Crimes Records Bureau

*"The World is a book, and those who do not travel read only a page."*
Augustine of Hippo

figures indicate 134,000 people died on our roads in 2010, and these are expected to increase with traffic and unreported road accident deaths. World Health Organization estimates that we lose US$20 billion due to road accidents annually, which they say is enough to feed 50% of our nation's malnourished children

Albeit the majority of goods are transported by road, the poor condition of vehicles, road and the congestion allows goods to only be transported at 30-40 kilometre per hour, even on the most advanced stretches of the highways; other obstacles and road traffic further reduces this average speed on poorer stretches of road.

The majority of our cities have grown rapidly and developed in an ad-hoc manner; there has been limited overall strategy or detailed planning; in general, we have underinvested or poorly planned; seeking short-term easier solutions rather than longer-term sustainable solutions. This poor approach and consequent infrastructure has led to major road traffic problems and its resultant impact on citizen productivity, effectiveness and health. Even as we begin to redesign older cities and towns, and build new *out-of-town* developments, the absence of a structured approach to infrastructure and environment will not resolve the road traffic problems; in fact this will further deteriorate. Government estimates say that our economic losses from congestion and poor roads will be US$15 billion a year by 2017 (INR32 per capita by 2014). Our major cities need to have transportation infrastructure to include road, rail and increasingly two-wheeler and bicycles, to improve the overall health of our citizens and improve the environment.

As we increase the number of roads and traffic, we need to ensure that the vehicles meet safety regulations, we have appropriate traffic regulations and these are enforced by our traffic and highway law enforcement officers.

*"The most important trip you may take in life is meeting people halfway."*
Henry Boye

# FARM TO KITCHEN

Poor infrastructure is now contributing to even larger problems, including inflation and the overheating in the economy. Inflation, has been driven in large part by the cost of food items, and was at near double digits by end 2011 and early 2012.

A 2011 study by Food and Agriculture Organisation of the United Nations showed that food wastage in Europe and North America was about 31-33% against 36% for the developing world. The difference came from where the wastage occurred; in developing countries, most of it was during harvest and distribution. Up to of 40% of our farm produce, including 215 million tonnes of fruit and vegetables, are lost annually, equivalent to 120 kg per year per capita, because they rot in the fields or are damaged (due to poor packaging, over packing, poor and delayed transport, poor transfer, handling and warehousing etc.) before they get to the kitchens of our citizens; this has contributed to rising prices for staples such as lentils and onions amongst many others. This can and must be reduced.

We also have too many stakeholders and participants between the farmer and the end consuming citizen, between 5-7 intermediaries. This is ineffective and inefficient; it does not make economic sense to have margins and profits at each of these 5-7 stages of handover, this coupled with transit damage further increases costs. This has resulted in many high profile farmer protests on food and grain, as it is being discarded or left to rot as it is uneconomic to sell and to move to the next person in the existing 'supply chain'. Our nation needs more organisations and individuals that will try to manage the 'end-to-end' supply chain for farm produce, from farm to kitchen, and in doing so, provide the farmers with a commercially competitive fair price for an agreed quality produce which is economically transported and distributed to the citizens at a lower end price. Organising this will help leverage scale, reduce waste and bring down costs; however, it

*"If you want to succeed you should strike out on new paths, rather than travel the worn paths of accepted success."*
**John D. Rockefeller**

will require infrastructure investment to help make happen. This is all possible.

An example is our continuing import of food stuffs because we cannot seem to economically process these ourselves, the value-added is lost to the off-shore providers. During the last two quarters of 2011, a slowdown in domestic oilseed crushing activity led to 73% increase in the import of vegetable oil to meet a deficit created by lower production from domestic sources. Data compiled by the Solvent Extractors' Association showed overall vegetable oil import rose 95% to 897,404 tonnes in April 2012 alone. There is an abundance of oilseed inventory in domestic warehouses for crushing; however, processors are not keen on procuring seeds at the current price, which makes crushing unviable for them.

# RAIL TRANSPORTATION

Indian Railways (IR) is the world's largest railroad operating under a single administration, with 1.4 million employees it is the world's 4th largest railway network after those of the United States, Russia and China. It spans a rail network of ~64,000 kilometres carrying more than 23 million commuters on 12,000 trains and 2.65 million tonnes of freight on 7,000 trains every day. It styles itself as the *"Lifeline of the Nation"*, and is closely linked to the average citizen, with its heavily subsidized fares; it offers 25%-75% fare concessions to 50 categories of travellers, from the physically and mentally impaired to patients travelling for medical treatment, war widows, the elderly and students, including those from overseas.

IR have undergone a transformation over a short period from a notoriously slow, inefficient and unprofitable operation to a profitable State-owned company with higher arrival and departure performance, electronic booking, web services, GPS tracking, new rolling stock, faster lines and new stations.

*"A lie can travel half way around the world while the truth is putting on its shoes."*
Charles Spurgeon

It had achieved this through:[130]

1—**Speeding things up:** Turnaround time between the end and beginning of each new trip (unload, repair, refuel and reload) has been reduced from 7.1 to 5 days for a freight train, which equates to 800 trains leaving each day against 550. Given that an additional trip can earn up to US$15 million, the improvement made a significant contribution to IR's revenue and profitability

2—**Increase Length of Freight trains:** IR placed more cars and hence more cargo on each train, adding up to US$1.5 billion a year in revenue.

3—**Increase Length of Passenger Trains:** IR increased trains from ~15 to 24 carriages realising at that length it could make a profit. By following a *"quicker, heavier, longer"* mantra, rail bosses have also been able to improve services.

4—**Special Trains:** IR began offering special express trains for tourists and commuters on certain routes such as New Delhi to Agra.

5—**Outsourcing:** Catering and other services are now outsourced improving service levels and reducing costs.

6—**Leverage Land Assets:** IR own ~1 million acres (420,000 hectares) of land along rail lines, around stations and shunt yards. Real estate developers are currently bidding to overhaul major stations and the provision of paid services at these stations.

Albeit, this change and progress has not been sustainable, these are the sorts of initiatives PSUs and other State-owned entities need to execute to become profitable commercial operations contributing to the financial success of the nation and therefore its citizens. IR had created a Vision 2020 document in 2009, which covered a wide range of issues relating to the sector

*"Travel teaches toleration."*
**Benjamin Disraeli**

as well as its priority areas. This is better than most other sectors, and unless IR supports this vision with a long-term working and implementation plan, it will not be able to improve efficiency and recover its market share.

While China has begun to earn billions of dollars exporting high-speed bullet train technology to the United States and Europe, and bidding to develop infrastructure of more industrialised nations in Europe and across the world, the struggle of IR to manage its financial woes and modernisation delays serves as a stark contrast in approach and outputs between the operators of the world's two largest railway networks.

We need to continue to build and enhance our national rail network, local rail services within primary, secondary and tertiary cities, suburban and rural links, increase electrification and ensure high speed lines and trains are installed to provide faster and safer commuter and freight transportation. Given its past performance, we should have full faith that with commitment and focus, IR will be able to achieve what the Delhi Metro achieved; delivery on time, to specification and on budget; a first for Indian infrastructure.

# SEA PORT TRANSPORTATION

Our maritime activities and trade are serviced by 13 major sea ports, 12 on the main land and Port Blair in the Andaman and Nicobar Islands. There are additional ~185 private smaller ports that cover our ~7,516 kilometre coastline that undertake a variety of activities, with 60 of these operational for goods handling, trading or fishing. We have moved towards private ports and ports built under PPP arrangements to help meet the need for more capacity and faster more effective and efficient port services. Some of these ports still operate manual labour for loading and unloading; however others have significantly improved their operations through automation as volumes have grown with the

"Strength does not come from physical capacity. It comes from an indomitable will."
Mohandas Karamchand Gandhi

economic growth of our nation; whilst others have focused on specific types of goods and industries etc.

Sea ports are the main trading routes for our nation, they account for ~90% of the volume and ~70% of the value of trade, and the main complaint heard by international and local investors and commercial organisations is the inefficiency these ports. The smaller private ports seem to be increasing their share of trade from 26% in 2004-5 to 34% in 2009-10. The often quoted statistic is that Shanghai's Port can turnaround a container ship in 8 hours, but the same ship in Mumbai can take 3 days. The further challenge we face is the infrastructure to and from the port. In many cases our exporters have trucks waiting outside ports for many days prior to goods being off-loaded, there are limited waiting, off and on-loading, warehousing and road side capacity and facilities to ensure the smooth movement of goods across our nation and to and from these ports.

Logistics and supply chain issues and costs now contribute a significant proportion to the total value of the goods and global supply chains now need to be ever more effective and efficient to be competitive, and in India it increases supply chain costs by 4-5%.[131] We are already losing out to our newer South-East Asian competitor nations for FDI, and this will become starker as our manufacturing costs begin to rise.

Similar to roads and railways, sea ports are plagued by poor leadership, lack of vision at the national level and poor implementation. Our ports need to significantly increase their capacity and in parallel they must improve their efficiency and effectiveness in ship turnaround times and further hand-off to rail, road and water connectivity.

There really seems to be no comprehensive policy for sea port development, and although a maritime policy for the nation was attempted in 2004, it was not finalised. Consequently, the sector has progressed poorly and individual State governments have created and established their own policies for developing ports and meeting their own priorities.

*"Civilization as it is known today could not have evolved, nor can it survive, without an adequate food supply."*
Norman Borlaug

For a nation that has 90% of its international traded goods passing through sea ports we have very poor planning, administration, understanding and control over these assets. The government has proposed a maritime agenda for 2010-20, which projects traffic, estimates capacity and identifies future priorities for the sector. These include leveraging land for optimising the through-put and revenue of ports; corporatisation of major ports; and the creation of an empowered sea port regulator with judicial powers to issue regulations and policy guidelines, who is able to take actions to improve competition, environmental practices, dredging and rail-road-water connectivity. However, as with many initiatives in our nation, there are no timelines, discussions are never ending, there is no agreement, no metrics and where there are plans the implementation is poor, and outcomes substandard to requirements. There are many published examples, of locally manufactured good destined for the international markets that have been delayed or damaged when going in and out of our sea ports.

More industrialised nations and those with large land mass are increasing the use of their waterways for the transportation of goods, as it is seen as more ecologically friendly and effective as industries and cities in these nations have grown from river banks. Our nation has an extensive network of inland waterways in the form of rivers, canals and backwaters. The total navigable length is ~14,500 km, out of which it is claimed ~5,200 km of rivers and 485 km of canals can be used by mechanised crafts. Freight transport by waterways is highly underutilised in our nation compared to other large countries. The total cargo moved by inland waterways is estimated only to be ~0.15% of the total inland traffic in India, compared to the corresponding figures of 20% for Germany and other European nations.[132]

We have a large land mass, which we need to maintain for agriculture and our environment; we can better utilise this form of transport to support industry and commerce along

*"To travel is to discover that everyone is wrong about other countries."*
Aldous Huxley

our waterways. Increasing our waterways transportation helps supporting the retention of water and its use for agriculture, reducing road traffic, accidents and the need for additional roads etc .

The Inland Waterways Authority of India has recognised five National Waterways:[133]

- Allahabad-Haldia stretch of the Ganges, and Bhagirathi-Hooghly river system, a total length of 1,620 km.
- Saidiya-Dhubri stretch of the Brahmaputra river system, a total length of 891 km.
- Kollam-Kottapuram stretch of the West Coast Canal, and Champakara and Udyogmandal Canals, a total length of 205 km.
- Bhadrachalam-Rajahmundry and Wazirabad-Vijaywada stretch of the Krishna-Godavari river system and the Kakinada-Pondicherry canal network, a total length of 1,095 km.
- Mangalgadi-Paradeep, Talcher-Dhamara stretch of the Mahanadi-Brahmani river system and the East Coast Canal, a total length of 623 km.

We need more of these waterways connecting our major rivers and supporting the transportation of goods, water and people across our nation.

# AIR PORT TRANSPORTATION

We currently have 449 airstrips and airports, and of these 125 are owned by the Airports Authority of India (AAI), of which 84 are operational. There are an additional six joint ventures under the PPP framework. These airports transported a total of 162.3 million passengers (121.5 million domestic and 40.8 million international) in the year to March 2012, these volumes have significantly increased over the last 10 years, and is expected to

*"The whole object of travel is not to set foot on foreign land; it is at last to set foot on one's own country as a foreign land."*

G. K. Chesterton

continue. Domestic passenger traffic is estimated to reach 160 million with 92 million international passenger movements by 2020, this will continue to expand to 448 million domestic and 249 million international by 2031; our government will need to sanction a larger number of regional and city airports to meet this demand.[134] Air transportation supports the fast and effective movement of people and goods across our nation, and internationally, supporting the further development of commerce and making efficient use of the time for our citizens and their businesses.

The largest international airports across the world support between 45-65 million passengers per annum. India has one of the largest diaspora across the world and an increasing number travelling to and from these locations. The majority of our international trading partners, diaspora, non-residents and citizens use foreign airlines and transit hubs to travel; in the last few years Dubai has from nowhere become a favourite transit point due to service, quality, cheap fares and shopping. Frankfurt, London, Amsterdam, Paris, New York, Chicago, Toronto, Hong Kong and Singapore are other transit points with national commercial air carriers to name a few. We have missed out in the last 20 years from creating and delivering a long-term strategy for linking the Indian National Airlines with our nationally owned airports to form a coherent hub and spoke or another strategy to ensure the revenues and incomes from our diaspora, and more importantly the *'share of wallet'* of transit passengers from Europe to South East, East Asia and Australasia, as they spend in our nation to benefit our citizens and industry. However, in order to realise this we need to have a service and quality mentality which is currently absent in the public and some parts of the private sector. Some private Indian airlines are beginning to fill this gap, but this still requires a coherent approach between the airlines and airports. Air India and the AAI can still do this if they are truly determined to succeed.

*"The person attempting to travel two roads at once will get nowhere."*
Xunzi

India's airport infrastructure sector faces the challenge of significant expansion as India's overall economy continues to grow, and as airports have been operating at their capacity. Development of the airports physical infrastructure still remains inadequate to sustain the growth momentum. Progress on these existing projects has been slow, and as could have been expected, been significantly more expensive than initially planned. This is true for both privatised and AAI airports. We have invested ~US$10 billion in the past five years on airport modernisation and a further US$30 billion will be required in the next ten years; we are building 14 greenfield airports and have approved 13 additional metro airports to provide a second location in our major cities.

The Airport City type projects are also being planned to combine infrastructure and urban development. These initiatives will include industrial complexes and information technology parks, logistics hubs, maintenance and repair operations, and include social infrastructure including housing, hospitals, educational institutes and shopping malls.

National economic growth has also resulted in a significant growth in Indian private airlines and they now account for the majority of air travel across the nation. With increasing service standards to international levels and new fleets of aircraft, these airlines are making an impact on the international travel market for key routes into India. There are also an increasing number of private aircraft and helicopters owned by the corporations and individuals. The launch of budget air lines and cargo carriers have made air travel affordable for more citizens, albeit, they only fly to major cities; these airlines have been more competitive and agile than the national Air India and Indian Airlines. The sector is competitive and these companies have borrowed heavily, resulting in near bankruptcies and mergers to gain economies of scale. By mid-2012, two major Indian private international airlines were cancelling and reducing routes; whilst the national carrier suffers from poor services, inefficiency, poor work practices and

*"Criticism may not be agreeable, but it is necessary. It fulfils the same function as pain in the human body. It calls attention to an unhealthy state of things."*
Winston S. Churchill

ineffective economic model is on life support from the nation's treasury.

The government has initiated several policies to ensure the time-bound development of world-class airports across India. This sector has a high demand for investments in aviation infrastructure, because there is a positive demographic and continued economic growth, which will lead to a continued increase in domestic and international passenger traffic. Plans have been approved for new airports in resort destinations and expanding cities. International traffic is also expected to increase with trade activity and tourism.

We need to ensure that the all our towns and cities that are planned to have airports have sufficient and regular air services for the benefits of local citizens. The economics of the private and national airlines need to be better understood to ensure rates, tariffs and taxes are appropriate to ensure competitive pricing and regular services.

# TELECOMMUNICATIONS

We have one of the most dynamic telecommunications markets in the world. From a nation that faced challenges in providing landline telecommunications, we have now leapt forward ahead of many nations to become a leading nation in the use of this technology. By September 2012 we had ~906 million connections, and had the second largest wireless network in the world after China. Overall tele-density reached ~77%.

Our government policy and regulatory authority has been embroiled in controversies on issues relating to the auction and allotment of 2G spectrum licences in 2007-8, where the Comptroller and Auditor General concluded that the government exchequer incurred a loss of between INR 67,364-1,76,645 crore. This typified the incompetence and corruption label that further reinforces our nation as a potential *'could have been'*; where licences had been issued on a single day, at a 2001 price when the market was at a nascent stage of development as opposed to an appropriate 2008 market price, when the sector had undergone significant transformation and growth. 70% of the 122 new licences were issued to companies that did not meet the basic eligibility conditions, facts were suppressed, incomplete information submitted with fictitious documents, licences were not awarded on a first come, first served basis as had been purported etc. This is where the corrupt Executive and Legislature meets corrupt commercial interests.

This sector continues to evolve as 3G and BWA spectrum auctions were undertaken in April-May 2010. In the 3G auction, the overall winning value was almost five times the reserve price and in the BWA auction it was more than seven times the reserve price. Almost all 3G auction winners have launched 3G services in their winning circles and are in the process of entering into roaming arrangements with other players in the remaining circles, thereby providing an all-India 3G network to their customers. Mobile number portability was also implemented across the nation by end 2011 to improve the quality of service to avoid loss of subscribers.

The government is also launching a New Telecom Policy to ensures a more transparent and stable operating environment. This includes the rapid growth of broadband. We need to ensure all schools, hospitals, government agencies and institutions have access to high speed broadband connections. In doing so, we will be able to take the next leap in the use and application of information and services for the faster development of our nation and its citizens.

A large proportion, if not the vast majority of our adult population has access to a mobile phone or the telephone network, and we need to further leverage this for the benefit of our citizens. We need to create and launch applications and services that each section of our communities will use for the development of their livelihood and betterment of their living

*"Knowledge will give you power, but character respect."*
**Bruce Lee**

standards. Telecommunications technology has now evolved where farmers and fishermen use the technology to better price and time the sale of their goods and produce, medical services and education can be better delivered using mobile and satellite communications, our military and security services can better monitor our borders and cities to ensure a safer living environment for our citizens. We need to continue to apply new and creative uses for this application and use of telecommunications to the betterment of life for our citizens.

*"Cultivation to the mind is as necessary as food to the body."*
Marcus Tullius Cicero

# Electrical Energy Assurance

*"A nation that can't control its energy sources can't control its future."*

**Barack Obama**

It is sometimes difficult to understand electricity measurement and other terms to describe the power output and capacities of electricity. Sixty Watts is an average light bulb. An electric Iron or microwave uses ~1000 Watts, a Kilo Watt, One Million Watts = 1 MegaWatt = 1MW and 1,000MW = Billion Watts = 1 Giga Watt (GW). Power and energy are two words that are sometimes confused. Consumption has a time component to it, so 1 MWh/yr = 1,000,000 Wh/(365.25 x 24)h = 114.07 Watts. As a broad explanation to get an idea of scale the table overleaf shows that we may be a major consumer; however, on a per capita basis we are one of the lowest in the world.

This is also a sector, which surprisingly, has little consistency in data; each information source provides slightly different data or data for different time-lines. There are also major gaps and sometimes confusion between what is Production Capacity, the Demand and the Supply of electricity and energy.

Depending on the data source, we are the world's 4th-5th largest generator and consumer of electricity at ~193 GW as of March 2012, having grown by over 9% on the previous year. We have a range of power generation modes; thermal power plants constitute 65% of capacity, hydroelectric about 22%, nuclear at less than 3%, and the remaining 11% (18.5 GW) is through new and renewable energy: wind, solar, biomass, waste-to-electricity, which is expected to grow significantly.

*"It isn't that they can't see the solution. It is that they can't see the problem."*
G.K.Chesterton

| Global 2010 Rank | | Electricty Net Consumption (Billion Kilowatthours) | Electric power consumption (kWh per capita) | Global 2010 Rank |
|---|---|---|---|---|
| 1 | United States | 3,886.40 | 13,393.90 | 9 |
| 2 | China | 3,633.79 | 2,943.53 | 62 |
| 3 | Japan | 1,002.38 | 8,394.12 | 16 |
| 4 | Russia | 861.47 | 6,451.87 | 28 |
| 5 | India | 698.82 | 616.20 | 110 |
| 6 | Germany | 549.12 | 7,215.42 | 22 |
| 7 | Canada | 499.92 | 15,137.59 | 6 |
| 8 | France | 470.95 | 7,728.55 | 21 |
| 9 | Brazil | 455.75 | 2,383.73 | 70 |
| 10 | South Korea | 449.51 | 9,744.46 | 13 |
| 11 | United Kingdom | 329.29 | 5,736.03 | 36 |
| 12 | Italy | 306.78 | 5,384.17 | 38 |
| 13 | Spain | 267.04 | 6,154.83 | 31 |
| 14 | Taiwan | 217.67 | | |
| 15 | South Africa | 214.98 | 4,802.54 | 42 |
| 16 | Australia | 213.54 | 10,177.49 | 11 |
| 17 | Mexico | 212.31 | 1,990.46 | 74 |
| 18 | Saudi Arabia | 190.88 | 7,967.00 | 21 |
| 19 | Iran | 182.70 | 2,652.31 | 65 |
| 20 | Turkey | 170.37 | 2,477.06 | 67 |
| 21 | Ukraine | 150.42 | 3,549.85 | 56 |
| 22 | Indonesia | 145.10 | 641.31 | 107 |
| 23 | Thailand | 140.84 | 2,243.40 | 71 |
| 24 | Sweden | 135.96 | 14,939.23 | 8 |
| 25 | Poland | 134.84 | 3,783.08 | 52 |
| | | | | |
| 71 | Iceland | 122.37 | 51,439.91 | 1 |
| 27 | Norway | 120.90 | 25,175.22 | 2 |
| 47 | Kuwait | 46.71 | 18,319.66 | 3 |
| 101 | Luxembourg | 6.44 | 16,833.91 | 4 |
| 34 | Finland | 84.83 | 16,482.79 | 5 |
| | | | | |
| 92 | Zambia | 7.96 | 623.14 | 108 |
| 107 | Bolivia | 5.83 | 616.42 | 109 |
| 93 | Guatemala | 7.95 | 567.31 | 111 |
| 132 | Nicaragua | 2.43 | 473.21 | 112 |
| 36 | Pakistan | 74.42 | 456.64 | 113 |
| 90 | Sri Lanka | 8.92 | 449.18 | 114 |

| Item | Power Consumption (Watts) |
|---|---|
| Light Bulb or Laptop Computer | 60 |
| Desk Top Computer | 200-500 |
| Television | 200-900 |
| Refrigerator Freezer | 600-800 |
| Iron or Microwave | 1000-2000 |
| Air Conditioner | 2000 |

Despite this we still have major electricity shortages and many other power issues to address; over one third (~300 million) of our rural population have no access to electricity, nor do 6% of the urban population. Our over-stressed power grid is one of the most obvious signs of poor infrastructure development. Of those who did have access to electricity, the supply was intermittent and unreliable through 'blackouts', 'brownouts' (an intentional drop in voltage in an electrical power supply dimming lighting system, and used for load reduction) and power shedding (an intentionally engineered rolling blackout where electricity is stopped for non-overlapping periods of time over geographical regions) which interrupts irrigation, manufacturing and services across the nation. Power failures happen even in the most developed areas of Delhi, Mumbai and Bangalore. Businesses, hospitals, communities and households have to maintain diesel generators, and some large institutions and housing blocks are now designed and built with large fuel storage tanks. These outages are not intermittent, but rather hour-long blackouts with multi-hour brownouts. Some industrial machines, computers, air conditioning, refrigeration and hospital critical equipment must be operational 24x7 to avoid danger and damage to people, goods and information. This is uneconomic as significant additional capital and operational costs are added, further reducing our longer term competitiveness and development. Across the state of Maharashtra, major cities lose power one day a week to relieve pressure on the grid. In Pune, a university city of 4.5 million

*"Continuous effort - not strength or intelligence—is the key to unlocking our potential."*
Winston S. Churchill

*"New opinions are always suspected, and usually opposed, without any other reason but because they are not already common."*
John Locke

citizens, lights go out every Thursday, forcing manufacturers to maintain expensive backup generators; many other cities and towns across the nation have variable black-out periods for electricity supply, whilst other parts of the grid provide power at obscure times when it is little use to the citizen. The place that remains in darkness the most is Bihar, our poorest state, which has more than 80 million people, 85% of whom live in households with no grid connection. Government officials were said to be shocked in 2007 when Intel Corp. chose Vietnam over India as the site for a new chip assembly plant; although Intel declined to comment, industry insiders say the reason was largely the lack of reliable power and water in our nation. This is one of many examples of businesses now looking at South-east Asia as a priority over ourselves for FDI. Gujarat is now focusing on green energy generation to become a power surplus state; albeit only 2-3GW, they are aiming to sell their electricity across the nation. Without reliable power our nation will never be able to manufacture and develop truly high-tech, leading edge, high-value products and services.

For decades, many countries have operated on the assumption that power from large electricity plants will eventually trickle down to small towns, villages and to villagers. The last miles are the most difficult and uneconomic, and in many parts of the world this has proven to be elusive. We need to create power generation models that economically meet the needs of isolated and small communities; we can do this through renewable and sustainable energy sources; this in turn has significant benefits ecologically, environmentally and for the communities themselves.

Lack of sufficient and regular electrical power also poses major problems for water management, for both fresh water and sewage treatment. Absence of power affects the supply of fresh water to both urban and rural communities, and this coupled with the inefficient electrical pumps used for ground water extraction and pumping further exacerbates the problems. Poorly maintained and poor quality inefficient water pumps have been identified as one of the major drain in our effective use of available electrical power. The majority of sewage water treatment plants are government-owned, and are inoperable due to the absence of reliable electrical supply (but also because they are not maintained). Studies have found that discharge of untreated sewage is the largest and single most important cause of surface and ground water pollution across our nation.[135]

The Indian electricity distribution network is inefficient compared to many other networks across the world. In 2010 our network losses (loss, theft and unmetered) were estimated to exceed 32%, compared to world average of less than 15%. Loss reduction technologies, if adopted, can add ~30GW of electrical power, while simultaneously reducing electricity cost and carbon footprint pollution. If losses remain at ~32%, we will need to add ~135 GW of power generation capacity, before 2017, to satisfy the projected demand after losses.[136] We will never be able to do this in an environmentally friendly way; there will be consequences, for both our land and our citizens. We will have to make compromises and take some difficult decisions.

The International Energy Agency estimates we need to add 600-1200GW of power generation by 2050, at investment of at least US$135 billion to provide universal access of electricity. This new capacity requirement is equivalent to the total power generation capacity of the European Union in 2005.[137]

Over 2010-11, our industrial demand accounted for 35% of electrical power requirement, domestic household use accounted for 28%, agriculture 21%, commercial 9%, public lighting and other miscellaneous applications accounted for 7%.

The electrical energy demand for 2016-17 is expected to be at least 1,392 Tera Watt Hours, with a peak electric demand of 218GW.

The electrical energy demand for 2021-22 is expected to be at least 1,915 Tera Watt Hours, with a peak electric demand of 298GW.

McKinsey, a management consultancy, claims that India's demand for electricity may cross 300 GW, earlier than most estimates, which will require ~400 GW of installed capacity. The extra capacity is necessary to account for plant availability,

*"Human history becomes more and more a race between education and catastrophe."*
H. G. Wells

215

infrastructure maintenance, reserve and losses. They identify four reasons for this additional growth:

1: Our manufacturing sector is likely to grow faster than in the past.
2: Domestic demand will increase more rapidly as the quality of life for more Indians improve.
3: About 125,000 villages are likely to get connected to the electricity grid.
4: Currently blackouts and load shedding artificially suppresses demand; this demand will be sought as revenue potential by power distribution companies.

The power sector is one of the major users of hydrocarbon *'energy fuels'* for the conversion to electricity. Our growing external dependency on Oil, Gas and Coal as an energy source has major global implications for our nation and the world energy markets. The liberalisation of our electricity market in 1990 has moved us forward; however, the power sector is now facing a serious crisis with implications for the country's overall economic growth and development.

Due to our growing external energy dependency and global emissions from the energy sector, the changes taking place are increasingly large enough to affect world energy markets. The technologies and fuel sources we use to meet the power gap will also have a significant impact on global resources and environmental issues.

We imported ~172 million metric tons of crude oil in 2011, a 5.2% volume increase, at a 41% value increase, which has continued to damage our nation's economic outlook as higher crude import costs also widened our fiscal deficit as we provide large subsidies to keep fuel prices artificially low. Our national budget deficit reached 5.9% of GDP in the year to March 2012, above a 4.6% target, an overshoot that Standard & Poor's, a global credit ratings agency said this was a *'matter of concern'*; it cut its outlook on our long-term debt to negative and warned of a possible downgrade to junk status, and as a result the INR

*"It takes as much energy to wish as it does to plan."*
Eleanor Roosevelt

continued to weaken, falling against all major currencies due to fears onthe widening trade and budget deficits. Concern over the mounting deficit has also scared investors, pushing the INR to record lows in 2012. We may be the first BRIC country to have a *'junk'* investment and credit status.[138]

Consumption of refined fuel products rose 4.9% last year to ~148 million tons, its fastest increase since 2007-08 on the back of a growth in vehicle sales and with power shortages boosting demand for diesel to run private generators. In May 2012 Oil Secretary G.C. Chaturvedi said, India's crude oil imports were expected to continue to increase as fuel consumption is planned to rise by more than 4% annually over the next 10-15 years. In volume terms our crude imports to fiscal year 2012 climbed to 172.11 million metric tons (3.45 million barrels a day) from 163.59 million tons (3.29 million barrels a day) a year earlier.[139]

We import 75% of our crude oil needs and this is expected to rise to 90% by 2020 according to a Tata Energy Research Institute (TERI) estimate. This is unsustainable in the medium to long-term due to its impact on the overall balance of payments, and secondly, because we continue to be players, pawns or hostages to the ever-changing script of global political oil theatre.

We are targeting to hold strategic petroleum reserves in the form of Crude Oil of about 40 million barrels, equal to little more than two weeks of supplies. It is estimated that we have only 9.8 million barrels of crude in our reserves, leaving us exposed to disruptions in Saudi Arabia, Iran, UAE and Nigeria currently our biggest suppliers. We need to wean ourselves off imported oil, begin to better extract our own, and find alternatives with a sense of urgency. We have proven reserves of 5.48 billion barrels of oil and are the world's 22nd largest holders; with ~1,241 billion cubic metres of natural gas.[140] However, these *'reserves'* still need to be efficiently and effectively extracted; existing fields are ageing and recent exploration has also been disappointing as these levels of reserves are insufficient to meet our energy and power needs.

Traditional fuels such as fuelwood, agricultural waste and biomass cakes are still used by nearly 2/3rd (~800 million) of our citizens for cooking and heating.[141] We need to reduce wood fuel

*"Do not mistake activity with achievement."*
John Wooden

217

use and provide better alternatives for our citizens as these traditional fuels will not sustain our environment, given the growth in demand and in population; other benefits will include improved health and living conditions for our citizens (from inhaling chemical fumes released from burning these materials). Alternatives are being planned and used, which need to be both economic and suitable for use by our rural and urban citizens; these include solar, wind, gas, clean burning fuel and other combustion technologies.

The energy situation in the nation is expected to get worse before it gets better to meet the demand of an economy forecast to grow at 9% per annum, our generation capacity will be *'ecologically unsustainable'* as 70% of this additional capacity is to be added through coal-based thermal power. The most serious bottleneck in generation will be the shortage of coal, *"The shortage would have been even more had all the planned coal-based power plants been commissioned on time."* By 2017, the coal shortage is forecast to be 200 million tonnes.

Our ability to deliver a plan is poor. On average, 50.5% of overall energy targets were met in the 8th, 9th and 10th Five Year Plans (1992-2007). The target for the 11th Plan (2007-2012) has already been revised downwards from 78.7GW to 62.3GW, and apparently only 50% of that revised target has been achieved.

According to a 2010 report prepared by audit and consulting firm KPMG on the power sector, the shortage of equipment (primarily in the core components of boilers, turbines and generators) is also a bottleneck and a significant reason for us missing our capacity targets.

We also need to urgently revise power tariffs upwards to viable and realistic levels. According to the Planning Commission, based on calculations of the financial performance of distribution companies in 20 major States, companies lose INR0.8-1 per unit of power supplied to consumers. On average our citizens pay much less for a unit of electricity; we charge an average of ~8 US cents per unit compared to 12-15 cents in Canada, South Africa and the USA, and 19-20 cents in much of Europe and the less industrialised nations.

*"In times of great stress or adversity, it's always best to keep busy, to plow your anger and your energy into something positive."*
Lee Iacocca

Ultimately, the issue is not just total power production and capacity but improved management and efficient and effective distribution. We not only need to increase the numbers of our citizens that have access to electricity, but to also have it delivered in a reliable manner, and have to manage our electricity production and distribution in a more professional manner to be able to achieve this at a lower unit production, distribution and delivery cost.

# THERMAL POWER

Our government expects that the rapid growth in electricity generation over the next 20 years will be largely met by thermal power plants. Thermal power plants convert energy rich fuel into electricity and heat. Possible fuels include coal, natural gas, petroleum products, agricultural and domestic waste, landfill gas and biogases. In some plants, renewal fuels such as biogas are co-fired with coal. Coal and lignite accounted for about ~55-57% of our nations installed power generation capacity.

Our electricity sector consumes ~80% of the coal we produce and a large part of our coal reserve is of poor quality and low natural fuel value; low calorific value, high ash content and low iron content. On average, power plants using our coal consume about 0.7 kg of coal to generate 1 kWh of electricity, whereas in the USA thermal power plants consume about 0.45 kg coal per kWh.[142]

The installed capacity of thermal power in India, as of June 30 2011, was ~116GW which is ~66% of total installed capacity. Current installed base of:

- Coal power is 96,743.38 MW which is 54.66% of total installed capacity
- Gas power is 17,706.35 MW which is 10.00% of total installed capacity
- Oil power is 1,199.75 MW which is 0.67% of total installed capacity

*"The person who knows one thing and does it better than anyone else, even if it only be the art of raising lentils, receives the crown be merits. If be raises all his energy to that end, be is a benefactor of mankind and its rewarded as such."* —Augustine Mandino II

Coal remains India's most important fuel for power generation. According to the Ministry of Coal, we are the 3$^{rd}$ largest coal user in the world, with an annual expected output of 574.4 million tonnes in 2012-13; an increase of 6.4%. In spite of this globally significant amount of production, we cannot meet domestic demand by 15-20%, and depend on imports to fill this gap which is expected to be 192 million tonnes to FY2013. Prakash Sharma, a Wood and Mackenzie coal analyst, has said that India would overtake Japan as the second-largest consumer of thermal seaborne coal by 2030, with imports growing five-fold to 400 million tonnes per year. We face the same issues as in crude oil.

We continue to face difficult issues in domestic coal that cover regulatory, political and logistical issues. Some claim our railways are congested and there is insufficient rakes to transport the coal from mines to the power stations and the industrial users, others claim there is insufficient production to meet demand, or that poor mining efficiency and effectiveness leads to higher priced coals making imports cheaper; this supports an argument for importing higher calorific value coal for improved productivity and effectiveness, as local coal is of poor quality. Some are of the view that we need to increase the licenses to mining companies to mine in our forests, protected and tribal areas, others that we need to increase the quotas to allow for more mining. All views may be correct from different perspectives; what would citizens wish our decision makers do?

Our nation had 1,330 billion cubic meters of proven natural gas reserves as of April 2012, world's 26$^{th}$ largest deposit. We extracted approximately 47.56 billion cubic meters of natural gas in FY2012 (8.9% reduction on the previous year), while consuming ~90 billion cubic meters. The electrical power and fertiliser sectors account for 2/3$^{rd}$ of natural gas consumption in India. Natural gas is expected to be an increasingly important component of our energy consumption as we diversify our energy sources and manage our overall energy security.

We already produce some coal-bed methane and have a major potential to expand this source of cleaner fuel. According to the preliminary estimates, India's shale-gas resources may be larger

*"We need to become energy independent or at least aspire to that."*
Thomas L. Friedman

than its conventional gas resources. Schlumberger estimates that India may have a 600-2,000 trillion cubic feet shale-gas resource, while the EIA estimates 63 trillion cubic feet. Industry observers and users claim that we have been slow to issue licensing for shale gas blocks and we have been slow to develop our natural gas resources due to regulatory challenges and bureaucratic red tape. These views may be correct; however, given our government and administrations capabilities and competencies to raise funds from 2G telecoms licences and the mining scams we have uncovered, it is possibly better at this moment to be cautious and steady rather than hasty.

# NUCLEAR POWER

As of 2011, we had 18 pressurised heavy water reactors in operation with 4.8 GW of installed electricity generation capacity; another four reactors are being constructed. Nuclear power provided 3% of our total electricity generation in 2011, and the target is to supply 9% of demand by 2032.

Our nuclear energy power stations have been developed through predominantly indigenous capabilities, competencies and technology, and are a major achievement following the high technology embargo after the Pokhran-I test in 1974.

Nuclear Power Corporation of India Limited is a public sector enterprise within the Department of Atomic Energy established to commercialise nuclear power in India through construction and operation of nuclear plants. It has plans to establish 63GW generation capacity by 2032 to provide an economically viable, safe, environmentally friendly, source of electrical energy:[19] everything is relative.

In 2011 potentially one of the largest reserves of uranium in the world, spread over 35 km, was found in Andhra Pradesh. Confirmed reserve of 49,000 tonnes could be as high as 150,000 tonnes of the mineral, making total national reserves of up to 175,000 tonnes; however, even these may not be sufficient to meet our future energy needs; we would still have to import the

*"Because we don't think about future generations, they will never forget us."*
Henrik Tikkanen

221

materials. The newly discovered ore is of lower grade than that from Australia.

Following the Japanese tsunami and earthquake, the damaged Fukushima Dai-ichi I Nuclear Power plant has had to be closed down. Leaks of radioactive materials resulted in an exclusion zone, which may exist for many years to come. Dai-ichi management and the operating culture of this reactor (and potentially other Japanese reactors) have subsequently been found to have been a major reason for some of the poor decisions and poor safety issues in the past, and immediately post this event. This event has stopped the Japanese nuclear energy expansion plans and paused or derailed those in some other countries who are not even in earthquake and tsunami zones.

Our nation will face a major power shortage for the next 30 years, and nuclear is just one of the modes of generation. If we can generate 10% of our total needs by nuclear, we would be in a fortunate position. Given our national record of poor maintenance and repair, corruption, inefficiency and ineffectiveness of processes and procedures; we need to ensure our nuclear power reactors are operated by professional staff designing and operating with the most rigorous, secure and safe practices and procedures. If we do not wish to go down the nuclear route, then we need to find suitable alternatives that have sufficient outputs to close this gap, within the necessary timeframes, which also avoid the risk and environmental footprint issues.

# RENEWABLE POWER SOURCES

As of December 2011, we had an installed capacity of about 22.4GW of renewal technology-based electricity, ~11-12% of our total. Under the 2010 Jawaharlal Nehru National Solar Mission, our government planned to generate 1GW of power by 2013 and up to 20GW grid-based solar power, 2GW of off-grid solar power and cover 20 million square metres with solar energy collectors by 2020. Gujarat, Rajasthan and others states have already begun to

*"Happiness belongs to the self sufficient."*
Aristotle

build and generate power from utility scale solar power generation plants with dedicated infrastructure.

According to the Ministry of New & Renewable Energy, as of end 2011, we had made significant progress in development of these sources; and the World Institute for Sustainable Energy estimated significant potential capacity as follows:

| Energy Type | Capacity end 2011 | Potential Capacity | Assumed Plant Load Factor |
|---|---|---|---|
| Wind | ~16 GW | 100 GW | 25% |
| Small Hydro | ~3.1 GW | 15 GW | 45% |
| Bagasse | ~1.7 GW | 5 GW | 60% |
| BioGas | ~1.5 GW | 16.8 GW | 60% |
| Solar | ~0.01 GW | 400 GW | 25-30% |
| Geothermal | | 10 GW | 80% |

We plan to add ~30 GW of installed generation capacity based on solar energy technologies by 2017.

# WIND POWER

As at August 2012, we had the 5th largest installed wind power capacity in the world, with 17.9GW, accounting for 8.5% of our total installed power capacity, and 16.5% of the country's new power capacity. The Indian Wind Energy Association estimates the 'on-shore' generation potential using existing technology, could be up to 89GW by 2020.

The earliest proponent of wind power was Tamil Nadu, which is also now the largest wind power State with ~40% of installed capacity. Our long coastline, geography and the regular trade winds makes some parts of our nation ideal for wind generated power. The deserts and coastline of north-western Gujarat and Rajasthan, the highland areas of Maharashtra, Karnataka, Andhra Pradesh and Tamil Nadu provide the most

*"Almost every way we make electricity today, except for the emerging renewables and nuclear, puts out $CO_2$. And so, what we're going to have to do at a global scale, is create a new system. And so, we need energy miracles."*

**Bill Gates**

suitable wind power locations; Gujarat is estimated to have a potential to generate 10.6 GW.

Depending on the take-up scenarios generated by the Global Wind Energy Council, wind power generation capacity could increase to between 66-191 GW by 2030. Indian firms such as Suzlon have made a major impact on the world stage through the technology, competencies and capabilities in this sector.

There are many hurdles that wind power stakeholders have successfully navigated in such a short time to get to the current level of development; however, this is only the beginning as with all other renewable energy sources, wind power expansion and increased capacity installation will require greater support from the citizens and nation to ensure greater political and regulatory support.

Albeit installed wind power capacity is high, the load factor of 25% is low, due to its reliance on regular strong wind, which inevitably raises challenges from other renewable sources for investment and development, when business cases are based on 'output' of power generated from installed capacity, and the cost and environmental impacts.

On-shore and off-shore wind power is a major alternative to thermal power generation, and it needs to be prioritised accordingly, to ensure it provides longer-term sustainable solutions for our nation.

# HYDRO POWER

As of September 2011 we had an installed capacity of ~38.6 GW, which is ~21% of our total electricity generation. Assessments of a variety of Hydro (large and small) initiatives indicate that 148-185 GW of capacity could be created through Hydro Power. We currently rank 5th in the world in terms of hydro power generation and North-Eastern India is seen as the appropriate landscape to generate hydro power.[143]

Large dams clearly promise the most significant hydro power generation capabilities; however, North-Eastern India is both

*"Should you find yourself in a chronically leaking boat, energy devoted to changing vessels is likely to be more productive than energy devoted to patching leaks."*
Warren Buffett

ecologically and geologically fragile, prone to earthquakes and with many potential tribal and cultural clashes. These issues are as important, if not more so, to be addresses even before the issues of land acquisition. The government has accelerated approval of a number of these projects circumventing the Forest Advisory Committee, which reversed a recommendation requiring cumulative impact assessments for three new hydro-electric plants.

## SOLAR POWER

Large parts of our Western and Southern States have the geography to take advantage of solar power for large scale generation. In November 2009 the government initiated steps to develop this large potential through launching its Jawaharlal Nehru National Solar Mission, and this was further supported by some states, such as Gujarat and Rajasthan, who developed their own plans to establish large-scale solar parks. The government wishes that we generate 10GW by 2017 and 20GW by 2022.

A key advantage solar and wind power brings is that individual homes, societies, localities and business parks are able to install such equipment to ensure they generate enough power to begin to support energy self-sufficiency. The efficiency of equipment can vary and initial capital costs were a hurdle; however, government subsidies and Solar Loan Programmes to support consumer financing for solar home power systems has helped increase take-up. It is estimated that well over 100,000 people have benefited from this scheme across the country. This type of local energy generation also reduces the costs of connecting these 'last mile' locations to the national grid, and it provides more immediate power for lighting and heating without the larger infrastructure requirements.

Land acquisition is always a challenge and some state governments are developing innovative methods to manage this, for example, by installing solar equipment above irrigation canals,

"It is science alone that can solve the problems of hunger and poverty, of insanitation and illiteracy, of superstition and deadening custom and tradition, of vast resources running to waste, or a rich country inhabited by starving people . . . Who indeed could afford to ignore science today? At every turn we have to seek its aid . . . The future belongs to science and those who make friends with science." —Jawaharlal Nehru

thereby generating 1MW solar energy whilst reducing water loss through evaporation by~237.7 gallons per annum.[144]

The improvement in technology and the reduction in prices of solar panels are making this form of power generation a viable alternative. Chinese manufacturers have helped lower solar panel costs, with firms increasing production of the panels and cutting all-in module costs to less than US$0.5 a watt by end 2015.[145] Making it potentially very competitive to other electricity generation forms. Developers of solar farms across India have shown a preference for the more advanced, thin-film solar cells offered by suppliers in the United States, Taiwan and Europe. We do not have a large solar manufacturing industry, but we are trying to develop one and China is also showing a new interest in ours as China's Suntech Power sold the panels used at the Azure installation in Khadoda, Gujarat.

We are still significantly behind European countries in the use of solar power, Germany had 28.4 GW and Italy 12.8 GW of installed solar power at the end of 2011. As a nation, we get more than 300 days of sunlight a year, and are therefore a more suitable location to generate solar power. With initiatives to install solar power and heating units on all Government buildings, schools, hospitals and other buildings, this could provide a continuous source of renewable and clean energy for our nation and citizens. Solar power units are used across the world to also provide single unit energy for equipment such as road lighting and water pumps amongst many other applications.

From a purely commercial and economic perspective solar power is now able to compete directly with coal and oil fired power generation, especially as equipment costs continue to reduce, efficiency improves and cost of coal and oil continue to rise. Effective and efficient implementation and regular execution of maintenance remains our main challenge

*"If you talk to a man in a language he understands, that goes to his head. If you talk to him in his language, that goes to his heart."*
Nelson Mandela

# OTHER SOURCES OF POWER

In this system biomass, bagasse (sugar cane waste), husks, forestry and agricultural wastes are used as fuel to produce electricity.

The Government have been promoting biomass gasifier technologies to generate up to 3 MW capacities in rural areas for at least 20 years, to use surplus biomass such as rice husk, crop stalks, small wood chips, and other agro-residues to generate electrical power. This has had some successes. We have also run many programmes to install small scale biogas plants for providing energy for cooking in rural areas. We have also installed ~4.44 million small scale biogas plants and added ~77,000 in 2012.[146] This has also been a success.

Due to our geology our nation also has potential resources to harvest geothermal energy. According to the Geological Survey of India in 2001, six geothermal regions have been identified as potential locations for energy production:

- **Himalayan Province:** Tertiary Orogenic belt with Tertiary magmatism

- **Areas of Faulted blocks:** Aravalli belt, Naga-Lushi, West coast regions and Son-Narmada lineament

- **Volcanic arc:** The Andaman and Nicobar arc

- **Deep sedimentary basin of Tertiary age:** Cambay basin in Gujarat

- **Radioactive Province:** Surajkund, Hazaribagh and Jharkhand

- **Cratonic province:** Peninsular India

We have over 340 hot springs across our nation, which were documented by the British in 1882. These are single locations sources or large tracts of geothermal activity. The thermal springs

*"Dream no small dreams for they have no power to move the hearts of men."*
Johann Wolfgang von Goethe

*"Nuclear power generation has been given a thrust by the use of uranium-based fuel. However, there would be a requirement for ten-fold increase in nuclear power generation even to attain a reasonable degree of energy self-sufficiency for our country." —Dr. Abdul Kalam*

in our peninsular region are more related to faults, which allow a downward circulation of meteoric water to considerable depths. The circulating water acquires heat from the normal thermal gradient in the area, and depending upon local condition, emerges out at suitable localities. It is claimed that India was one of the first nations to review and recognise the potential of geothermal power, but alas we are yet to implement any significant plants and realise the benefits.

We are fortunate to have a number of high potential geothermal regions. Many nations across the world that have such geology are using technologies to heat whole communities and generate power. Individual homes are also able to economically drill to provide heating to reduce main grid power consumption for water and home heating.

A December 2011 government report identified the six most promising geothermal sites for development of geothermal energy, in order of importance and priority, with Gujarat already taking a lead in to start harnessing this source:

- Tattapani in Chhattisgarh
- Puga in Jammu & Kashmir
- Cambay Graben in Gujarat
- Manikaran in Himachal Pradesh
- Surajkund in Jharkhand
- Chhumathang in Jammu & Kashmir

Our nation is surrounded by sea on three sides and therefore its potential to harness tidal wave energy is significant. More industrialised nations across Europe have begun to invest significantly in Tidal Wave energy for power generation as a major source of renewable and sustainable energy.

Tidal energy can be extracted from the oceans in several ways. In one method, a reservoir is created behind a barrage and then tidal waters pass through turbines in the barrage to generate electricity. This method requires mean tidal differences greater than 4 meters and also favourable topographical conditions to keep installation costs low. One report claims, barrage technology could harvest about 8GW from tidal energy in India, mostly in Gujarat in the Gulf of Khambhat and the Gulf of Kutch. The Ganges Delta in the Sunderbans, West Bengal is another possibility, where in December 2011, the Ministry of New & Renewable Energy and the Renewable Energy Development Agency of State of West Bengal jointly agreed to establish our nation's first 3.75MW mini tidal power project at Durgaduani. Gujarat is planning to establish Aisa's first commercial tidal power station with 50MW capacity.

As a nation we have a potential 8GW Tidal Energy generation capability in the Gulf of Cambay, Gulf of Kutch and in the Sunderbans region of the Gangetic Delta. Another tidal wave technology harvests energy from surface waves or from pressure fluctuations below the sea surface. A report from the Department of Ocean Engineering Centre, Indian Institute of Technology in Chennai, estimates the annual wave energy potential along the Indian coast is between 5MW to 15MW per meter and our first sea surface energy harvesting technology demonstration plant has been built in Vizhinjam, near Thiruruvananthpuram.

The third approach to harvesting tidal energy consists of ocean thermal energy technology. This approach tries to harvest the solar energy trapped in ocean waters into usable energy through the thermal gradient between the warmer surface water and the cooler deeper levels of the ocean. Initial tests have been undertaken near Kerala and Lakshadweep; however, this technology is still in its early stages of application and commercial viability.

Each method has its advantages and challenges; however, this is another source of sustainable renewable energy and as such, further effort and focus needs to be applied to create practical economic solutions for the benefit of the nation and its citizens.

*"In times of crisis, actions are the strongest words."*
**Winston S. Churchill**

# CONCLUDING COMMENTS

We need to produce and use energy more efficiently and in between these two, transport it more effectively. We need to find alternative methods of *'supply'* through central, local or regional generation in parallel we need to reduce *'demand'* and use of energy through low energy consumption equipment and to change the outlook on our behaviours. Forced *'black-outs'* and *'brown-outs'* are already making us think and act differently; if we apply our national creativity and innovative thinking to generate ideas and build new 'disruptive' technologies and equipment, we will be able to meet our energy needs without significantly damaging our environment or ruining our national balance sheet through payments for imports of hydrocarbon fuels.

A positive development towards energy efficiency has been made with the launch of the National Mission for Enhanced Energy Efficiency (NMEEE), which is one of the missions under the National Action Plan on Climate Change, aiming to create and promote efficient and cost effective strategies and initiatives to reduce demand and promote energy efficient processes, products and services. Over the next five years it aims to avoid adding 19.6GW of capacity and reduce Carbon Dioxide emissions.

To provide for implementation of these initiatives the Government has set up Energy Efficiency Services Ltd. a joint venture with equity participation by four central Public Sector Units; Rural Electrification Corporation, Power Finance Corporation, Power Grid Corporation and NTPC Ltd., our largest power company.

One of the main initiatives under NMEEE is aimed at improving energy efficiency in nine industrial sectors; aluminium, cement, chemicals, fertilisers, iron and steel, pulp and paper, railways, textiles and thermal power plants. Government units in each of these sectors will be given individual energy efficiency improvement targets to reduce their specific energy consumption by a fixed percentage. The key to any national or government

*"I cannot teach anybody anything; I can only make them think."*
Socrates

initiative is implementation in a time-bound fashion that delivers to its committed targets.

Key challenges for our electrical power sector include building competencies and capabilities in Project Management and Implementation, ensuring quality and regular maintenance and repair of equipment, ensuring availability of fuel quantities and qualities, land acquisition, environmental clearances at State and Central government level, and training of skilled and semi-skilled manpower to prevent talent shortages for developing, operating and maintaining the latest technology plant and equipment.

*"The greatest sin is to think yourself weak"*
Swami Vivekananda

# Water & Agriculture
# Assurance—Water

*"Water, like religion and ideology, has the power to move millions of people.*
*Since the very birth of human civilization, people have moved to settle close to it. People move when there is too little of it. People move when there is too much of it. People journey down it. People write, sing and dance about it. People fight over it. And all people, everywhere and every day, need it."*

**Mikhail Gorbachev**

*"We never know the worth of water till the well is dry."*
**Thomas Fuller**

A number of studies have shown South Asia as one of the flashpoints over water resources in the future, particularly in the wake of climate change and a burgeoning population. A recent assessment by American intelligence agencies has said South Asia will be one of the regions in the world where *"water would be used as a weapon of war or a tool of terrorism"*. It is believed by many strategic analysts that the bitterest conflicts in the next fifty years will not be over oil, but water. The supply of water has begun to be raised as an issue in the more industrialised nations and has begun to influence national and international policy. Visible climate and weather change has started to affect rainfall in various parts of the world and our nation, and these changes are likely to be more pronounced in the future. Global warming has led to the well-documented variations in annual monsoons and reduction in the size of our nation's glaciers in the Himalayas, whose snowmelt feeds the nation's major rivers. Water is becoming, and has already in certain parts of the world, become a valuable resource and commodity which is critical for ensuring political, social and economic stability. How we ensure water security, availability and distribution will be critical for the future of our nation; more especially as our population continues to increase in parallel to our industry and agriculture demanding more water.

Fresh and clean drinking water must be recognised as a resource that must be available to all citizens; it is a national asset that should be fairly and equitably available as a basic requirement to life, and therefore water problems can be difficult to resolve as some citizens will have access to more, as it is provided naturally through rivers, rain and groundwater, whilst others will have difficulty to access sufficient clean water. It is similar to other utilities such as roads, rail, sea and air ports which is a common need by all citizens, and also like electricity and telecommunications as it is specific to the user and driven by how much the citizen uses and needs; however, it is also different from all these in that it is essential to life and a natural resource belonging to the nation, that needs to be made available to all citizens.

Large parts of our nation are already water stressed as they have insufficient water. Conflicting views on water policy, availability and use have increased at all levels within our society, with our neighbouring countries, between our states, regions within states, political parties, castes, interest groups and individual farmers. It has begun to threaten our short and long-term economic growth, social stability, security and environment.

Like many other utility and data recordings across our nation, there are no consistent records for the use and availability of water, and all estimates, figures and analyses vary; neither is there a single central entity to manage water. The Ministry of Water Resources and the Central Water Commission clearly recognise that much needs to be done to improve the management of water resources across our nation. The challenge is not only having the ideas and initiatives, it is also in the clarification of governance and legislation of water ownership, water rights and in the effective implementation of these initiatives.

As a nation we have ~17% of the world's population, but only 4% of world's renewable water resources and 2.6% of world's land area. In 2010 we had 230 million citizens who were without clean water for domestic use; that included 10% of our urban population (28 million out of total of ~280 million) and 27% of our rural

*"We're in a giant car heading towards a brick wall and everyones arguing over where they're going to sit."*
David Suzuki

population (202 million out of total ~740 million). Our demand for clean water has been estimated to increase from 519 bcm (billion cubic meters) in 1990, to 693 in 2010, 942 in 2025 to 1,422 bcm by 2050, and increase of more than 200% from 2010, driven by population, industry and agriculture. However, current estimates are that we receive on average ~4,000 bcm of annual rainfall, as our basic water source, out of which only ~1,869 bcm flows through our rivers and aquifers, and of this, only ~1,123 bcm is potentially usable, of which, some claim only a very small proportion of this is actually used. Our distribution of rainfall is geographically highly uneven, and this is expected to get worse with climate change; ~28% of our land mass receives high rainfall in excess of 1,150 millimetres (mm), and 30% is particularly dry with less than 750 mm of rain per annum; ~40 million hectares of agricultural land is drought-prone, and floods affect ~7.5 million hectares of agricultural land; so in large parts of our nation water is only available throughout the year from ground water wells, which need recharging to ensure sustainable long-term availability.[147]

50% of our irrigation water, 85% of drinking water, and 33% of domestic water in cities comes from groundwater through wells, and in 2008-9, 61% of farmland was irrigated through groundwater.[148] 29% of our groundwater blocks are now in need of improvement and better management of the resource. Our groundwater quality and quantity is fast reducing.

Our individual citizen's availability of clean water significantly reduces as our population increases and this is further limited as we have an uneven distribution of this water over both time and location, resulting in frequent floods in some parts of the nation and frequent droughts in other parts.

A 2008 water survey report by the International Water Management Institute stated that the average consumption of water for agriculture during 2015-2050 was projected to increase by 80% and our water-intensive crops (wheat, rice and sugar cane) would require increases of 91%. Our current structure of agriculture would need more water than our current water reserves, so our water footprints will be depleting sooner than either China or the USA, with our largest ground water basin, the Ganges, depleting by at least 50-75% of its reserves. The threat to our food supply, due to and from, our own agricultural sector is clear

According to the Food and Agriculture Organization of the United Nations, and the Central Water Commission, a per capita water availability of less than 2,000 cubic meters per annum is defined as a water-stressed condition, and the per capita availability below 1,000 cubic meters per annum is termed as a water-scarce condition. Due to a three-fold increase in our population from 1951 to 2010, our average per capita availability of water has decreased from 5,177 cubic meters per annum in 1951 to 1,588 cubic meters per annum in 2010. Ministry of Water Resources estimate the per capita water availability in 2025 and 2050 to come down by almost 36% and 60% respectively from 2001 levels. This clearly indicates that at a national level we are water-stressed. However, this is worse at local and regional levels. Nearly 900 million (75%) of our citizens live in water-stressed regions (less than 2,000 cubic metres per annum) of which one third, 25% of all our citizens, ~300 million, live in water scarce areas (less than 1,000 cubic metres per annum).[149] This is both unsustainable and unacceptable.

The Water Resources Group estimated in 2009 that if the current pattern of demand continues, about half of the demand for water will be unmet by 2030. Our nation is divided into twenty river basins, out of which fourteen basins are water-stressed; this is not only due to increased demand but also because of the poor quality of the available water caused by pollution from untreated municipal sewage, industrial effluent, fertiliser and pesticide penetration into rivers and groundwater.

Agriculture is the largest consumer of water, accounting for almost 89% of total consumption, followed by industry and energy at 7% and domestic users at 4%. Agriculture is also the most highly inefficient user of water, with our agricultural water and crop productivity being lower than many less developed and more industrialised nations. Our industry and domestic use is also inefficient. Key is increasing the effectiveness and efficiency of water use in agriculture and to improve productivity from the water used.

*"The gap in our economy is between what we have and what we think we ought to have, and that is a moral problem, not an economic one."*

Paul Heyne

Whilst in 2012 water availability was not an issue for industry, in ten years the situation will probably be akin to the national power grid where there are rolling *'blackouts'* and *'brownouts'*, as water reservoirs run dry and must be refilled. Likewise, industry will need to have reservoirs of freshwater onsite to provide continuous water just as they currently need diesel generators. This will further add additional cost for doing business in our nation, on top of the other infrastructure challenges.

The Water Resources Group has evaluated various options for managing supply and water productivity to reduce our *'water gap'* by 2030. The most cost effective options are to improve the utilisation and effectiveness of water used in agriculture. Actions such as changes in crop selection, cropping patterns, better irrigation techniques, water-saving innovations, micro-dams to support water retention and recharge of ground water, and improving the productivity of *'rain fed'* agriculture are some practical actions that we can begin to implement. Rainwater harvesting offers a very promising solution through *'check dams'*; estimates indicate that currently only ~6% of the available surface and groundwater is being captured, and decentralized water harvesting could capture five times more water.

Small, local water saving initiatives and water management techniques and technologies has been proven to be the most effective way to improve agricultural productivity and water use. These *'demand-side'* initiatives are essential to increase awareness and these need to be expanded to industry and domestic users. The *'supply-side'* initiatives should focus on the major infrastructure projects to balance national availability of water throughout the year, such as waste water treatment, canals, river-linking and dams. As with road and rail, we need to change our approach and mindset to the quality of our planning and building operations, providing sufficient financial resources for repair and maintenance, to avoid the *'build-neglect-rebuild'* behaviour we exhibit.

Our nation's fragile resources are therefore further stressed and are faster reduced in both quantity and quality. Clean water supply, water quality and waste water treatment all needs to be managed at a national level with a singular national strategic resource strategy

*"The rights of every man are diminished when the rights of one man are threatened."*
John F. Kennedy

and plan, with inputs from all states. Co-ordination, planning and execution should also be centrally controlled with participation and ownership from the individual states.

# IRRIGATION

We have got ourselves into a position of needing to reverse some decisions made in our *'Green Revolution'* to ensure we increase water availability and agricultural productivity. These are now politically sensitive decisions and we do not have the leadership, management or administration capable or able to take these hard decisions.

It is stated that around the year 1900 our nation was the *'irrigation champion'* of the world. Where the colonial government recognised the potential of large-scale gravity driven canal irrigation as an economic enterprise and built canals as a business on a large scale. Canals were therefore, in a far better condition due to repair and maintenance, productivity impacts and providing financial returns of 8-10% for their investors; and 100 years later, we may have continued to build canals, however, we have neither maintained them, nor provided economic returns relative to the scale of the initiatives. The colonial irrigation management was a low cost, high-input-high-output model, delegating and employing aggressive revenue management for large irrigation systems whilst ensuring water availability. This led to farmers focusing on high-value produce and better focus on water management. Some lessons need to be applied to our present predicament.

Our over-designed water management systems have been built to justify higher returns; however, they have failed as they are rarely able to deliver water to more than half of their command area. Farmers at the upper-end over-appropriate water to cultivate high-value crops, leaving little for tail-end farmers. As a result, farmers in the periphery started relying on groundwater, which also gives them greater control of timing their water use. The rise in use of groundwater irrigation has then led to a decline in use of canals; however, this is a short-term benefit and we are seeing the first stages of consistent agricultural productivity

*"We forget that the water cycle and the life cycle are one."*
Jacques Yves Cousteau

decline in the last decade due to the poor availability and management of water.

The government's *'Green Revolution'* policies provided farmers cheap and unmetered electricity and subsidised credit for irrigation wells. Groundwater irrigated farms performed better compared to surface irrigation in cropping intensity, input use and yields; and it was also seen as being more equitable than surface irrigation. As a result of the poor performance of public canal irrigation and the relative advantages of groundwater use, wells have become the predominant means of irrigation. However, excessive and over use of groundwater has created more serious long-term problems. Lack of regulation and its indiscriminate extraction has led to a lowering of the water table and increasing salinity and water quality problems in the six States that account for half the food grain production in the nation (Punjab, Rajasthan, Haryana, Gujarat, Tamil Nadu and Uttar Pradesh); with a continuing decline in the net irrigated command area under canals. The ~20 million water pumps are also large users of electricity, as discussed earlier, and the vast majority are inefficient, further compounding the national energy problem. The water table in the North has dropped from 60 feet ten years ago to over 300 feet today, nearly depleted, and ground water aquifers have also increased in excessive salinity, especially in coastal regions.[150]

Decentralised traditional methods of rainwater harvesting has significant potential for replenishing and recharging groundwater and the *'check dam'* scheme in Gujarat is an excellent example of small local dams being constructed by public and non-governmental organisation (NGO) to store water during monsoons, which not only recharges groundwater, but also fills up wells for drinking water and use during the dry season; claiming to capture more water and are a major alternative to conventional river basin water resource development. Locally built tanks have provided excellent storage and minimised water losses in Rajasthan. Drip irrigation and rotational cropping etc. are all excellent initiatives to manage our agricultural water resources better whilst increasing agricultural productivity

We need to provide better canal based irrigation to farmers and reduce the impact on our ground water. We need to better connect our major rivers to ensure increased water availability across our nation. We need to reduce the number of water pumps being used and charge appropriate energy costs to farmers. We need to move towards larger farms to make more effective and efficient use of our land and resources. We need to delegate decisions and activities to Water User Association levels. We need to use check-dams, large tanks and other methods to better capture and use water at a local level. We need to recycle more water; we need to reduce excessive fertiliser and pesticide use; we need to reduce chemical pollution and untreated sewage, as this is further damaging our eco systems and our water resources.

# RURAL DRINKING WATER

The major problem with rural drinking water is its availability and quality. Government initiatives, such as Bharat Nirman have not been able to supply sufficient good quality water to rural citizens. The majority of rural drinking water is supplied by groundwater; however, declining water tables and deteriorating quality of groundwater has rendered these initiatives unsustainable. The Planning Commission has found that where access has been given to many rural communities to ground water aquifers for drinking, they have used the same sources for irrigation and have begun to dangerously deplete the source.

Management and administration need to be delegated to local user groups such as *Panchayati Raj, Gram Sabhas and Gram Panchayats*, and these need to be provided with the legal, financial, regulatory and water standard authority to ensure supply, operation, maintenance and revenue responsibilities to provide equality and accountability in decision-making.

*"Invention is the most important product of man's creative brain. The ultimate purpose is the complete mastery of mind over the material world, the harnessing of human nature to human needs."*
Nikola Tesla

# URBAN DRINKING WATER

*"The two defining issues of this century are both universal but felt locally: the global water crisis and the resources boom."*

Jay Wilson Weatherill

The urban water supply sector across our nation continues to be plagued with severe deficiencies in terms of availability, quality and equity of services. According to the Ministry of Urban Development and United Nations population records, our urban population is expected to increase by over 60%, reaching 575 million by 2030 from an estimated 325 million in 2005. Urban infrastructure needs to significantly improve for all our existing cities, and planning and construction needs to start for the inevitable expansion without which our cities will become a quagmire of humanity eventually leading to decay and destruction.

As with other utilities, only a few cities across our nation have a water consumer database, asset register, records of water provided and consumed and revenue accounts. It is therefore, difficult to make assessments or comparisons, which is very concerning given the urban water supply shortages across our nation. These utilities face challenges in investment and not surprisingly inadequate repair and maintenance, which has led to inadequate coverage, irregular and inequitable supply, deteriorated infrastructure and unsustainable water sources. These are driven by a lack of governance: poor leadership and direction, weak management and administration, poor capabilities and competencies, operationally inefficient with losses due to leakage, theft and non-payment, financial weakness, political interventions in levying and recovering tariffs, absence of clear targets to monitor and evaluate performance.

Around 90-95% of urban Indian households now have access to water; however, access to piped water is 75%, and 55% have direct connections. Complex administrative connection procedures, poor quality of piped services, accompanied by relatively high connection costs, are factors which further inhibit direct connections even where a water network exists.

Our water providing authorities need to address the long-term supply and sustainability issues as a matter of urgency, and in doing so, need to improve the medium-term outlook.

We need to have a major improvement in operational efficiency through increasing coverage, metering and reduction in non-revenue water. We need to revise water tariffs to an appropriate level based on rationalised cost structures that are needed to achieve cost recovery, repair and maintenance and provide for incremental costs and margins. We need to better allocate public funds to achieve desired outcomes, and base performance on outcomes of service, supply and quality measures.

# INDUSTRIAL WATER

Supplying the rising water demand and pollution caused by the discharge of waste water are the two major issues that currently dominate the industrial water sector. 70% of the wastewater generated by industry is discharged untreated due to the absence of effective regulation and the lack of enforcement of existing regulation. Some estimate that each litre of discharged waste water further pollutes 5-8 litres of river or ground water. Some companies that supply and bottle carbonated drinks can use 5-6 litres of clean water for each litre of drink they produce. Water has to be priced and valued accordingly.

As in agriculture, water productivity in industry is low. This could be due to inefficient use of water and low water pricing. Water only forms a small proportion of the total costs of operation for industry and water charges are generally very low. Some research has indicated that industry may be willing to pay more for the water it receives, and therefore a potential upward revision should be viewed as a viable option.

A major hurdle in industrial water management is the involvement of multiple agencies and of institutions. Ministry of Water Resources, Ministry of Commerce & Industry, Central Ground Water Board / Authority, Central Pollution Control Boards, State Pollution Control Boards, Central Water Commission. There is too much bureaucracy, discussion, deliberation and policy generation and not enough effective decision making and implementation. Unless all aspects of water

*"Water is the driving force in nature."*
**Leonardo da Vinci**

241

use by industry are regulated by fewer agencies or even a single agency, it will not be possible to achieve either water conservation or pollution controlin our nation.

# WASTE-WATER AND SEWAGE (RECYCLING AND POLLUTION CONTROL)

According to a UNICEF and WHO joint monitoring programme report on drinking water and sanitation, 60% of the world's open defecators live in India; defecating on streets, shorelines, river edges, car parks or in fields, 626 million people. Though growing rapidly at 20 million new latrines per year, our sanitation coverage is below 50%. At the current rate, according to the joint monitoring report, India will reach its millennium development goals only by 2054. We need to improve the environment by building more latrines. Even the cheapest public latrines cost INR 1 per visit per person per day in rural and INR 2 in urban areas. Waste-water as sewage, clean water, our environment and healthare are all linked in the way our citizens behave and excrete their natural body fluids and contents.

Water pollution is becoming a serious problem across our nation with almost all rivers, lakes and water bodies being severely polluted; ~70% of our surface water and a growing percentage of our groundwater reserves are contaminated by biological, toxic, organic and inorganic pollutants, causing environmental and health hazards. Most of the polluted stretches of rivers are located in and around large urban areas with municipal sewage contributing ~75% and industrial pollution about 25%. In many cases, these water sources have been categorised as unsafe for human consumption as well as for other activities, such as irrigation and industrial needs. This is beginning to severely impact the water availability and further compounds water scarcity whilst damaging our ecosystem.

WHO estimated in 2007 that the lack of water, sanitation and hygiene results in the annual loss of 400,000 lives; while air

*"Filthy water cannot be washed."*
**African Proverb**

pollution contributed to the death of 520,000 people across our nation. Environmental factors contribute to 60 years of ill-health per 1,000 citizens in India compared to 54 in Russia, 37 in Brazil and 34 in China. The socio-economic costs of water pollution are extremely high: 1.5 million children under five years die each year due to water related diseases, 200 million man-days of work are lost each year, and our nation loses about INR 366 billion (3.95% of GDP) each year due to water related diseases.

Groundwater Fluoride problems exist in 150 districts in 17 states across our nation, with Orissa and Rajasthan being the most severely affected, in drinking water this causes fluorosis resulting in weak bones, weak teeth and anaemia. Arsenic, a poison and a carcinogen, has been found in the groundwater of the Ganges delta causing health risks to 35-70 million citizens in West Bengal, Bihar and neighbouring Bangladesh. In 2004 researchers calculated the cost of industrial water pollution reduction to be ~2.5% of industrial GDP, and that found the cost of avoidance to be 1.73-2.2% of GDP. The social and health benefits would far exceed the financial benefits of such an initiative.

There is a large gap between the generation and treatment of domestic and industrial wastewater across our nation. Central Pollution Control Board studies indicate that there are 269 sewage treatment plants across our nation, of which only 231 are operational. It is estimated that we only have capacity to treat 19% of our sewage and a negligible amount of our industrial waste water; so not only do we lack sufficient sewage and waste-water treatment capacity but also that the sewage and waste water treatment plants that we do have are not always operational (either through lack of electrical power or poor repair and maintenance). This sewage and waste-water either seeps into the soil or evaporates; it accumulates causing unhygienic conditions and releases heavy metals and pollutants that drain into surface and groundwater. Reliable generation and supply of electricity is essential for managing our water pollution and associated environmental issues, as discussed in the earlier section.

Waste-water recycling has begun to offer a viable and practical alternative and solution for water shortages. The costs of

*"Water belongs to us all. Nature did not make the sun one person's property, nor air, nor water, cool and clear."*
**Michael Simpson**

recycling have significantly reduced especially for large industrial use. There are a growing number of cases where large industries, forced by lack of fresh water supply from municipalities, have resorted to waste-water recycling. The cost of recycled water to industry may be slightly higher than the current municipality tariffs for freshwater; however, the reliability of supply and the potential increase in municipality rates would make it economic for industry to recycle wastewater. These entities could also begin to process waste for local companies and for municipality sewage as costs will further be reduced through economies of scale. Additional capital costs can be supported through State and Central grants, such as the Jawaharlal Nehru National Urban Renewal Mission.

The use of sewage-treated recycled water by large industries should be compulsory, and eventually industry should recycle all their water needs. Tariffs should reflect the opportunity cost of freshwater to incentivise a shift to using recycled water.

In view of the population increase, demand of freshwater will become unmanageable and waste-water management plans do not address this increasing pace of wastewater generation. We need to also leverage our nation's talent and capabilities to support development of technologies to treat waste water and sewage. Tata Chemicals launched *a water filter appropriate for the needs of the country*. The technology uses burnt rice husks with nano-silver as a filter for water, making it 99.8% free of harmful bacteria and also some viruses. Burnt rice husk is available in huge quantities in India and used as a fuel thereby using natural and readily available low cost resources.

There is an urgent need to generate water from all available resources including wastewater by recycling, reuse, recharging and storage. There is urgent need to build sewage systems and wastewater treatment facilities to augment water supplies.

*"Rivers, ponds, lakes and streams, they all have different names, but they all contain water. Just as religions do, they all contain truths."*
Muhammad Ali

# RIVER LINKING PROJECT: GBM BASIN

In 2002, the government announced plans to *"free India from the curse of floods and droughts"* by linking major rivers in the region to reduce persistent water shortages. The basic idea is to take water from areas where authorities believe it is abundant and divert it to areas where it is less available. The Ganges, the Brahmaputraand and the Meghna (GBM) river system basins are made up of the catchment areas of 1.75 million square kilometres stretching across five countries: Bangladesh, Bhutan, China, India and Nepal. While Bangladesh and India share all the three river basins, China shares only the Brahmaputra and the Ganges basins, Nepal only the Ganges basin, and Bhutan only the Brahmaputra basin. The three river systems contribute an annual discharge of 1,350 bcm (billion cubic meters), of which the Ganges contributes ~500bcm, the Brahmaputra 700 bcm and the Meghna 150 bcm. The countries sharing the GBM basins have a number of water management issues due to gross inequalities in the availability and distribution of water through floods, droughts and seasons. This poses a threat to infrastructure, property, agriculture, navigation and the ecosystem.

The National River Linking Project (NRLP) aims at transferring water from the Ganges and Brahmaputra basins to the water deficit areas of Western and Southern India. The overall goals of the NRLP are to increase water availability for irrigation, increase hydropower production potential and reduce the effects of flooding. Through this project the National Water Development Agency aims to improve food security and self-sufficiency by increasing the area of arable land, increase in electricity production, and reduction of reliance on coal as an energy source, as well as managing flooding in the Ganges basin. The Peninsular component of the NRLP will consist of 16 links and the Himalayan component of the NRLP will consist of 14 links. These will have storage reservoirs on the main Ganges and theBrahmaputra rivers, and interlink the Ganges and Yamuna to transfer the surplus flow to the drought prone areas of Haryana,

*"Civilisation did not come with fire. It came with the discovery of how to use fire to heat water."*
**Laura Anne Gilman**

245

Rajasthan and Gujarat, and also provide irrigation benefits to large areasin southern Uttar Pradesh and southern Bihar.[151]

The NRLP has faced a lot of review and scrutiny. Conflict between *'donor'* and *'receiver'* states has not been an issue; however, major opposition has come from 58 water professionals who sent a letter and memorandum to the Prime Minister to reconsider the project. The validity of the basic principle of having *'surplus'* water in some rivers, on which the NRLP was conceptualised, was questioned by some researchers on the argument of the need for a balance between the natural flow and ecosystem requirement. Drought mitigation was seen as a local problem requiring local solutions. While efficacy of the project in flood control remains doubtful, large-scale constructions of dams, reservoirs, and conveyance systems are likely to cause environmental impacts and displacement problems.

In early 2012 India's Supreme Court ordered the government to implement the project *"in a time-bound manner"*. The court also appointed a committee to plan and implement the project. The judges had said the project had been long delayed, resulting in an increase in its cost as the project had remained on paper for ten years

The challenge we will face is the perennial large project dilemma in our nation, of political, administrative and commercial corruption, incompetence and poor planning, use of sub-standard materials and equipment etc. Maybe we could deliver this project in the same fashion as we delivered the Delhi Metro. Maybe we could find the professionals that could emulate this achievement, to deliver on time, on budget and without any hint of corruption, whilst managing to reduce the ecological and environmental consequences.

## CHINESE WATER DIVERSION PLANS: TIBETAN PLATEAU

The Chinese government has been considering a plan to dam or redirect the southward flow of water from the Tibetan plateau, the starting point of many international rivers, including major rivers

*"In the world there is nothing more submissive and weak than water. Yet for attacking that which is hard and strong nothing can surpass it."*

Lao Tzu

like the Brahmaputra, Yangtze, Mekong and international cross-border rivers like the Indus, Sutlej, Arun and Karnali. The plan includes diverting the waters of the Yangtze, the Yellow river, and the Brahmaputra to China's drought-prone Northern areas, through huge canals, aqueducts, and tunnels. One of the water diversion routes, more specifically the southern component of the route cutting through the Tibetan mountains, will divert waters of the Tsang-po for a large hydroelectric plant and irrigation use. The planned water diversion will have adverse consequences in the downstream areas, resulting in loss of land and ecosystems due to the submergence of a huge area in the Tibetan region and pose a serious threat to the flood management, dry season water availability, and ecosystem preservation of northern India and Bangladesh.

As with increased communication and collaboration across the military and national border controls, we also need to ensure regular communication and information sharing with China on this issue to ensure they recognise, understand and appreciate our predicament and the affects and consequences it will have on our nation and its citizens.

## CONCLUDING COMMENTS

Multiple factors are converging to ensure that our nation will suffer severe shortages of freshwater in the years to come. Our population is growing rapidly, and as the poor majority of our population gain access to running drinking water, freshwater usage will significantly increase. Our industrial base is also rapidly expanding and requires increased clean water for operation, and as our farm yields are declining due to poor farm and crop management and pesticide use, these will need increased irrigation.

Several reforms are required to improve the performance of water utilities. International experience suggests that effective leadership, political will, improvement in management practices, corporatisation, measures for demand side management and

*"The fall of dropping water wears away the Stone."*
Titus Lucretius Carus

wastewater reuse, and full cost recovery are amongst the necessary elements for the successful transformation of utilities.

The impending water crisis is already evident in several parts of our nation. The 2012 Draft National Water Policy from Ministry of Water is a sound initial document. Policy makers could consider additional factors presented here. A radically new approach to water management and use is required. We need to act decisively to protect our water resources and use them prudently. It must be understood by the general public and at all national management and administration levels that our water availability is limited and will be exacerbated by climate change. We also need to recognise and manage the inter linkages between Infrastructure (Energy), Agriculture and Environment and that Water is the common factor across each.

## We need to ensure:

- A single Central governing body with regulatory and legal authority to manage and decide on all water resources, including clean and waste water management.
- A single Central governing body that interfaces with Agriculture, Industry and Environment to ensure aligned and consistent approach to water management.
- A single Central governing body that will not be affected by political influences and intervention.
- A single Central governing body that sets measurable performance standards and reports these as its accountability to the citizens.
- A single Central governing body that enforces financial and legal penalties for failures to meet standards, pollution and activities affecting water as a national security resources.
- Improved governance, competence and capabilities of all water management utilities.

*"Thousands have lived without love, not one without water."*
W. H. Auden

- Increased water data and information management to support informed decision making (sources, users, quality, quantities, usage, assets etc.).
- Reduced water consumption per unit of output in agriculture and industry.
- Increase defficiency and effectiveness of water used in agriculture to increase yield.
- Increased reservoir and groundwater storage.
- Increased use local user groups to decide and manage water resources.
- Increased use of check dams and other methods to increase rain water usage.
- Clean water for all: Piped water availability to rural and urban citizens and households.
- Latrines available to all households and used by all citizens.
- Increased wastewater treatment and recycling.
- Increased sewage treatment.
- Increased use of recycled water.
- Compulsory use of recycled water for industry.
- Compulsory treatment of waste water by industry.
- Diversion of excess flood waters for storage and agricultural use.
- Creation of new tools and technologies for reducing evaporation.
- Creation of new tools and technologies for conversion of sea and brackish water to fresh water.
- Improve repair and maintenance of irrigation and water processing equipment
- Water rates are set at realistic financial levels to cover investment, waste, losses, repair and maintenance requirements and cost recovery.
- Increase in water rates for agriculture and industry.
- Realistic electricity rates for agriculture.
- Realistic water rates for domestic users.
- Realistic water rates for industrial and commercial users.

*My parents told me, "Finish your dinner. People in China and India are starving."*
*I tell my daughters, "Finish your homework. People in India and China are starving for your job."*

Thomas L. Friedman

*"When the last tree is cut and the last fish killed, the last river poisoned, then you will see that you can't eat money."*

**John May**

# Water & Agriculture
# Assurance—Agriculture

*"Agriculture not only gives riches to a nation, but the only riches she can call her own."*

**Samuel Johnson**

Between 30-80% of food produced is lost before it reaches our kitchens; Indian agricultural productivity has continued to sharply decline since 2000, and is a major contributor to rural poverty, where 72% of our citizens live. The 1968 *'Green Revolution'* saw an increase in our basic grain production; however, agricultural productivity has now failed to keep up with our population increase. India ranks second to China in population, but produces only 33% of China's rice yield and about 50% of Vietnam and Indonesia's productivity; we have very low agricultural productivity across all major food items, and in some cases we only produce 20% compared to the best-in-class farming examples; these include Fruit, Vegetables, Milk, Wheat, Sugar Cane, Mangoes, Cotton, Tomatoes, Onions, Peas and Groundnuts. We lag the world in agricultural productivity in all items that are the basic food stuffs for Indian citizens.

Agriculture contributes a significant 21% of our GBP and we need strong rural and agricultural leadership to ensure we will be able to feed our growing population. We now need a new *'Evergreen Agricultural Revolution'* to improve productivity and output across all food items on a sustainable basis.

We are one of the largest food producers in the world, with 158 million hectares of arable land; however, 50% of our agricultural land is dependent on rain and is a major contributor to this poor productivity. A 64% deficiency in monsoon rainfall

250

has a potential 2-5% impact on GDP and resulting inflation.[152] Our GDP and balance of payments continues to decline as we import more food stuff. Prices of commodities will continue to increase due to higher demand and less availability due to population growth. We have failed to balance the domestic demand and supply situation.

Food production has been one of the major concerns in India for successive governments. Major agricultural changes and policies have been initiated to increase productivity and growth; however, the result seems to be slower agricultural growth. We lack an overall vision for the sector and professional implementation and sustainability of initiatives. Perennial concerns are availability of water, storage and fair distribution of water, water pollution and land pollution, absence of farming technology and equipment, insufficient research into seed and ways of farming, soil and farm management, planting cycles etc. it also does not help that the majority of farmers are currently illiterate.

With increasing population growth our per capita land availability declined from 0.35 hectares in 1951, to 0.14 in 2001 and is projected to be 0.09 by 2050; however, per capita agriculture land has been maintained at 0.14 hectares in 2001 and 2011 through increasing the areas of land under agricultural from ~135 hectares in 2001 to ~160 million hectares in 2011.[153] We not only need to increase the area of land under agriculture, but more importantly, grow more on the land we already have. We should not sacrifice fertile forests and jungles for agriculture, but to reclaim the deserts, fallow, barren, waste and brackish lands for appropriate agriculture, whilst maintaining our existing environment. If we can increase our existing agricultural land productivity to world class standards, and reduce our wastage, then we should not have a problem for food security and supply. Our vision and objective should be to meet the food needs of our increased population through productivity improvements rather than increasing the land under agriculture.

*"Bring diversity back to agriculture. That's what made it work in the first place."*
David R. Brower

The causes for low productivity of Indian agriculture can be divided into three broad categories:

## 1—Ownership& Behavioural Factors

- **Overcrowding in Agriculture:** The area of agricultural land per farmer has declined despite an expansion of area under cultivation. A hereditary practice of handing farms down generations has resulted in too many small farmers with too small a farm.

- **Size of Holding:** The small size of farm and agriculture holdings, with an average of less than 2 hectares makes efficiency and productivity very difficult. Machinery and technology cannot be used effectively on the smaller holdings, and these small holdings are very inefficient users of labour, resources and energy. Of 15 major agricultural nations surveyed from the years 1970 to 2000, India was the only one with a reduced average farm size. 80% of farm holdings were less than 2 hectares in size, with 62% averaging less than half a hectare.

- **Labour Resources:** In some parts of the country, there is a shortage of permanent farm labour as the traditional labour is moving towards higher paid and better work conditions in urban factories and offices.

- **Owner Profiles:** In some parts of the country, the younger generation of land owners are not wishing to pursue a challenging career in farming, leaving many farms operated by the increasing less productive older generation owner farmers; this coupled with labour shortages results in a *'hobby farming'* approach and attitude.

- **Discouraging Rural Atmosphere:** Some rural farmers are still tradition-bound, uneducated, superstitious, uninformed, unadventurous and conservative. Their general attitude of maintaining the status-quo in tried and tested practices maintains a less developed

*"I have always said there is only one thing that can bring our nation down, our dependence on foreign countries for food and energy. Agriculture is the backbone of our economy."*
John Salazar

agricultural system. Some farmers do not seem to be prepared to accept new tools and techniques, and as a consequence, improvements in agriculture become difficult. It is still seen as a *'way of life'* rather than a business.

## 2—Structural & Institutional Factors

- **Pattern of Land Tenure:** Agricultural land ownership structure does not support or incentivise the farmer to be progressive. Significant tracts of land are owned by landlords and landowners who have a considerable influence over their lands. The farm tenant therefore, has little incentive for improvement and to be more production or creative in what and how he cultivates. High rents can be demanded by local and non-local *'absentee landlords'*; coupled with the seeming apathetic attitude of the farm tenants, productivity increases are difficult.

- **Education & Information:** There seems to be no impetus to farming education and agricultural information and initiatives resulting in a stagnation of ideas, creativity, risk and initiatives to improve agricultural productivity.

- **Inadequate Irrigation Facilities:** There is poor infrastructure to provide for water outside the monsoon season, irrigation is insufficient in many parts of the country and is still irregular and ineffective in its use of water.

- **Groundwater Pumping:** The short-term benefits of bore and tube wells is recognised. However, over-extraction has now meant that farmers have to dig deeper, to over 300 feet in some instances to access water for their crops, and water tables are dropping as much as 3 feet every year. This is expensive financial burden. Water pumps can cost up to US$4,000 and this is also an additional cost that takes away from other investments, increases

*"The more we pour the big machines, the fuel, the pesticides, the herbicides, the fertilizer and chemicals into farming the more we knock out the mechanism that made it all work in the first place."*

David R. Brower

debt, and uses large amounts of electricity that is provided to farmers at a subsidised rate.

- **Poor Financial Management:** Farmers in many parts of the nation are subsistence farmers; they do not have access to cash-flow management services and are generally debt driven. Capital and equipment purchases are financed by traditional banks; however, as this is not fully geared towards farming needs and stretched, they have invariably turned to *'unofficial'* local lenders who charge up to 24%, at least double the banks' interest rate, in some regions. During the profitable years of the *'Green Revolution'* farmers increased their debt to improve their life styles, borrowing to buy many traditional non-farming assets; and now as costs increase and margins reduce, this has driven farmers further in debt, and in many cases to unserviceable levels for a lifestyle can cannot be funded by agriculture, leading to a *'vicious cycle of debt'*. Suicide by farmers in the press is the only visibility many citizens have of the end-result of this damaging *'chain-reaction'* spreading across our nation.

- **Poor Soil Management:** Deeper drilling has resulted in extraction of brackish water in many regions. In land closer to the shore, it is the result of salt water replacing fresh water that has been extracted, and often drilling taps brackish underground pools, and the salty water poisons the crops, leaving weak crops and a whitish salt residue across the soil, causing plant injuries as the root cannot take the nutrients from the soil.

- **Poor Incentivisation:** Studies show that intensive farming methods, which government policies subsidise, are also destroying the soil. The high-yield crops require significant amounts of nutrients such as nitrogen, phosphorous, iron and manganese, which then makes the soil anaemic. Farmers claim that they now use three times as much fertiliser as they used to, to produce the same amount of crops, further draining finances whilst damaging the soil and environment and eco-system.

*"All serious daring starts from within."*
Eudora Welty

Studies have also shown that excessive use of fertilisers and pesticides have killed many soil based animals that support agriculture and pollination. In some regions worms, which help aerate the soil, and small birds and mammals have disappeared.

- **Poor Soil Management and Crop Alignment:** Improved information and education to improve soil quality and support aligning the most appropriate crops and farming techniques for the types of local soils and weather conditions would increase productivity.

- **Poor non-agricultural services:** Lack of finance, marketing and selling channels and storage facilities are also responsible for poor agricultural development. Co-operatives and other institutional agencies have not been able to eliminate the village money lenders. Storage facilities for farmers are also very limited in availability. 21 million tons of wheat are lost each year due to inadequate storage and distribution systems.

- **Poor Supply Chains:** There are too many intermediaries within the food Supply Chain within our nation. Margins and costs are added at each stage across 5-7 *'middle men'* from farmer to kitchen table. This does not provide the farmer with a fair price for their produce, and increases damage and losses through multiple handling; further reducing productivity.

## 3—Technological & Natural Factors

- **Poor Tools & Techniques:** The tools and technique used by traditional farmers are outdated and inefficient; they have not been able to adapt to progressive techniques to increase yields from the land, poor quality seeds and traditional wooden ploughs and bullocks are still used. There is also insufficient information, education, support and Research & Development to improve agricultural productivity. Our use of land and

*"The food that enters the mind must be watched as closely as the food that enters the body."*
Patrick Joseph 'Pat' Buchanan

255

water productivity is poor. We produce 0.2-0.26 kg of rice per cubic metre of water; which is half that of China, and 0.32-0.42 kg of cereal per cubic metre of water, just one-third of China.

- **The *'Green Revolution'*:** Higher yield seeds required more significant amounts of water than the rainfall could provide; and as canal irrigation infrastructure and management was weak, this resulted in bore holes and the other subsequent knock-on chain reaction damaging affects to farming and agricultural productivity.
- **Effect of Nature:** Indian agriculture is heavily dependent on the monsoon, and rainfall dictates the scale of output; this can lead to both droughts and floods.

The Punjab State Council for Science and Technology states that farmers are committing ecological and economic suicide, through national policies that reward farmers for the very practices that destroy the environment and trap them in debt.

Our initial *'Green Revolution'* over 40 years ago, persuaded farmers to grow only high-yield wheat, rice and cotton instead of their traditional mix of crops, this worked, and our farmers complied; however, this has had both short-term positive and longer-term negative effects, which we are only beginning to recognise. We now need to urgently launch a new revolution, an *'Evergreen Agricultural Revolution'* that is sustainable, a programme that evolves with time and is evergreen, to ensure we maintain food self-sufficiency and are also able to export food to other nations. The challenge our nation will face in this is that there is no single perfect farming system, anywhere across the world that produces high yields, provides for a sound economic return for farmers, protects and enhances the environment, whilst still producing quality food at affordable prices. However, the advantage we have is that we have a large geography with a range of weather and soils that could support us creating a strategy and approach to farming and agriculture that progressively moves us towards this.

*"We may find in the long run that tinned food is a deadlier weapon than the machine-gun."*
George Orwell

We need more innovative ways of minimising the use and consumption of water. We need to apply a range of approaches and strategies and have leading edge applications such as *'Bio intensive'*, *'hydroponics'* etc.; growing basic staples and grains, as well as high-value and low-water produce; we need a better informed, educated and trained next generation of agriculturist to support us meet the needs of the nation, farmers and citizens.

*"A riot is the language of the unheard."*
**Dr. Martin Luther King, Jr.**

# Environment Assurance

*"What we are doing to the forests of the world is but a mirror reflection of what we are doing to ourselves and to one another."*

**Mohandas Karamchand Gandhi**

Our environment is inextricably connected to our other infrastructure demands and requirements; transportation, energy, water and agriculture. Our nation has one of the most widely diverse environments that few others on Earth can experience: from the Himalayas in the North, the long coastline touched by the Arabian Sea on the West and the Bay of Bengal in the East, to the islands of Andaman, Nicobar and Lakshadweep, we have deserts in Rajasthan and Gujarat, teak forests in Central India, and thick towering rainforests in the Northeast.

Across our nation there is an ever growing list of environmental problems, including pollution, deforestation, mineral extraction, wildlife protection; and this is increasing due to the effects of increased population and industrialisation with its longer-term catastrophic consequences.

## POLLUTION

We have covered some of the effects of pollution in the earlier sections. Pollution is seriously damaging our living environment and the eco-system that support us. Water pollution is killing our rivers, lakes, water resources and affecting the life forms within these environments. Our air is being polluted through increased industrialisation and traffic, to a level where our local television and publishing news reports the level of air pollution within our cities; this does not even happen across many more industrialised

*"Here is your country. Cherish these natural wonders, cherish the natural resources, cherish the history and romance as a sacred heritage, for your children and your children's children. Do not let selfish men or greedy interests skin your country of its beauty, its riches or its romance."* —Theodore Roosevelt

nations. Our soil is being polluted by both industry and agriculture which is causing long-term damage to our useable living space. Our management of waste and use of chemicals and pharmaceuticals has also caused major damage to our eco-system. The use of plastics is beginning to be recognised as a major problem. Simple steps can be implemented by all citizens to improve our own living environment and eco-system.

As an example of the cascading domino type affect, simple lateral *'pollution'* type problems can have on our specific national ecosystem: The use of Diclofenac, a Non-steroidal anti-inflammatory drug, used by humans and on animals has caused catastrophic damage to our ecosystem.[154] Diclofenac is responsible for bringing three South Asian species of *Gyps* vultures to the brink of extinction. This is a pharmaceutical drug that is used in the more industrialised nations, but is has not caused any damage to their ecosystem as it has to ours; a lesson we must take-away as each ecosystem has its own characteristics and must be assessed accordingly. Diclofenac had been used by humans and farmer for cattle across our nation to reduce inflammation; however, this drug accumulates in the liver. Vultures were our key mechanism to remove dead carcases and carrion across our nation, they cleaned our environment effectively and efficiently of decay and disease. Diclofenac has been found to kill 95% of our vultures in a matter of less than ten years. The population crash was first noted in the late 1990s, with even small-scale usage of the drug having catastrophic consequences to these birds. This has led to an increase of rotting carcases and carrion across our nation, increasing diseases and giving rise to feral dog populations which have grown in significant numbers through the availability of an abundant food source. These dogs in turn have now formed packs and are beginning to cause major personal safety and health issue for citizens across the nation; something vultures never did. Many children and adults have been attacked by these dogs and rabies is now again on the increase. The direct human affect has also been on our Parsee citizens as their cultural practices of disposing of their deceased has been affected by the absence of vultures and the affect of human remains with Diclofenac

*"It is horrifying that we have to fight our own government to save the environment."*
Ansel Adams

residues. They are also now beginning to address this issue as a matter of urgency.

Our government has, relatively quickly, banned the manufacture and sale of Diclofenac for veterinary use in 2006 because of its toxicity to these critically endangered vultures, and our scientists have begun a breeding programme for these birds. Further measures in 2008, placed additional restrictions on Diclofenac for animal use, with contravention punishable with imprisonment. It may be a bit too little too late, but we are trying. However, our own citizens are working against our own environment for short-term personal profit and gain. A study published in 2011 in the journal *Oryx* had found that over a third of Indian pharmacies continue to sell Diclofenac to livestock farmers. Farmers are purchasing widely-available human Diclofenac illegally in conveniently large bottles to treat their cattle. This must be stopped and we need to apply the rule of law and begin long imprisonment penalties to stop this brazen illegal behaviour. Our laws are useless unless applicable. Lead author and principal conservation scientist at the Royal Society for the Protection of Birds, Dr. Richard Cuthbert has also stated, *"The ban is still quite easy to avoid because human formulations are for sale in large vials, which are clearly not intended for human use. Preventing misuse of human Diclofenac remains the main challenge in halting the decline of threatened vultures."* The report's co-author, Dr. Vibhu Prakash of BirdLife Partner the Bombay Natural History Society said, *"While the increase in meloxicam brands* (an alternative which does not affect vultures) *and availability is encouraging, firm action at Government level against pharmaceutical companies and pharmacies that are breaking the law by manufacturing and selling Diclofenac for veterinary use is urgently needed if we are to save vultures from extinction."* However, until production and sale of veterinary Diclofenac is stopped, we cannot guarantee these birds have any future in the wild and we will face its devastating ecological consequences.

The reduction of worms in our soils, and other insects and small birds in some parts of our nation is due to the over use of

*"A nation that destroys its soils destroys itself. Forests are the lungs of our land, purifying the air and giving fresh strength to our people."*
Franklin D. Roosevelt

fertilisers and pesticides, and this will cause long-term damage to our environment well before we get to 2050.

Waste dumps in large cities across our nation and around the world have also been found to pollute the soil and grounds water with a cocktail of chemicals and buy-products of the waste. Recycling and incineration can support our environment and power needs.

# DEFORESTATION

In 1952 the National Forest Policy of India aimed to bring one-third of our land mass under forest cover. They had recognised the essential need for forests to maintain biodiversity, ecology, environment and a comfortable living and working environment. We should aim to realise and maintain this.

Forests and trees cover 78.29 million hectares of our nation, ~23.8% of our geographical area; however, this includes only 2.7% of tree cover. This report claims an increase of 1,128sq. km (1,128,000 hectares) of forestry from 2009 after it allowed for *interpretational changes* in the 2009 report; without those *interpretational changes*, there was a net reduction of 367sq.km of forest cover. The Hilly areas of our nation have seen a reduction of 548sq. km and the Tribal Areas have seen a decrease of 679 sq. km. The Northeast of our nation contains 25% of our current forests, and these have seen a 549 sq. km reduction.[155] There is therefore, a potential total reduction of 1,594 sq. km. in only 2 years.

The concern with some of these statistics and research is that there is significant encroachment in forests, hills and the tribal areas, which is well documented in newspaper articles and journals; and although these statistics may not reflect the full extent and overall reduction in areas classified as forests, it does not account for the reduction in tree density; forests are becoming less dense as foliage and old trees are removed by illegal traders, mining, encroachment and for fuel use. Many believe that the total number of trees has been significantly reduced. Major areas

*"We do not inherit the earth from our ancestors; we borrow it from our children."*
**Chief Seattle**

we classify as Forests and Jungles are no more than glorified shrub lands dispersed with trees.

It is estimated that we use around 9 million cubic meters of wood per annum; around 3 million of this is legally sourced for residential, commercial and industrial use, and 6 million is imported. By 2020 we are expected to have a timber deficit of 20-70 million cubic meters.[156] This does not allow for unauthorized and unrecorded removal of trees from our forests and protected areas, which has not been estimated by any source.

Deforestation affects our whole environment in all parts of our nation and affects the whole water cycle; fewer trees result in:

- A warmer and drier climate
- Less rainfall due to less evaporation through photosynthesis and respiration
- Less rain water retention in the soil, which leads to reduction in the ground water table
- Reduces soil quality (increased salinity and reduced nutrients)
- Increased soil erosion and landslides etc., which leads to
- Increased flooding
- Reduced wildlife and bio-diversity
- An increase in carbon dioxide and reduction in oxygen in the atmosphere

# MINING

There is mixed progress in our balancing the need of minerals from mining and the management of the environment. We have been displaying a *'yo-yo'* or *'pendulum'* type behaviour where we approve a project and then stop it. We pass laws but are unable to enforce these. We claim that we have prevented or halted a project but they still continue. Our behaviours seem to illustrate a *'go-pause-go'* type of approach where time allows resistance to fade and collective memories to be erased, as new issues come across the horizon.

*"Happiness is when what you think, what you say, and what you do are in harmony."*
Mohandas Karamchand Gandhi

It is prudent to move slowly on environmental and forest clearances, which have affected the development of hydropower and new coal based Ultra Mega Power Projects. It is essential that an independent holistic environmental impact assessmentis completed for all projects including detailed impact on bio-diversity and thorough analysis and prognosis of effects downstream.

The Ministry of Environment and Forests has quite rightly declared 47% of the coal mining areas as *'No-Go-Areas'*, which means that no coal mining can be done in these areas. The Planning Commission has estimated that the gap between demand for coal and supply of domestic coal is likely to widen further to 200 million tonnes in the 12ᵗʰ Five Year Plan, so we will be unlikely to meet our energy capacity needs unless we import coal and oil or expand existing, and create new and renewal forms of energy generation.

Illegal mining is potentially a larger fraudulent issue than many other *'scams'* undertaken by our corrupt politicians and businessmen. These involve encroachment of forest areas, underpayment of government royalties, conflict with tribal citizens and illegal use of tribal lands and land-rights. The knock-on effects of both legal and illegal mining have led to increasing insurgencies, Naxalite resistance, local uprisings and increased criminalisation of our local citizenry, which in turn begins to distort our democracy by mixing political and mining interests. The Goa and Karnataka State governments alone could have lost ~INR36,000 Crore through the illegally extracted iron ore. According to a former Mining Secretary quoted in The Hindustan Times on 17ᵗʰ March 2012 on condition of anonymity, *"annual illegal mining should be worth over INR100,000 Crore."*

China currently accounts for 86% of our iron ore exports. It is claimed that the sale value is US$136 per tonne for ore that is bought with a US$1 royalty fee from our government. Other lucrative minerals include manganese, bauxite and cadmium. According to Ramesh Gauns and Claude Alvares of the Goa Foundation, *"For this exorbitant profit, miners extract much more*

*"Progress is measured by the speed at which we destroy the conditions that sustain life."*
**George Monbiot**

*than permitted"*, and former Lokayukta Justice Santosh Hedge also found that iron ore excavated in Karnataka's Bellary district was five times the legally permitted levels.

The complicity of local officials and politicians has been established. *"A fixed bribe is paid for each illegally mined truck leaving a mine,"* Hedge says, with half of the ore exported from Karnataka being illegal. Once the mineral is out of the mining area, its export is extremely easy because ports are only concerned with payment of duty, not the mineral's source. *"About 43% of iron ore being exported from Goa was illegal,"* according to the Public Accounts Committee of Goa Assembly. Illegal mining of minor minerals, for which permission is given by State governments, is higher than it is for the major minerals. As at March 2012, 9,390 mining leases had been issued across our nation by the Indian Bureau of Mines. There has been a steady increase in the illegal mining cases registered across our nation, by September 2011 there were 47,254 registered cases related to illegal mining activities. This is another blatant disregard of our laws and the environment on an epidemic scale.

Many honest, law-abiding, public-spirited citizens and organisations have raised their voice against illegal mining and quarrying, and have paid the ultimate price. On March 9, 2012, Indian Police Service (IPS) official Narender Kumar Singh was run over when he tried to stop a lorry carrying illegally mined stones in Morena, Madhya Pradesh. On March 11, 2012 Sathish Kumar, a 21-year-old student, was crushed to death allegedly by a tipper lorry carrying illegally quarried sand at Mittadarkulam in Tamil Nadu's Tirunelveli district. On March 10, 2012, criminals in Madhya Pradesh allegedly fired at a Vigilance Team led by a sub-divisional district magistrate, who was to decommission a bridge as the structure was apparently being used to transport illegally mined sand from Madhya Pradesh to neighbouring Uttar Pradesh. In June 2011, Swami Nigamanand was allegedly poisoned for undertaking a fast in Haridwar, Uttarakhand, against illegal mining of stones in the river Ganga. In July 2010, Rights to Information activist Amit Jethwa was shot dead (a police officer and a forest guard were arrested in connection with his

*"God forbid that India should ever take to industrialism after the manner of the West . . . keeping the world in chains. If [our nation] took to similar economic exploitation, it would strip the world bare like locusts."*

Mohandas Karamchand Gandhi

death) for exposing illegal sand mining in the Gir forests of Gujarat, the world's only habitat for Asiatic lions. In August 2007, Sudalaimuthu of Harikesanallur, district secretary of the Democratic Youth Federation of India, was murdered by illegal sand quarry miners. In December 2004 R. Venkatesan, a deputy tahsildar died in the line of duty when reportedly boarding a truck carrying illegally mined sand. J.B. Dabral had been forced to leave his home in Tehri Garhwal, Uttarakhand, after receiving threats from local logging criminals for trying to halt their activities, he said *"They are after my life because I have filed Public Interest Litigations in the Supreme Court to halt illegal felling of trees."* He did not get support from the potentially compromised local bureaucrats and administration. Many other civil society activists protesting against illegal mining in Uttarakhand have been receiving threats.

Most of these cases highlight inaction by local State authorities and governments. In some cases local officials leak information about complaints to the illegal miners thereby compromising the citizens' personal security. It is a prime reason for many activists being killed or assaulted. A sad fact is that this illegal activity involves the full and willing participation of many local citizens, who will actually be the ones to suffer and lose the most in the long-term, and they are perpetuating this illegal action by contributing as co-conspirators. These are just a few examples of where honest law abiding citizens who have the nation and the citizens interest at heart are murdered in the pursuit of short-term profits. It has not yet stopped the mining, and thankfully, nor has the resolve of the honest concerned citizens.

The damage caused by these mining activities is beginning to take a visible effect on our citizens and population. The Centre for Science and Environment reported an increase in cases of asthma near mining sites in Madhya Pradesh and Chhattisgarh. The Damodar river region in Jharkhand has 46% of our nation's coal deposits, and is dangerously contaminated with heavy metals, resulting in local citizens having an average age of only 49 years compared to 65 for the rest of the nation. In 2009 all tigers

*"If all mankind were to disappear, the world would regenerate back to the rich state of equilibrium that existed ten thousand years ago. If insects were to vanish, the environment would collapse into chaos."*
Edward Osborne Wilson

were lost in the Panna reserve possibly due to its rampant illegal mining. According to the Lokayukta Justice Santosh N. Hegde's report in early 2012, he said that sloth bears and medicinal plants had also disappeared from Karnataka's mining districts, and the entire system of rain had changed in the Bellary district, and the area surrounding the mine is now stripped of greenery and has no agricultural activity.

The common denominator in illegal mining, scams and other illegal activities are elected and non-elected public servants (local and national politicians and bureaucrats) working in collaboration with either corrupt businesses or existing criminals; often all three working together. Why do our citizens continue to vote for politicians that are criminals and are looting the national assets?

The Hindustan Times details examples of Mining scams across 11 States and the involvement of local politicians, administrators and criminals. If proven guilty, all these individuals and their associates need to be removed from society and all their assets transferred to the Central Government for redeployment across the *'Foundation Pillars'* for the benefit of the nation and all its citizens.

# CONCLUDING COMMENTS

There are significant differences between the market price of ore and the royalty required by the government, especially as commodity prices have been increasing rapidly. There are also weak measures and controls on the volumes and weights of ore extraction. It makes sense to link royalties to a percentage of the market rates which are reviewed and set on a regular monthly basis, and to add Environmental and Forest taxes as an additional levy, in conjunction with a simple volume and weight assessment per number of trucks and mined volumes. A *'windfall tax'* should also be retrospectively enforced on all businesses and shareholders of mining operations that have been assessed to have *'profited'* through illegal activities. Our laws also need to be strictly enforced.

*"I submit to you that if a man hasn't discovered something he will die for, he isn't fit to live."*
Dr. Martin Luther King, Jnr.

Based on these experiences, the determining factors for a successful fight against illegal mining or any other protest could be:

- A charismatic leader to personify the fight.
- Strong support from the civil society.
- Digital and traditional media involvement for large scale awareness and increased pressure.
- A political regime, democratic enough to bring legal consequences and conclusion.

In a 2012 annual survey from Behre Dolbear Group Inc., a International Minerals Industry Advisor of where *'not to invest in'* our nation ranked a poor 16 (tied 15th) out of 25 global mining countries in which *'not to invest in',* based on points assessment of economic, political, social, corruption, currency and taxation.

It seems that running an illegal business in our nation is not difficult. All a citizen has to do is to share a proportion of the profits with those in power and eliminate or discredit whoever protests against this. This has a short-term win-win situation for all those involved; however, mining and pollution have a long-term adverse effect on the environment and socio-economic condition of locals. It is well-documented in news and publications that Maoists and Naxalite insurgencies in tribal areas have been given local citizen support because miners and politicians were not giving or investing a sufficient proportion of their profits to local tribals, for them being allowed to mine, legally or illegally, in the tribal areas.

In April 2012, Dinsha J. Patel, Minister of Mines in the upper house of Parliament reported that a Special Task Forces for inspection of mines completed inspections in December 2011 at ~454 mines in States including Karnataka, Andhra Pradesh, Odisha, Jharkhand and Gujarat, and suspended 155 mines under the Mineral Conservation and Development Rules, on the grounds of serious violations of law; it has further recommended to the State governments to cancel eight mining leases. The current Central government had admitted in Parliament that mining activity has increased significantly in the states of Orissa,

*"Be a yardstick of quality. Some people aren't used to an environment where excellence is expected."*
**Steve Jobs**

Jharkhand, Andhra Pradesh, Karnataka and Goa because of higher demand of iron ore; however, they fell short of stating that a large proportion of the mining may actually be illegal. The cases of Bellary mines in Karnataka and illegal mining in Goa had national headlines prominence and raised awareness and consciousness on the environment.

The Central government expresses its helplessness stating that mining is a local State subject whereas the States claim that the Centre sets the regulations govern mining across our nation. This has left concerned citizens in a limbo, as only illegal miners benefit from this lack of leadership, management and decision making. We need a stronger Centre to set policy and implement this policy with authority and conviction, as with all the other *'Foundation Pillar'* priorities. What is refreshing to read is that social activists are enthusiastically engaged across the nation in a common movement against the dangers of illegal mining.

# WILDLIFE

Our nation provides a home to very diverse and rich wildlife which includes over 172 endangered species, and we have made great efforts since independence at preserving their natural habitats as well as their population numbers. We have 2,356 recorded species of amphibians, birds, mammals and reptiles according to the World Conservation Monitoring Centre and of these, 18.4% are endemic only in our nation and 10.8% are threatened.

*'Jungle'* is a Hindi word for wilderness and was adopted into English; and over time this has begun to be synonymous with lush tropical forests across the world. Our nation has rainforests, moist and dry deciduous forests, thorn forests, deserts, mangroves, grasslands, and coniferous forests and a variety of freshwater and marine habitats. Our diverse geography and landscapes are home to many critically endangered species, including the Asiatic lion, Asian elephant, tiger, white-rumped vulture, Asian one-horned rhinoceros and water buffalo amongst many others. We also have a significant number of species of deer,

antelopes, wild dogs, cats, bears and primates including macaques, gibbons, lorises and the golden langur, one of the world's rarest monkeys. We also have a diverse reptilian, amphibian and bird populations, some of which are still being discovered in 2012 and are new to science.[157]

Our nation is home to 60% of the world's tigers, 65% of its elephants, 80% of the Asian rhinos and 100% of Asian lions and these large animals migrate from one jungle area to another to sustain their population and feeding requirements.[14] We must maintain their habitat; encroachment of human activities has significantly shrunk and destroyed their natural habitats. This has endangered not only the smaller avian, reptile and mammal population but also eroded endemic flora and fauna. Our conservation efforts have supported Tigers, Elephant, Olive Ridley Turtles and Vultures; we have launched Wildlife Conservation programmes and Coastal and Marine Biodiversity initiatives; created National Parks, sanctuaries, protected 'no-go' areas, set-up UNESCO World Heritage Programme sites and have passed legislation to protect against trade in endangered species, controlling poaching, illegal extraction and trade in Wild Flora and Fauna. This is all excellent, and a few programmes have been a great success; however, this is still insufficient as the implementation in many initiatives has been incomplete, poor and weak.

For a nation of citizens that have a culture of valuing and respecting nature and all life, we are now travelling down a slippery slope of beginning to kill these animals; we are now getting nearly weekly reports of elephants, leopards, large cats and other protected animals poisoned, being killed, or being injured by our citizens as they come into contact with us. This is so sad. Large animals need space to live, move, breed and feed. Inevitably, with fast shrinking habitat they will come into conflict with human beings. This is exacerbated by human development proliferating without understanding or care into their migration paths, breeding grounds and core habitats. There are parts of Central and Eastern Africa where the wildlife has been decimated and poaching was rampant, and to some extent, still continues illegally; whilst some nations like South Africa, Botswana and

*"The man who makes no mistakes does not usually make anything."*
**Edward John Phelps**

Angola have taken a positive view that protection of this wildlife, flora and fauna can have a constructive effect on the citizens, eco-system and economy. We need to adapt these types of solutions for our nation.

It is stated that the postings of government officers to Wildlife and Forest type duties is seen as a *'dumping'* grounds for unwanted officers and staff of other departments, and as such the personnel neither have the interest, aptitude nor training in wildlife and environment management. Once in post these individuals are claimed to make endeavours to move to other postings. We need to ensure that all officers posted to Wildlife and Forest type duties are trained prior to their taking up these posts, and that only officers who are interested and have a personal commitment to nature and conservation should apply and be given positions. The average age of the Wildlife and Forest guards is claimed to be over 40 years of age, and 50 years in some States, and this can be a physically stretching role.[158] There has been a significant increase in tourism, illegal activities such as felling of trees, poaching, encroachments; and we need to ensure that we increase the calibre and quality of our recruits and officers to ensure compliance and implementation of protection initiatives, laws and regulations.

A possible solution is that we should re-enforce the protection of these natural habitats with our armed security services. When not otherwise employed on the prime task of national security they can support the protection of our nation through the protection of its natural environment. This is a sound proposal. As we move towards a *'more focused front-line'*, *'technologically advanced'*, *'higher firepower per personnel'* set of armed services, we may have a large number of serving personnel that could support on a more regular or semi-permanent basis. Our armed services:

- Are already deployed in areas that are critical to wildlife protection and ecological diversity, such as our borders and other insurgency affected areas (Rann of Kutch, the Thar Desert, the Himalaya, the tropical rain forests of North East India, Western Ghats and the Andaman and Nicobar Islands etc.).

*"The most absurd and reckless aspirations have sometimes led to extraordinary success."*
Marquis deVauvenargues

- Active involvement would not only prevent poaching and habitat degradation by others, but also prevent illegal transportation and movement of wildlife.
- Are predominantly recruited from rural areas, potentially already giving them a better appreciation, understanding and recognition of the importance of nature, wildlife and the environment.
- Have the competence and capabilities to undertake surveys and research in remote areas and to prevent illegal traffic in wildlife and products.
- Are one of the largest landowners in the nation with establishments in different ecosystems and environments which are already protected from intrusion.
- Already have a special unit called the *'Environment and Ecology Cell'*, which deals with conservation aspects. It could liaise and lead the states and other protection agencies to agree a clear strategy and implementation plan.
- Are organised, structured, trained, motivated, and disciplined to do this. They have the communication skills and mobility capabilities ideally suited for environmental protection.

## CONCLUDING COMMENTS

The Indian Constitution Article 48-A and 51-A specifies that *"it shall be the duty of every citizen of India to protect and improve the natural environment including forests, lakes, rivers, and wildlife and to have compassion for living creatures."* Even under tremendous development pressures, our nation is home to an impressive array of wildlife, flora and fauna. This is mainly due to the cultural and religious significance we place on these, combined with a relatively robust legal and constitutional framework for wildlife protection, an active judiciary, and a proactive civil society sector. It could be much worse, and then again, it could be so much better.

*"Democracy cannot succeed unless those who express their choice are prepared to choose wisely. The real safeguard of democracy, therefore, is education."*

**Franklin D. Roosevelt**

271

To avoid the *'build-neglect-rebuild'* syndrome applying to our conservation movement to support the environment, we should ensure:

- Under the leadership of the Central government, and with participation from the State governments, a potential rationalisation and redistribution of protected area boundaries across our nation (Wildlife Reserves, Conservation Reserves and Community Reserves), and add other larger human settlement-free habitats to these protected areas. This could involve redistribution of boundaries and human resettlement in consultation with local citizens.

- Each protected area would have a focused rationale for its existence, maintenance and a strategy and management plan developed accordingly i.e. conservation of endangered species, representative wildlife habitat; tourism; catchment area; protection of bird life and swamps, etc.

- Each protected area would have a structured governance and leadership that is mandated and measured to develop, maintain and operate that environment to agreed standards. A Chief Warden or similar post will be personally held accountable for their protected area.

- Each protected area should have a comprehensive management plan which would be measured, monitored and periodically revised.

- Each protected area would be under the direct control of the Central Government and the State Governments must support prevention of all illegal activities banned under the Wildlife (Protection) Act.

- Sufficient financial investments and resources need to be available to ensure operation of the areas.

- Improved data, information and records must be kept to monitor and support research, analysis and decision-making; a consistent protocol for data input, access, maintenance, storage and retrieval will be implemented.

- Funds generated by tourism will not go to the public exchequer, but be reinvested for eco-development of the local communities, especially in the tribal areas.

- The protected areas will employ only personnel with interest, capabilities and competencies in wildlife management.

*"Kindness is a language which the deaf can hear and the blind can see."*
Mark Twain

272

- The forest service supported by the armed services will be mandated, trained and armed to combat wildlife and environmental crime.
- The broad recommendations of the Subramaniam Committee report of 1994, especially the formation of the wildlife crime unit and the provision of legal training and support to wildlife law enforcement agencies will be implemented.
- No electric lines be laid over, across or under national parks and sanctuaries and those that exist will be safeguarded against vandalism and misuse, as there have been numerous instances of wild animals being deliberately electrocuted by cutting overhead wires, amongst them elephants, rhinos and tigers. Livestock and humans have also perished. Ecologically sensitive areas should also include areas such as elephant corridors, important bird areas etc.
- Buffer zones will be created around of protected areas and be designated as ecologically sensitive areas with a view to restrict activities.
- Clear boundaries will be erected around all areas to avoid human-animal conflict.
- Compensation mechanisms in areas of man-animal conflict must be reviewed and schemes implemented to pay appropriate immediately damage.
- Universities, schools, non-government and International organisations should be encouraged to participate in regular monitoring of birds and other wildlife within (under supervision and license) and outside protected areas.
- Reintroduction of species should be undertaken with professional participation across all interested stakeholders.
- In areas prone to organized or large scale violations or insurgency, special protection staff or para-military forces will be deployed to prevent illicit felling, encroachment, infiltrations, smuggling and poaching, especially on the international borders and in insurgency affected areas. These will be treated as violations and all trespassers will be treated with unreasonably excessive lethal force.

*"I wake up each morning determined to change the world and also to have one hell of a good time. Sometimes that makes planning the day a little difficult."*
**E. B. White**

**The 'Foundation Pillar for Infrastructure, Agriculture & Environment' could read that we will:**

1. Ensure a holistic approach to Transportation and Infrastructure, so our road, rail, air and water transportation strategies and plans are synchronised with one-another, to create a singular improved delivery for our citizens.

2. Provide the quality and scale of road, rail, air and sea transportation for our citizens to meet the longer-term needs in the continuing development of our nation.

3. Provide for a faster, more efficient and effective infrastructure and transportation network across our nation for the movement of citizens, good and services.

4. Balance the needs of infrastructure development with that of the environment and our eco-system.

5. Always prioritise on the side of environment and eco-system over infrastructure unless essential for the health of citizens and security of the nation.

6. Be pioneering, resourceful and innovative in the utilisation of our land for development of our infrastructure.

7. Design and build our infrastructure in the most efficient manner and be more effective in its use and application.

8. Build a simplified food supply chain to reduce wastage and losses from the 'Farm to the Kitchen'.

9. Reduce the number of intermediaries, and thereby the costs and margins, in the food supply chain to provide farmers with appropriate prices for their produce.

10. Aim to generate more electrical power through renewable sources through being more pioneering, resourceful and innovative in the development of technologies and equipment to support us towards energy self sufficiency.

11. Aim to generate more electrical power locally and closer to the end user, using renewable sources, to reduce losses and high infrastructure costs.

*"I know God will not give me anything that I can't handle. I just wish that he didn't trust me so much."*
Mother Teresa

12. Aim to reduce electrical power demand through better and more creative energy efficiency and use of lower power consumption equipment and appliances.

13. Aim to better utilise and develop our own hydrocarbon fuel (oil, gas and coal etc.) resources to support us towards energy self-sufficiency.

14. Aim to reduce our imports of hydrocarbon fuels to support the environment and the national balance of payments though faster and further development of local renewable energy sources.

15. Aim to significantly increase rain water retention by building more local *'check dams'*, tanks and other methods to provide year round water for all citizens.

16. Provide water links from regions of high water availability to low water availability to provide year round water for all citizens.

17. Provide sufficient waste water and sewage treatment plants across the nation to increase health and water recycling and reduce disease and environmental damage.

18. Set national standards for all industrial and domestic use of clean water and waste water.

19. Set national standards for air, soil and water quality.

20. Institute a set of laws and penalties, that are enforced, for the protection of our environment.

21. Price all utilities and fuels (water, fuel, gas and electricity) at market rates, for Industry and Domestic users, to support more effective use of these scarce resources and increase the drive towards energy and operational efficiency.

22. Develop and build better competencies and capabilities in the professional management, implementation, operation and maintenance of all infrastructure and utilities across our nation.

23. Drive a new *'Evergreen Agricultural Revolution'* that is sustainable and evolutionary to become self-sufficient in the majority of food produce.

*"What is not good for the hive is not good for the bee."*
Marcus Aurelius

24. Increase agricultural productivity and efficiency to world class standards across our major range food produce.

25. Maintain our existing acreage of agricultural lands and not encroach any further into forests and other protected areas.

26. Develop our deserts, barren and waste lands for both agriculture and human habitation rather than encroach any further into forests and other protected areas.

27. Establish clear protected areas for wildlife, flora and fauna and have professional governance and warden control operation for all these areas.

28. Provide armed services capabilities and competencies for the protection of our wildlife, flora and fauna.

29. ....................................................................................

30. ....................................................................................

31. ....................................................................................

32. ....................................................................................

Etc...................................................................................

*"I never see what has been done; I only see what remains to be done."*
**Siddhārtha Gautama Buddha**

# IDEAS, INSPIRATION, INFORMATION SOURCES & REFERENCES

I take this opportunity to thank all the individuals, institutions and publications mentioned below for their work, support and contribution in further educating and informing me. There are many other and multiple sources of information I had used, and these are not presented here for brevity, and are available on request, or are detailed on www.FoundationPillars.in

Reading feeds the mind!

Widely used sources to corroborate facts:
*   The World Bank Data Catalog
*   Encyclopaedia Britannica
*   World Health Organisation (WHO). Global Health Observatory Data Repository: http://apps.who.int/ghodata/
*   Planning Comission of India website (http://planningcommission.nic.in)
*   'India Infrastructure Report—2011: Infrastructure Development Finance Company. Oxford University Press

## LIST OF REFERENCES:

1   King Asoka, the third monarch of the Maurya Dynasty in India: *14 Rock Edicts at Girnar & 7 Pillar Edicts*, circa -257 BC.
2   "Beyond BRICs", *Financial Times* Emerging Markets Section. BRIC Acronym created by Jim O'Neill, global economist at Goldman Sachs, in 2001 to highlight his thesis that Brazil, Russia, India and China could become among the four most dominant economies by the year 2050 due to their inherent economic potential.

3    Richard M. Langworth, ed. *Churchill by Himself. The Life, Times and Opinions of Winston Churchill* (Ebury Press, London) Richard M. Langworth, email and phone discussions, May 2012

4    Martin Gilbert, *Winston S. Churchill Vol. 5* "The Birla-Churchill Meeting, August 1935" (London: Heinemann, 1977)

5    Sir Winston Churchill, speech at the Albert Hall, London, 18 March 1931.

6    Pandit Jawaharlal Nehru, *The Discovery of India,* 1946 (Reprint Penguin, India)

7    www.bharat-rakshak.com

8    Shashi Tharoor, *The Great Indian Novel,* (Arcade Publishing, New York, 1989 & 2001)

9    Stephen Ross, compiled, *The Harvest Field Statistics—2013.*

10   Jon Clifton, *150 Million Adults Worldwide Would Migrate to the U.S.:* Gallup Survey April 20, 2012

11   *Global Humanitarian Assistance—India: Country Profile,* January 2012 (Development Initiatives, Somerset, UK) Data based on CIA World Fact Book, http://www.indexmundi.com

12   Indian Election Results, http://www.indian-elections.com/india-statistics.html

13   Matt Rosenberg, *India's Population: India Likely to Surpass China in Population by 2030.* 01 April 2011

14   Trading Economics, http://www.tradingeconomics.com/india/gdp

15   *Supplementary Notes,* Government of Indian Press Release, 20 March 2012, New Delhi

16   *Human Rights in India, Status Report 2012, Updated & Revised,* (with first & second UN Universal Periodic Review Recommendations), (Working Group on Human Rights in India and the UN, December 2012)

17   *Poverty Estimates 2009-2010,* Planning Commission, Government of Indian; Report,19 March 2012, New Delhi

18   South African President attends 3rd BRIC Leaders Conference on 14 April 2011 in Sanya, a resort in China's southern island province of Hainan.

19   Fareed Zakaria, *Is India the Broken BRIC?,* CNN World Report, 21 December 2011

20   Nirmala M Nagaraj, 'India ranks 171 out of 175 in public health spending, says WHO study', *The Times of India,* 11 August 2009

21 Parliament of India, Rajya Sabha, http://164.100.47.5/Newmembers/memavgage.aspx

22 Andrew MacAskill and Kartikay Mehrotra, *Jailed Lawmakers Rule in India as Crime Brings Few Punishments*, Bloomberg, 05 March 2012, http://www.bloomberg.com/news/2012-03-04/jailed-lawmakers-rule-in-india-as-crime-brings-re-election-not-punishment.html

23 S. G. Deogaonkar, *Parliamentary System in India* (Concept Publishing, New Delhi, 1997)

24 Balmiki Prasad Singh (Union Home Secretary (1997-99), *The Challenge of Good Governance in India: Need for Innovative Approaches*, (Oxford University Press).

25 Second Administrative Reforms Commission, *e-Governance: Initiatives in India, Chapter 4*, 11th report, December 2008.

26 *Study on EWRs (Elected Women Representatives) in Panchayati Raj Institutions*, (June 2010, Ministry of Panchayati Raj, Government of India).

27 *Civil Services Survey: 2010*, 12 April 2010, Ministry of Personnel, Public Grievances and Pensions Department of Administrative Reforms & Public Grievances, Government of India.

28 *62nd (2011-2012) Annual Report*, Union Public Services Commission, New Delhi.

29 Commitment and Pledge made on December 16, 1950 (The day after his death) by 1500 Officers of IAS & IPS at Sardar Vallabhbhai Patel's Residence: *Freedom Fighters of India*, Volume 2, Lion M. G. Agrawal, (2008, ISHA Books)

30 Dean Nelson, 'Indian civil service issued honesty guidelines', *The Telegraph*, UK, August 14 2012;

http://www.telegraph.co.uk/news/worldnews/asia/india/9474691/Indian-civil-service-issued-honesty-guidelines.html

31 Political and Economic Risk Consultancy, Ltd., 28 Queen's Road, Central, Hong Kong

32

    1. Narendra Kumar (08 March 2012):
http://articles.timesofindia.indiatimes.com/2012-03-16/india/31200535_1_stone-laden-tractor-trolley-tractor-trolley-ips-officer

2. Yeshwant Sonawane (25 January 2011) http://www.ndtv.com/search?q=Yashwant+sonawane

3. Jagadananda Panda (31 July 2009) http://www.telegraphindia.com/1090802/jsp/nation/story_11311451.jsp

4. K.C. Surendra Babu(05 January 2005) http://news.outlookindia.com/items.aspx?artid=271545

5. G. Krishnaiah (05 December 1994) http://www.telegraphindia.com/1120711/jsp/bihar/story_15713478.jsp

33 Literacy Rates Census 2011, part of Census 2011, the 15th National census survey conducted by the Census Organization of India http://www.census2011.co.in/literacy.php

34 Emily Jansons, 'Philanthropy in its infancy in india', *The Hindu Business Line* (18 Dec, 2012) http://www.thehindubusinessline.com/opinion/philanthropy-in-its-infancy-in-india/article4214008.ece

35 *Children in India 2012—A Statistical Approach*, Social Statistics Division, Central Statistics Office, Ministry of tatistics and Programme Implementation, Government of India, Sep 2012.

36 *Improving India's Education System through Information Technology*, (IBM, Bangalore, 2005)

37 David P. Baker & Gerald K. LeTendre, *National Differences, Global Similarities: World Culture and the Future of Schooling*, (Stanford University Press)

38 Anubhuti Vishnoi, 'Grim Details in CBSE Survey on Sanitation in Schools', *The Indian Express*, 16 January 2012, http://www.indianexpress.com/news/-grim--details-in-cbse-survey-on-sanitation-in-schools/900119

39 'Higher Education in India: Issues, Concerns and New Direction', Recommendations of the UGC Golden Jubilee Seminars, University Grants Commission, Delhi, Government of India

40 Philip G. Altbach & Pawan Agarwal, 'Scoring higher on education' *The Hindu*, 12 February 2013; http://www.thehindu.com/opinion/op-ed/scoring-higher-on-education/article4404687.ece.

41 Dharmakirti Joshi et al, 'Skilling India: The Billion People Challenge', A report by CRISIL Centre for Economic Research, November 2010

42 FICCI Higher Education Summit 2012.

43 Helen Clark, 'Our World in 2050: More Equitable and Sustainable—or Less?', 07 November 2012, UNDP; http://www.undp.org/content/undp/en/home/presscenter/speeches/2012/11/07/helen-clark-our-world-in-2050-more-equitable-and-sustainable-or-less-.html

44 Examples: http://www.TheGlobalTutors.com, http://www.TutorChapter.com, http://www.TutorVista.com

45 World Health Organisation (WHO). Global Health Observatory Data Repository
http://apps.who.int/ghodata/

46 Human Development Reports from the United Nations Development Programme (UNDP) http://hdr.undp.org/en/statistics/

47 'Access to Healthcare: Challenges and Solutions', July 2010, PricewaterhouseCoopers, India

48 Op.cit. World Health Organisation (WHO).
Op.cit 'Access to Healthcare: Challenges and Solutions', July 2010, PricewaterhouseCoopers, India

49 Ajay Mahal, Bibek Debroy, and Laveesh Bhandari, 'India Health Report 2010', (Business Standard Books, 2010)

50 Op.cit. World Health Organisation (WHO).
Op.cit. 'Access to Healthcare: Challenges and Solutions', July 2010, PricewaterhouseCoopers, India

51 Op.cit. 'India Health Report 2010'.

52 Richard Skolnik, 'Essentials of Global Healthcare', (Jones and Barltett Publishers, 2008)

53 'A Brief Report on Healthcare, Telemedicine & Medical Tourism in India', August 2012, ASA & Associates, KS House, Shahpur Jat, New Delhi, 110049, India

54 World Health Organisation (WHO) Immunisation Profile: India 02 October 2012 data http://apps.who.int/immunization_monitoring/en/globalsummary/countryprofileresult.cfm?c=ind

55 'Soon, one out of 5 diabetic patients will be Indian: Dr Reddy', 25 July 2012 http://www.firstpost.com/economy/soon-one-out-5-diabetic-patients-will-be-indian-dr-reddy-390525.html

56 Malathy Iyer, 'One in three Indians is overweight, shows study' The Times of India, aper., 02 November 2012, http://articles.timesofindia.

indiatimes.com/2012-11-02/india/34877095_1_obesity-and-diabetes-ideal weight-anoop-misra

57  TB Facts Organisation; http://www.tbfacts.org/tb-statistics-india.html

58  Kounteya Sinha 'India in grip of obesity epidemic', The Times of India, 12 November 2012,; http://articles.timesofindia.indiatimes.com/2010-11-12/india/28245306_1_obesity-india-and-china-overweight-rates

59  Op.cit. 'India Health Report 2010'

60  Paul H. Keckley, 'Medical Tourism: Consumers in Search for Value', (Deloitte Center for Health Solutions, 2008)

61  Press Release (No.191/2012), Information Note to the Press, Telecom Regulatory Authority of India, New Delhi, 09 October 2012

62  Itishree Samal, 'Apollo to open 1,000 telemedicine centres', The Business Standard, 07 April 2011; http://www.business-standard.com/article/companies/apollo-to-open-1-000-telemedicine-centres-111040700024_1.html

63  'Can Telemedicine Alleviate India's Health Care Problems?' Indian Knowledge @ Wharton, Health Economics, 08 March 2012, http://knowledge.wharton.upenn.edu/india/article.cfm?articleid=4675

64  op.cit 'Medical Tourism: Consumers in Search for Value', Deloitte Center for Health Solutions

65  'Healthy Business: Will Medical Tourism Be India's Next Big Industry?' Indian Knowledge @ Wharton, Health Economics, 02 July 2011, http://knowledge.wharton.upenn.edu/india/article.cfm?articleid=4615

66  Sreenivas Janyala 'It saves 200 lives per day, if it can wade through 35,000 prank calls', The Indian Express, 04 June 2010, http://www.indianexpress.com/news/it-saves-200-lives-per-day-if-it-can-wade-through-35000-prank-calls/631707/0

67  op. cit. 'Access to Healthcare: Challenges and Solutions', PricewaterhouseCoopers.

68  'Law and Justice: A Look At The Role And Performance of Indian Judiciary', Address delivered at the Berkeley Seminar Series on Law and Democracy held at University of California, Sept. 2008, Professor N. R. Madhava Menon, Former Director, National Law School, Bangalore and Kolkata, and National Judicial Academy at Bhopal; http://indiandemocracy08.berkeley.edu/docs/Menon-LawANDJustice-ALook%20.pdf

69  Maheshwari and Co, *An Overview of delay in Judicial System*, http://www.maheshwariandco.com/repository/articles/downloads/delay_in_judicial_system.pdf

70  *'Judges of the Supreme Court of India and the High Courts'*, 2009, Government of India, Ministry of Law and Justice, Department of Justice

71  All India Prison Officers Association; http://aipoa.com/doc/File909.pdf

72  'Study: Indians Turning Away From Courts' *The Wall Street Journal*, India, 09 April 2012; http://blogs.wsj.com/indiarealtime/2012/04/09/indians-turning-away-from-courts-study/

73  Justice Ruma Pal, speaking at the 5th Tarkunde Memorial Lecture, 10 November 2011; http://theradicalhumanist.com/index.php?option=com_radical&controller=article&cid=431&Itemid=56

74  *Laws to Implement On Corruption Convicted People.* http://www.indiaeyewitness.com/Channels/Issues.asp?category=Law%20Order

75  BBC News. 'India Anti-Corruption Chief PJ Thomas Forced To Resign', 03 March 2011, Soutik Biswas, Delhi, India; http://www.bbc.co.uk/news/world-south-asia-12631887

76  'Corruption in India: A million rupees now -
Congress drags its feet over tackling graft. It may pay a high price', *The Economist* (Asia). 10 March 2011, http://www.economist.com/node/18338852

77  Bhaskar Dutta and Poonam Gupta, *'How Indian Voters Respond to Candidates with Criminal Charges: Evidence from the 2009 Lok Sabha Elections'*, October 2012, Working Paper # 2012-109, National Institute of Public Finance and Policy, New Delhi, India

78  Pankaj Sharma and Varad Choudhary 'Law And Order Of India in The Hands Of Criminals', *DNA*. 01 April 2012, New Delhi; http://www.dnaindia.com/india/report_law-and-order-of-india-in-the-hands-of-criminals_1669956

79  Shyamlal Yadav 'A Lot to Hide', *India Today,*. 27 March 2008; http://indiatoday.intoday.in/story/A+lot+to+hide/1/6290.html

80  Kuldip Nayar, 'India's 'black money' in Switzerland', *The Express Tribune (International Herald Tribune).* '18 July 2011, http://tribune.com.pk/story/212295/indias-black-money-in-switzerland/

81  T. C. A. Ramanujam, 'Primacy of constitutional rights vs Judicial overreach', *The Hindu Business Line*, 23 July 2011, http://www.thehindubusinessline.com/industry-and-economy/taxation-and-accounts/article2285531.ece?homepage=true

82  Dhananjay Mahapatra, 'BMW hit and run case: R K Anand fined, told to help poor' *The Times of India*, 22 November 2012, http://articles.timesofindia.indiatimes.com/2012-11-22/delhi/35301390_1_r-k-anand-sanjeev-nanda-legal-aid

83  Dean Nelson, 'India's All-Female Police Force To Tackle Women Drink Drivers', *The Telegraph,* 15 November 2011, New Delhi, http://www.telegraph.co.uk/news/worldnews/asia/india/8891090/Indias-all-female-police-force-to-tackle-women-drink-drivers.html

84  'Social audits in India—a slow but sure way to fight corruption' *The Guardian,* http://www.guardian.co.uk/global-development/poverty-matters/2012/jan/13/india-social-audits-fight-corruption

85  ibid

86  Yukti Choudhar, 'The Lokpal and Lokayukta Bill, 2011: Who will guard the guards?', *India Law Journal,* http://www.indialawjournal.com/volume5/issue_3/article4.html

87  'Corruption in India: A rotten state', *The Economist.* 10 March 2011 http://www.economist.com/node/18332796

88  Diana Rodriguez, et al., Small Arms Survey, Issue Brief 'India Armed Violence Assessment: India's Sates of Armed Violence—Assessing the Human Cost and Political Priorities", September 2011, http://www.india-ava.org/fileadmin/docs/pubs/IAVA-IB1-states-of-armed-violence.pdf

89  ibid

90  The Global Armed Violence Prevention Programme (AVPP), Phase 1, WHO & UNDP Phase 1, 2nd June 2005; http://www.who.int/violence_injury_prevention/violence/activities/avpp.pdf

91  Ministry of Home Affairs, India, Annual Report 2011-2012 http://mha.nic.in/pdfs/AR(E)1112.pdf

92  Anuj Chopra, 'Alienation: Business in the Red Corridor', *Forbes India—Independence Day Special* 18 April, 2011,

http://forbesindia.com/article/independence-day-special/alienation-business-in-the-red-corridor/27682/1?id=27682&pg=1

93  op. cit. Small Arms Survey

94  India Government Budget; http://www.tradingeconomics.com/india/government budget

95  Update on India General Anti-Avoidance Rilcs (GAAR), 16 January 2013, Pricewaterhouse Coopers; http://www.pwc.com/en_GX/gx/tax/newsletters/pricing-knowledge-network/assets/pwc-india-gaar-update.pdf

96  'Country Reports on Terrorism 2011', United States Department of State Publication Bureau of Counterterrorism, USA, July 2012; http://www.state.gov/documents/organization/195768.pdf

97  ibid

98  op. cit. Small Arms Survey

99  'Naxals kill 15, inure five in Orissa', IBN Live, 16 February 2008 http://ibnlive.in.com/news/naxals-kill-15-injure-five-in-orissa/59087-3.html

100 *Annual Report 2010-2011*, Ministry of Home Affairs, Government of India http://mha.nic.in/pdfs/AR(E)1011.pdf

101. Amartya Sen, 'Violence, Identity and Poverty', *Journal of Peace Research,* 2008, DOI: 10.1177/0022 343307084920, Published by Sage Publications on behalf of International Peace research Institute, Oslo, Norway.

102 Priya Yadav, 'Another report says 73.5% Punjab youth drug addicts', *The Times of India,* 14 October 2012

103 Manan Kakkar, 'Law enforcement in India to get a major IT upgrade', *ZD Net news*, 03 August 2011, http://www.zdnet.com/blog/india/law-enforcement-in-india-to-get-a-major-it-upgrade/651

104 *Crimes in India 2011, Statistics*, National Crime Records Bureau, Ministry of Home Affairs, Government of India, New Delhi, http://ncrb.nic.in/CD-CII2011/Statistics2011.pdf

105 Dr. Birendra Kaur, 'Alarming Statistics', *Abstracts of Sikh Studies*: Jan-Mar 2008/53940NS, http://www.dise.in/Downloads/Use%20of%20Dise%20Data/Dr%20Birendra%20Kaur.pdf

106 '14,231 custodial deaths from 2001 to 2010',. Asian Centre for Human Rights Press Release. 21 November 2011, CHR Index: PR/IND/07/2011 http://www.achrweb.org/press/2011/IND07-2011.html

107 '60% of complaints against police found false: National Crime Records Bureau', *DNA*, 28 March 2010. http://www.dnaindia.com/india/report_60pct-of-complaints-against-police-found-false-national-crime-records-bureau_1364350

108 Prison Statistics India 2011, National Crime Records Bureau, Ministry of Home Affairs, Government of India, http://ncrb.nic.in/PSI-2011/Full/PSI-2011.pdf
International Centre for Prison Studies. World Prisons Brief http://www.prisonstudies.org/info/worldbrief/wpb_stats.php?area=all&category=wb_poptotal

109 'What do the rulers of China fear? 'Shuanggui', *Herald Tribune*, 15 June 2012 http://www.heraldtribune.com/article/20120615/ARCHIVES/206151023

110 Malavika Vyawahare, 'India's Police Force Lags Much of the World', *The New York Times*, 6 January 2013, http://india.blogs.nytimes.com/2013/01/16/india-has-one-of-the-lowest-police-population-ratios-in-the-world/

111 'Background paper on SIPRI military expenditure data, 2011', Stockholm International Peace research Institute (SIPRI). Press Release 17 April 2012. http://www.sipri.org/research/armaments/milex/sipri-factsheet-on-military-expenditure-2011.pdf

112 Global Fire Power (07 February 2013) http://www.globalfirepower.com/countries-listing.asp

113 C. Raja Mohan, 'India's new role in the Indian Ocean', India Seminar, http://www.india-seminar.com/2011/617/617_c_raja_mohan.htm

114 Joachim Hofbauer, et. Al., 'A New Analysis of Defense Budgets in Asia', 02 November 2012, CSIS, http://cogitasia.com/a-new-analysis-of-defense-budgets-in-asia/

115 *Annual Report 2010-2011*, Ministry of Defence, Government of India. http://merln.ndu.edu/whitepapers/India_Annual-Rpt_ENG_2010-2011.pdf

116 James Lamont, *Financial Times* Special Report: Aerospace. 'Stealth fighters: India and Russia form ground breaking partnership but US rival tries to muscle in', 11 November 2011, New Delhi

117 Dean Nelson, 'Pakistan expanding nuclear arsenal to deter US attack', *The Telegraph,* 07 December 2012, http://www.telegraph.co.uk/news/worldnews/asia/pakistan/9729884/Pakistan-expanding-nuclear-arsenal-to-deter-US-attack.html

118 Vijay Goel, and Himanshu Pimpalkhute 'Indian defence sector offers investment opportunities', *The In-House Lawyer Magazine,* February 2008, Singhania & Co LLP; http://www.singhania.com/Publication/IHL157_india2.pdf

119 ibid

120 Ajai Shukla, 'End this MMRCA hara-kiri', *Business Standard,* 01 November 2011, http://www.business-standard.com/article/opinion/ajai-shukla-end-this-mmrca-hara-kiri-111110100011_1.html

121 Op. Cit. James Lamont, New Delhi

122 Sandeep Unnithan with Kaushik Deka, 'Not ready for war', *Indian Today,* 29 October 2011, http://indiatoday.intoday.in/story/indian-army-war-readiness-against-china/1/157763.html

123 Frank Jack Daniel, Reuters News. 'Analysis: India's military build up may be too little too late?', 03 February 2013, New Delhi, Additional reporting by Arup Roychoudhury in New Delhi and Sanjib Kumar in Port Blair, http://www.reuters.com/article/2012/02/03/us-india-defence-idUSTRE8120LH20120203

124 Dr. Pushpita Das, 'India's Internal Security: The year that was, the year that may be', Institute for Defence Studies & Analyses, 13 December 2011, http://idsa.in/system/files/IB_IndiaInternalSecurity.pdf

125 *"Infrastructure Funding Requirements and its Sources over the implementation period of the Twelfth Five Year Plan (2012- 2017)",* Planning Commission, Government of India; http://planningcommission.nic.in/aboutus/committee/wg_sub_infrastructure.pdf

126 Annual Report 2011-2012, Ministry of Urban Development, Government of India; http://www.urbanindia.nic.in/quickaccess/ann_report/2011_2012/AR2011-12_English.pdf

127 *Position Paper on the Power Sector in India,* Department of Economic Affairs, Ministry of Finance, Government of India, December 2009 http://164.100.52.24/pdf/ppp_position_paper_power_122k9.pdf

128 Save the World's Forests. Japan's Forests

http://www.saveamericasforests.org/JapansForests/JapansForests.htm

129 '95 NHAI projects delayed due to law & order problems: Govt', *The Indian Express*, 22 March 2012, http://www.indianexpress.com/news/95-nhai-projects-delayed-due-to-law---order-problems-govt/927089

130 Simon Robinson, 'Working on the Railroad', *Time Magazine*, 28 February 2008, http://www.time.com/time/magazine/article/0,9171,1717905,00.html

131 Manu Balachandran, 'India's plan of doubling port capacity a distant dream now', *The Economic Times*, 08 October 2012,
http://articles.economictimes.indiatimes.com/2012-10-08/news/34322932_1_port-projects-mega-container-vizhinjam-port

132 *Development of Coastal Shipping. TCS Report,* Chapter 7: *Inland Water Transport*
http://www.dgshipping.com/dgship/final/tcsrep/chapter_7.htm

133 ibid

134 Report of Working Group on Civil Aviation Sector, National Transport Development Policy Committee, June 2012, Ministry of Civil Aviation, Government of India

135 . Kala Seetharam Sridhar and Surender Kumar, 'India's Urban Environment: Air/Water Pollution and Pollution Abatement', *Economic & Political Weekly*, distributed by Contify.com
http://www.epw.in/system/files/pdf/2013_48/06/Indias_Urban_Environment.pdf

136 Powering India: The Road to 2007, McKinsey & Company, http://www.mckinsey.com/locations/india/mckinseyonindia/pdf/Power_Report_Exec_Summary.pdf

137 ibid

138 Kartik Goyal, 'S&P Says India May Be First in BRIC to Lose Investment Grade', Bloomberg 11 June 2011, http://www.bloomberg.com/news/2012-06-11/s-p-says-india-may-be-first-bric-nation-to-lose-investment-grade.html

139 ibid

140 Basic Statistics on Indian Petroleum & Natural Gas, 2011-12. Ministry of Petroleum & Natural Gas. Government of India. http://petroleum.nic.in/petstat.pdf

141 US Energy Information Administration (eia). *Analysis India*. 21 November 2011
   http://www.eia.gov/countries/cab.cfm?fips=IN

142 Electricity Conservation. Thermal Power Plant
   http://www.kvcperi.com/temp1/thermal.html

143 EAI. India Hydro Energy; http://www.eai.in/ref/ae/hyd/hyd.html

144 GigaCom. 'A solar canal rise in india', 23 April 2012, Ucilia Wang
   http://gigaom.com/2012/04/23/a-solar-canal-rises-in-india/

145 Clean technical. Solar PV close to 50c/Watt', 24 July 2012, Giles Parkinson
   http://cleantechnica.com/2012/07/24/solar-pv-close-to-50cwatt/

146 Ministry of New & Renewable Energy. Government of India
   http://www.mnre.gov.in/mission-and-vision-2/achievements/

147 *India's Draft National Water Policy (2012)*: 29 June 2012. Ministry of Water Resources, GOI
   http://www.igovernment.in/site/india%E2%80%99s-draft-national-water-policy-2012-ministry-water-resources-goi

148 Vikram Utamsingh, Ramesh Srinivas, *'Water sector in India: Overview and focus areas for the future PanIIT Conclave 2010'*, KPMG India,

149 *India Infrastructure Report—2011: Water: Policy and Performance for Sustainable Development*; Infrastructure Development Finance Company, Oxford University Press, India.

150 Charles Runckel, *Business In Asia*. *'Infrastructure India: A long road ahead'*, Runckel & Associates; http://www.business-in-asia.com/asia/infrastructure_india.html

151 Upali Amarasinghe, *'The National River Linking Project of India, Some Contentious Issues'*, IWMI-TATA Water Policy Program. Water Policy Research. http://www.iwmi.cgiar.org/iwmi-tata/pdfs/2012_Highlight-16.pdf

152 M.Rajeevan, *'Prediction of Seasonal Mean Monsoon Rainfall'*, India Meteorological Department. National Climate Centre, India Meteorological Department, Pune, India

153 *'Utilisation of Land resources for Urban Sector in India'*, Town & Country Planning Organisation, Ministry of Urban Development, Government of India

http://www.landuseindia.in/live/hrdpmp/hrdpmaster/hrdp-asem/content/
e48335/e48799/e48940/e51439/e51483/8.UtilisationofLandResourceforUr
banSectorinIndia-PolicyRequirements_KKJ.pdf

154 BirdLife International. *'Diclofenac—the mystery solved'*,
http://www.birdlife.org/action/science/species/asia_vulture_crisis/
diclofenac.html

155 Ministry of Environment and Forests. Press Release 07 February 2012
http://pib.nic.in/newsite/erelease.aspx?relid=80170

156. T. R. Manoharan, *'Supply Determinants of Timber Trade in India'*. WWF &
GOI 2011,
http://planningcommission.nic.in/reports/sereport/ser/ser_timber300511.
pdf

157 'New type of legless amphibian discovered in India', *The Telegraph,*. 23
February 2012
http://www.telegraph.co.uk/earth/wildlife/9097531/New-type-of-legless-
amphibian-discovered-in-India.html

158 *'Evaluation reports of Tiger Reserves in India'*, Project Tiger Directorate,
Ministry of Environment and Forests, Government of India
http://projecttiger.nic.in/Report-2_EvaluationReportsofTRinIndia.pdf